Cistercian Studies Series: Number Sixty-five

NOBLE PIETY AND REFORMED MONASTICISM

The Letter of St Stephen Harding to Abbot Thurstan
and the Community of Sherborne.
Jesus College, Oxford, MS 34 (Q.B. 17), f. 108ᵛ.

CISTERCIAN STUDIES SERIES: NUMBER SIXTY-FIVE

NOBLE PIETY AND REFORMED MONASTICISM

Studies in Medieval Cistercian History VII

Edited by E. Rozanne Elder

CISTERCIAN PUBLICATIONS INC.

KALAMAZOO, MICHIGAN

1981

Available in the Commonwealth and Europe from

A. R. Mowbray & Co Ltd
St Thomas House Becket Street
Oxford OXI 1SJ

Papers presented at the Cistercian Studies Conference and Sesquemillenial Conference in Honor of St Benedict of Nursia under the sponsorship of the Institute of Cistercian Studies, as part of the Fifteenth Annual Medieval Studies Congress, Western Michigan University, Kalamazoo, 1–4 May 1980.

Composition by Linda Hensley
Printed in the United States of America

Table of Contents

Preface   vi

Noble Piety and Reformed Monasticism:
The Dukes of Burgundy in the Twelfth Century
    Constance B. Bouchard   1

Notes Towards the Exegesis of a Letter by
Saint Stephen Harding
    Chrysogonus Waddell, OCSO   10

Anthropology and Sanctity in the *Vita Prima Bernardi I*
    Richard M. Peterson   40

Early Citeaux and the Care of Souls
    Bede K. Lackner, O. Cist.   52

Maternal Imagery in Twelfth-Century Cistercian Writings
    Caroline Walker Bynum   68

Caesar of Heisterbach and the Cistercians
As Medieval People
    Brian Patrick McGuire   81

The Alleged Greek Sources of William of St Thierry
    David N. Bell   109

A Twelfth-Century View of the Imagination:
Aelred of Rievaulx
    Marie Anne Mayeski, CSJ   123

Conrad of Bavaria--the Pilgrim Prince
    Conrad Greenia, OCSO   130

Baldwin of Ford and Twelfth-Century Theology
    David N. Bell   136

Classical Reminiscences in Gilbert of Hoyland
    Lawrence C. Braceland, SJ   149

Table of Abbreviations   167

Preface

Through the essays in this volume, we glimpse the world of the early Cistercians, perceived both from without and from within the cloister. We discern part of the attraction the austere white monks had for powerful donors and champions and we hear them justifying their reform ideals to the dubious and the sympathetic. We see the threads which drew the Cistercians subtly into, and which held them to, the surrounding world and the gregorian church. We discover some of the sources--patristic and pagan--of their spirituality and witness its continuity into the third and fourth generations.

These papers were originally presented over several years at the Conference on Cistercian Studies, part of the annual International Medieval Studies Congress at Western Michigan University. Since the Cistercian sessions began in 1971, many familiar faces have returned, and many new scholars appeared, to share their research, their expertise, and their enthusiasm for Cistercian studies. The early fears of the organizers, that an annual conference would 'eat up' materials faster than scholars could research and write them, has proven happily unjustified. The exchange has instead stimulated new research and drawn scholars from many disciplines to explore areas of Cistercian studies.

We express our gratitude to all who participate in the annual Conference, and especially to the authors of these papers, who have in some cases waited patiently a very long time to see their work published.

E. R. E.

NOBLE PIETY AND REFORMED MONASTICISM:
THE DUKES OF BURGUNDY IN THE TWELFTH CENTURY

Constance B. Bouchard

In 1079, Hugh I, duke of Burgundy, resigned the duchy and retired to the abbey of Cluny, seeking the salvation of his soul.
The abbot of Cluny, his great-uncle, welcomed him and made him a
monk immediately, without making him go through any period of novitiate. When pope Gregory VII heard that Hugh had entered the monastery, he wrote the abbot a very sharp rebuke for encouraging this
act of piety, saying that when Hugh left his duchy, he had left
100,000 Christians without a protector.[1] In spite of the papal rep-
letter, however, the duke remained at Cluny, and his younger brother
Odo took over the governance of the duchy.

Although the pope might have been expected to rejoice that the
duke had entered the cloister rather than continue his grandfather's
wars, and that he had sought to save his soul by adopting the monastic life, Gregory instead considered that this powerful secular figure could better help the cause of Christianity by remaining a layman in the world than by living as a Cluniac monk. At a time when
a large number of laymen were entering the cloister in a search for
salvation, the pope believed that certain members of the nobility
should seek their salvation through their activities in the world.

Hugh's successors as dukes of Burgundy better illustrate the
type of christian activity that Gregory seemed to find appropriate
to a powerful member of the nobility. None of them entered the
cloister; they expressed their piety by going on pilgrimage or Crusade, defending the burgundian churches against their enemies, and
especially through their gifts to reformed monastic houses. These
dukes seem to have embraced a model of the powerful layman's christian duty similar to that advocated by the pope, a model which it
will be the purpose of this paper to explore. Rather than personally embracing a life of apostolic poverty and prayer, such persons
could more appropriately demonstrate their piety by using their
wealth and power to serve and protect those living the *vita apostolica*, with their own salvation to be won in turn through the grateful prayers of holy men and women.

The twelfth-century dukes maintained close ties with the important reformed houses of their duchy. Cluny and Cîteaux, the two
great centers of monastic reform, were located in Burgundy, about
fifty miles apart. The dukes established close ties with both of
these monasteries and with their daughter-houses as well. Princi-
pally, the ties were established through the variety of gifts they
made to the monks. Information on the dukes' relations with the
monasteries of Burgundy comes primarily from these monasteries'

cartularies, which record the donations of the dukes and other members of the nobility.[2] The large variety in the type of gifts made suggests that the dukes were acting from a broad principle of support for these monasteries, rather than a narrower belief that specific sorts of gifts should be made.

The most important type of gift which the dukes made was a donation of land, generally land abutting some that the monks already held. But land was by no means the only gift. At the end of the eleventh century, the dukes often gave to the local monasteries churches that had been in their control. For example, Hugh I gave Cluny the chapel of his castle at Avallon to be made into a Cluniac priory, shortly before retiring to Cluny.[3] Frequently a gift consisted of an annual income which was paid sometimes from the duke's tolls on nearby bridges or the market dues he collected, sometimes from the produce of his estates. Such an annual income was given most often in return for the monks' annual prayers for the duke's soul. Many examples could be given. To cite just one, in 1189 Hugh III gave the monks of Cluny an annual rent of ten pounds from his tolls at Dijon, in return for their prayers for his soul and those of his ancestors.[4] Another gift the dukes sometimes made was to free the monks of a particular house, or sometimes an entire order, from the requirement of paying certain tolls and taxes on ducal roads or in his markets. Before Hugh III left for the Holy Land, he freed the entire Cistercian Order from the obligation of paying such dues.[5] Another type of gift consisted of peasants; generally the dukes transferred to the monks their rights to collect the annual head tax and proceeds of justice from these peasants. For example, in 1197 Odo III granted the Cluniac priory at Avallon a number of peasants (called *homines*) with all their descendants.[6] One of the most important gifts that a powerful layman could make to a monastery, however, a gift that popes, monks, and the dukes themselves seemed to consider the duty of a powerful layman, was to offer a monastery protection against its enemies.

Pope Gregory VII, when reprimanding the abbot of Cluny for allowing Hugh I to become a monk, had said that a duke's christian d duty was to protect churches and the poor, by which he meant God's poor, the monks of local houses. This same attitude was expressed seventy-five years later by pope Eugenius III at a time when the counts of Nevers were attacking the cluniac abbey of Vézelay. Eugenius wrote to duke Odo II in 1150 that since 'divine dispensation' had made him great, it was his duty in return to 'defend all clerics from the attacks of the wicked.' He called Odo the only person on whom he could rely to protect the monks of Vézelay, even though at the time Eugenius wrote Odo was actively assisting the count in his attacks on the monks' herds.[7] Here the pope was quite explicit on the model of christian behavior he expected in the duke. In appealing to the duke's piety, he seems to have believed that the duke held the same model.

Other ecclesiastics also considered the dukes, by virtue of
their power in the world even if not their personal attributes,
the best guarantors of ecclesiastical rights and property. The
burgundian churches often asked the duke to witness gifts made
these churches by other laymen, as a guarantee that the original
donor or his heirs would not try later to recover the property.
For example, in 1197, when a certain knight of Beaune gave all his
possessions there to the cistercian house of Bussière, Odo III was
made *defensor* and *adjutor* of the gift.[8] Similarly, the dukes were
often asked to witness any mediated agreement which ended a quar-
rel between a church and a member of the local nobility. In one
instance, after the bishop of Langres had settled a prolonged quar-
rel between the lords of Montréal and the abbey of Cîteaux around
1175, he asked his nephew, duke Hugh III, to confirm this agreement
as a guarantee that it would be observed.[9]

Lest it appear from the eagerness of the burgundian churches
to make the dukes guarantors of their possessions that the dukes
were uniformly beneficient to the monasteries of their duchy, we
should note that contemporary documents also reveal that the dukes
sometimes made claims of their own on ecclesiastical possessions.
Odo II aided and abetted attacks on several other houses in addition to assisting the count of Nevers in his depredations on Vézelay, in spite of the pope's statement that he was the only hope for
the burgundian churches. Hugh III often prefaced charters in which
he made a donation to a monastery with the statement that he was making it for the good of his soul *and* in recompense for all the injur-
ies he had done to the monastery. When preparing to go to Jerusalem
in 1170/1, for example, he made gifts to the churches of St Bénigne
of Dijon and St Lazaire of Autun specifically to compensate for having earlier seized some of their property.[10] But for the most part,
the dukes appear to have fulfilled the expectations of the local
churches, and they supported the wellbeing of these churches. They
were themselves motivated by the same model of a nobleman's behavior toward churches that made the burgundian monasteries look to them
consistently for assistance. Indeed, Cîteaux found dukes Hugh II
and Odo II so generous that they included them with the abbots and
bishops of the order among the 'brothers' commemorated on a special
feast day of 11 January.[11]

The dukes were not the only members of their immediate families
to initiate gifts to burgundian monasteries. Their brothers, sisters,
and wives were major benefactors of many houses. They, like the dukes
themselves, became closely associated with houses of reformed monasticism without actually entering the cloister. During the twelfth
century, the dukes counted among their brothers four bishops of burgundian sees, two of Langres and two of Autun. These bishops appear
very frequently in the cartularies of Burgundian monasteries, helping

found them, **bestowing** gifts, and confirming the gifts of others.
The dukes' wives, especially when widowed, often went to a number
of different monasteries, making gifts at each to insure prayers
for their late husbands on the anniversary of their deaths. Odo
II's niece Mathilda, married in succession to the counts of Issou-
dun, Nevers, Flanders, and Dreux, and having children by the first
three, was especially generous during her long lifetime to the burgundian houses, where she established anniversaries for her parents,
her four husbands, and her children, several of whom pre-deceased
her. Odo II's brother, **Hugh** Rufus, was especially generous to Cîteaux and to the Cluniac house of St Bénigne of Dijon. Often when
these family members made a gift to a monastery, they specified
that they were confirming and adding to a gift previously made by
a parent or brother.[12] They were conscious of a continuity in the
family's relations with certain houses and intended to continue the
tradition.

Beyond their wives and blood relatives, the dukes were related
by **marriage** to many of the other chief benefactors of burgundian
monasteries, both houses that were special **beneficiaries** of the
dukes' generosity and some which the dukes themselves rarely patronized. Among the relatives of the dukes were the lords of Semur, who
were devoted to Cluny. Duke Hugh I's grandmother, Helias, came from
this family. Family members in the mid-eleventh century founded the
Cluniac priory of Marcigny, to which many of them retired. The family produced abbots for Cluny and the cluniac houses of Vézelay and
St Germain of Auxerre.[13] Another family generous to the burgundian
monasteries was the royal house of Spain and Portugal. Hugh I's
aunt Constance married Alfonso VI, king of Spain. Alfonso became
a major benefactor of Cluny shortly before marrying his burgundian
bride. His and Constance's descendants continued to send regular
shipments of bullion across the Pyrenees to Cluny for many years,
gifts which made up a major part of Cluny's income in the twelfth
century.[14] Hugh I's brother Henry married a daughter of this same
Alfonso VI by an earlier alliance, and became prince of Portugal;
his descendants on the throne of Portugal were nearly as generous
to Cluny as were their cousins on the throne of Spain. Before marrying Alfonso VI, Constance had been briefly married to count Hugh
of Chalon a member of the family into which Odo II's brother, Hugh
Rufus, later married. The counts of Chalon were responsible for the
foundation of La Ferté, the first daughter-house of Cîteaux. Within
a few years of its foundation, the monks of La Ferté had received so
many additional gifts from duke Hugh II that they felt obliged to
draw up a **pancarte** to summarize them all.[15] Hugh I's sister Beatrix
married the lord of Vignory, from a family which can most easily be
traced through the eleventh and twelfth centuries by the record of
their generosity to the Cluniac house of St Bénigne of Dijon.

Though the cluniac and cistercian orders were thus well served
by the dukes of Burgundy and their relatives by blood and marriage,

other monasteries not belonging to these two orders also established close ties with the dukes. Reynald, a brother of Hugh I, himself became abbot of Flavigny, a very old burgundian monastery which
was rarely patronized by the dukes.[16]

Feudal dependents as well as relatives of the dukes of Burgundy
are often found in the documents as principal benefactors of Burgundian monasteries, another instance of how the dukes could establish
ties with reformed monasteries of Burgundy even if they themselves
did not take the initiative in founding or endowing them. For example, the monastery of Cîteaux was founded in 1098 not by the dukes
but by their vassals, the viscounts of Beaune, who owned the valley
in which the New Monastery was located. Members of the family of the
dukes of Burgundy quickly appeared on the scene, however: the duke's
brother, bishop Robert of Langres, approved the establishment of the
New Monastery within his diocese, and the duke himself, Odo I, paid
the viscount of Beaune a large sum of money to give the monks of Cîteaux the remaining parts of the valley in which they had settled.[17]
The duke's generosity to Cîteaux seems inspired by the holiness of
the monks' life, not by any recognition that this was to become one
of the most important of the monasteries of Burgundy; the house remained small and poor until after Bernard's arrival there fourteen
years after its foundation. The fact that Odo paid the viscount to
give the monks the rest of the valley, rather than giving them some
land of his own, indicates that he made this gift with a careful
consideration of what would be in the monks' best interests, rather
than merely seeking self-aggrandizement by giving a gift larger than
that of his vassal. The lords of Vergy, again vassals of the dukes,
were also generous to Cîteaux in the early days of its foundation;
at the end of the twelfth century, duke Odo II married Alix of
Vergy, a descendant of these benefactors.

The dukes were thus related by blood or feudal tie to some of
the principal benefactors of the monasteries of Burgundy as well as
being benefactors themselves. This does not seem to have been a conscious family policy, because the families into which the dukes married were making gifts to local monasteries and producing abbots for
these houses at the time they became linked to the ducal family. The
case of the lords of Vergy, who were united by marriage to the dukes
of Burgundy only after a century of generosity to Cîteaux and enmity
to the dukes is only an extreme example. Rather than the dukes themselves being **responsible** for the patronage of the reformed burgundian houses by many members of the upper nobility, generosity to monasteries seems to have been a feature of most of the members of this
class.

The dukes stand out from the rest of the burgundian nobility,
however, by the fact that they extended their generosity to a number
of monasteries. Most other families would choose one house and make
gifts only to that house for generation after **generation**. Generally,

the house would be located very near their own center of power.
The dukes, wealthier and with authority extending over the entire
duchy, appear in the cartularies of numerous houses.

It is especially striking that the dukes were generous to both
Cluny and Cîteaux. They gave land, churches, and annual rents to
both of these centers of reformed monasticism. Other burgundian
noble families, if they made pious gifts to more than one monastery,
generally chose two cluniac or two cistercian houses, or perhaps one
from these orders and another associated with neither order. The
differences between Cluny and Cîteaux were widely understood at the
time--Cluny appeared very wealthy, and the monks spent most of their
day in liturgical observance, while Cîteaux had been founded in a
conscious attempt to follow strictly the benedictine Rule in poverty
and manual labor. These different interpretations did not appeal
equally to different patrons. The dukes of Burgundy, however, seem
not to have given up their long-standing support for the Cluniacs
with the advent of the Cistercians at the beginning of the twelfth
century. True, the dukes went through a period in the middle of the
twelfth century during which they **rarely** appear in Cluny's charters,
even though they were at this same time very generous to Cîteaux and
her daughter-houses, La Ferté and Clairvaux. But the dukes did not
consciously turn against the Cluniacs, for they continued their generosity to the Cluniac house of St Benigne of Dijon throughout the
century, and Hugh III again made numerous gifts to Cluny after an
hiatus during the reigns of Hugh II and Odo II. The gap in the mid-
twelfth century records of ducal gifts to Cluny may be due to the
rise of the Cistercian order--although the dukes were wealthy, there
were limits to the number of different houses they could patronize
at the same time, and their enthusiasm for the holiness of the Cistercians doubtless diverted funds that might otherwise have gone to Cluny
--but they continued to patronize the cluniac house located in Dijon,
their capitol, and began again to make gifts to Cluny herself in the
later twelfth century, when the distinctive poverty and manual labor
of the Cistercian order was becoming decreasingly evident.

Popes, like Gregory VII and Eugenius III, preferred that the
dukes stay active in the world rather than withdraw from it, and
most of the dukes seem to have agreed. Although Hugh I retired to
Cluny and his brother Reynald was abbot of Flavigny, no male members
of their family entered the cloister during the twelfth century.
Henry, Hugh II's brother, is sometimes said by modern authors to
have entered Cîteaux, but all the evidence in the primary documents
indicates that he lived a knightly life. Only one of the female members of the family is known to have become a nun at an early age:
Aremburg, one of the four daughters of Hugh II, who entered **Larrey**,
a house associated with St Bénigne of Dijon.[18] Other female members
of the family often retired to the cloister when widowed, most often
the house of Fontevrault, which became in the twelfth century a haven

for noble widows, but only after a long and active life.

Yet without becoming monks and nuns themselves, members of the family of the dukes of Burgundy were able to become associated with the spiritual benefits of the monastic life through their gifts to religious houses. They made gifts to a large number of houses, but most often to Cîteaux and Cluny, abbeys where the monks' strict adherence to the Rule made the sanctity of their life undoubted. They especially wished to become associated with the monks' prayers when they felt the nearness of death: when they themselves were dying, when a close friend or relative had just died, or when they were preparing to go to Jerusalem, a trip from which many Crusaders never returned. The largest number of different houses received donations at times of death, as when Hugh III established anniversaries at more than half a dozen burgundian churches in 1187 for the soul of his vassal and friend, Girard of Réon.[19] The fact that the dukes were often most generous when they felt death near is a strong indication that they made their gifts in hopes of a reward in the next world, rather than out of any hope for political gain in this one.

To go on Crusade was usually spoken of in the documents in the same terms as going on pilgrimage.[20] Odo I and Hugh III went to Jerusalem, Hugh II made a pilgrimage to Santiago de Compostella, and Odo III went on the Albigensian Crusade. That this method of seeking sanctity was closely linked to the practice of making gifts to burgundian monasteries is seen in the fact that dukes often spent months before their departures endowing monasteries. Before Odo I left for Jerusalem in 1101, he made a number of gifts to Molesme, the mother-house of Cîteaux, to Cluny, and to St Bénigne of Dijon.[21] The twelfth-century dukes, if they did not die overseas as did the two who went to Jerusalem, usually asked to be buried at Cîteaux, again to be close to the monks and their prayers.[22] With numerous burgundian houses available, the dukes made the greatest number of their gifts to Cluny and Cîteaux, houses where the sanctity of life guaranteed the effectiveness of the monks' prayers.

Popes and monks in the twelfth century considered that laymen, living in the world, could make a vital contribution to the church by supporting monastic houses. The duke, too, believed in the importance of the upper nobility's support for reformed monasticism. They acted on this belief and hoped in return for eternal salvation.

La Jolla, California

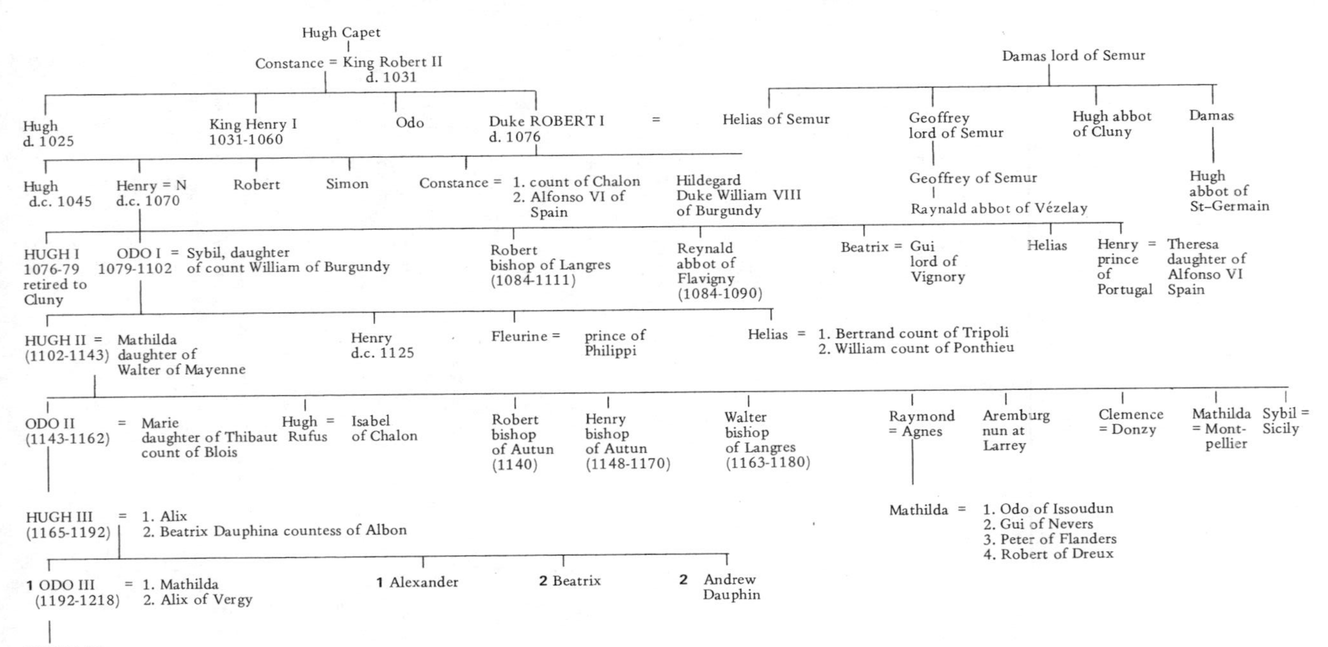

The dukes of Burgundy in the eleventh and twelfth century. Dukes' name in capitals.

NOTES

1. Erich Caspar, ed., *Das Register Gregors VII (MGH Epistolae Selectae*, Vol. 2[1]) pp. 423-24, no. vi, 17.
2. The charters in which the twelfth-century dukes figure may primarily be consulted in the editions of Ernest Petit, *Histoire des ducs de Bourgogne de la race capétienne*, Vols. 1-3 (Paris and Dijon, 1885-1889); J. Marilier, *Chartes et documents concernant l'abbaye de Cîteaux, 1098-1182* (Rome: Editiones Cistercienses, 1961); Auguste Bernard and Alexandre Bruel, *Recueil des chartes de l'abbaye de Cluny*, Vols. 4-5 (Paris, 1888-1894).
3. Maximilien Quantin, *Cartulaire général de l'Yonne*, Vol. 1 (Auxerre: Perriquet, 1854) pp. 192-95, no. 100.
4. Bernard and Bruel, eds., *Chartes de Cluny*, 5: 704-5, no. 4339.
5. Marilier, ed., *Chartes de Cîteaux*, pp. 155-56, no. 192.
6. Petit, ed., *Ducs de Bourgogne*, 3: 350, no. 953.
7. R. B. C. Huygens, ed., *Monumenta Vizeliacensia: Textes relatifs à l'histoire de l'abbaye de Vézelay* (Turnhout: Brepols, 1976) pp. 336-37, no. 39.
8. Petit, *Ducs de Bourgogne*, 3: 351-52, no. 955.
9. Marilier, *Chartes de Cîteaux*, pp. 170-71, no. 211.
10. Urbain Plancher, *Histoire générale et particuliere de Bourgogne*, Vol. 1 (Dijon, 1739) pp. lii-liv, nos. 82, 85.
11. Jacques Laurent and Pierre Gras, eds., *Obituaires de la province de Lyon*, Vol. 2 (Paris: Imprimerie Nationale, 1965) p. 612.
12. Bernard and Bruel, eds., *Chartes de Cluny*, 5: 718-19, no. 4358.
13. For this family, see Jean Richard, ed., *Le cartulaire de Marcigny-sur-Loire (1045-1144)* (Dijon: Société des Analecta Burgundica, 1957).
14. Georges Duby, 'Le budget de l'abbaye de Cluny entre 1080 et 1155,' *Hommes et structures du moyen âge* (Paris: Mouton, 1973) p. 67.
15. Georges Duby, ed., *Recueil des pancartes de l'abbaye de la Ferté-sur-Grosne* (Paris: Faculté de Lettres de l'Université de Paris, 1953) pp. 214-15.
16. *MGH SS*, 8: 285, 475, 503.
17. Marilier, ed., *Chartes de Cîteaux*, pp. 39-41, 50, nos. 15, 16, 23.
18. Petit, ed., *Ducs de Bourgogne*, 1: 480-81, no. 198.
19. Bernard and Bruel, eds., *Chartes de Cluny*, 5: 672-73, no. 4313. Petit, ed., *Ducs de Bourgogne*, 3: 270-76, 302, nos. 760-62, 765-66, 769, 772, 842. These churches included the monasteries of Cluny, Cîteaux, Maizières, Bussière, and Quincy, the cathedral of Chalon, the nunnery of Tart, and the priory Notre Dame of Beaune.
20. Petit, ed., *Ducs de Bourgogne*, 1: 416-17, no. 99.
21. *Ibid.*, pp. 418, 422-25, nos. 102, 108. Plancher, ed., *Histoire de Bourgogne*, 1: xxxiii-xxxiv, no. 46.
22. Marilier, ed., *Chartes de Cîteaux*, pp. 159-60, no. 198.

NOTES TOWARDS THE EXEGESIS OF A LETTER BY SAINT STEPHEN HARDING

Chrysogonus Waddell, OCSO

Letters by Saint Stephen Harding are not easily come by. The *registrum* of his official correspondence disappeared from Cîteaux so completely and at so early a date,[1] that not even a Manrique or a Henriquez--geniuses in the art of retrieving *deperdita*--were able to find so much as a few authentic fragments to incorporate into their mammoth collections of *cisterciana*. A few authentic texts by Saint Stephen can be classified, at least in loose terms, as 'letters': the *monitum* dated from Christmas Eve of 1109, and written for the celebrated Bible-manuscript which today so rightly goes by the name, the 'Stephen Harding Bible';[2] or the similar *monitum* which prefaced the early Milanese-Cistercian hymnal.[3] There are, however, two *bona fide* letters with Saint Stephen's name in the superscription, the one addressed to Louis the Fat, the other to Pope Honorius II. But the first of these is written in the name of Stephen, the assembly of Cistercian abbots, and the brethren of Cîteaux; while the second specifies as senders, along with Stephen, Hugh of Pontigny and a certain abbot of Clairvaux called Bernard. Since both letters have come down to us only through their inclusion in collections of Saint Bernard's letters,[4] the presumption seems to be that the first abbot of Clairvaux ghost-wrote them both. There is, however, one letter, a single letter, which is both a real letter and a letter indubitably written by Saint Stephen Harding himself.

It is a remarkable letter. The text has been printed on three different occasions, but in two different transcriptions. In an article of 1936, 'An Unpublished Letter of St. Stephen,' C. H. Talbot shared with readers of *Collectanea O.C.R.* his recent exciting discovery.[5] While working with the Rievaulx manuscripts at the Jesus College Library, Cambridge, he had come across, in a collection of *varia*, a copy of a letter by one *frater Stephanus cisterciensis ecclesiae servus* addressed to *T. venerabili abbati scireburniae.* He identified the text, 'written in a small neat hand,' and dating, it would seem, from the 'end of the XII century,'[6] as a letter from the third abbot of Cîteaux to Thurstan, abbot of the community at Sherborne in Dorset. Ancient as Sherborne was, the community had had no abbot of its own until 1122. Till that time the abbey had been united with the bishopric, so that the bishop of Sherborne (and, from 1075 onwards, the bishop of Old Sarum) had also been abbot of Sherborne. The dissociation of offices had taken place in 1122; and since the first abbot serving under the new arrangement was in office from 1122 till around 1142, and since his name was Thurstan, the two immediate emergents were these: 1) Stephen's letter must

have been written between 1122 and 1134, the date of his death;
2) the addressee was Abbot Thurstan.

Two further details enabled C. H. Talbot to suggest tentative-
ly an even more specific date:

1) Stephen refers to the existence of forty *turbae* or communities of Cistercians; if Stephen is precise in meaning forty rather
than 'about forty,' and if Janauschek is correct in his chronology
of Cistercian foundations, then Neuberg in Alsace is abbey Number
40,[7] and the date we are looking for is 1131. If Stephen is using
more-or-less numbers, however, then we should be a bit more vague,
and settle for something like 1129-1134.

2) Stephen mentions yet another helpful circumstance: he is
soon to go the way of all flesh; and this would suggest a date
closer to 1134 than to 1122. All in all, 1131, give or take a year
or two, is then the likely date. But why was the letter written?
'Under what circumstances the letter was written, it is not easy
to surmise,' writes Talbot; and he continues: 'The history of Sherborne is so fragmentary, that I have been unable to discover any
particular event with which it might be connected.'[8] He notes,
too, that the text of the letter 'adds nothing in particular to
our knowledge of the Saint or of the Order.'[9]

A quarter-century later the letter was printed in a quite different transcription with a title all but identical as that of the
earlier article by Talbot 'An Unpublished Letter of St Stephen Harding,' by D. L. Bethell. It appeared in the 1961 autumn issue of
Downside Review[10] with fewer helpful introductory notes and in a
less accurate transcription than was the case of the earlier *Collectanea* version. But at least this later publication brought the
letter to the attention of a new circle of readers.

In the same year, 1961, the Abbé Jean Marilier reproduced the
Talbot transcription in his own *Chartes et documents concernant
l'abbaye de Cîteaux 1098-1182*.[11] He summarized the text as a 'Letter of Abbot Stephen Harding to T[hurstan], abbot of Sherborne; he
reminds him that he himself had been a monk of Sherborne before
crossing the sea [to the tombs of the Apostles at Rome, and before
entering Molesme], and he exhorts the religious of his former monastery to virtue.'[12]

Thus far the printing-history of the letter. What has been
its impact on the scholarly world? Nil, so far as I can determine.
Writers interested in things Cistercian have, of course, referred
to the text in connection with Saint Stephen and early Cîteaux. But
there seems to be an understandable though tacit disappointment that
the text sheds so little specifically new light on the life and mission of Saint Stephen. Expunge our document from the dossier of
Stephen Harding source material, and it would make no real difference to what has been written about him in the last four decades.
It would seem that C. H. Talbot was right: the letter 'adds nothing

in particular to our knowledge of the Saint or of the Order. . . .'
The purpose of the brief notes which follow is chiefly to call
attention anew to a text which, bland and minuscule though it seems
to be, has much to tell us about the experience and inner life of
one of the most remarkable of all Cistercians. Convinced at last
that the best way of ensuring the serious exegesis of the text at
some future date by a scholar more competent than myself, would be
to provide a preliminary study, I offer the reader the following
notes. If I cannot honestly adopt as the **title** of this study, 'The
Exegesis of a Letter by St Stephen Harding,' I can at least settle
for 'Notes *towards* the Exegesis of a Letter by St Stephen Harding.'
The reader is forewarned of the provisional and sketchy nature of
these **notes**.
In his recension of D. L. Bethell's presentation of the letter,
Fr C[harles] D[umont] suggested that, though there were now two different transcriptions of the text in print, perhaps a third would
not be superfluous in view of the important divergences between the
two transcriptions.[13] We shall begin, then, with the third trans-
scrition. A phrase-by-phrase commentary will follow. By way of
summing up, the English version used in the commentary will be
pieced together and revised as a first draft of a translation.

I.   TRANSCRIPTION

The volume in which our unique text is found is a commonplace
book from Rievaulx, which includes among other things a catalogue
of the abbey library, the Cistercian *Consuetudines*, Saint Bernard's
Prologue to the reformed antiphonary and the treatise *Cantum quem*,
and even some notes on prosody. All this material is datable to
the twelfth and thirteenth centuries; and an analysis of the manu-
script--Ms 34 (Q.B. 17)--may be found in M. R. James, *A Descriptive
Catalogue of the Manuscripts in the Library of Jesus College, Cambridge* (Cambridge, 1895) pp. 43-56. The manuscript was given to
Jesus College Library by Thomas Man, Fellow of the College (B.A.
1674, M.A. 1678, M.Div. 1687) and later vicar of Northallerton,
where he collected a sizable collection of **mediaeval** manuscripts.
We do not know where the Rievaulx manuscript was between the disso-
lution of the monasteries and the time it came into Man's possession.[14]
The end of the twelfth century date proposed by C. H. Talbot
seems more likely than the mid-twelfth century dates suggested by D.
L. Bethell.[15] I am not sure, however, that I would describe the
hand, as Talbot does, as 'neat.' In spite of the preliminary tracing of lines in dry-point, the lines of the written text run crooked;
letters are unevenly spaced; and the general impression is that of
a competent but somewhat undisciplined scribe whose style was a bit
on the nervous side. He was however, very much an Englishman. No
expatriate monk from across the Channel would use the long-tailed *r*

and the kind of *s* that soars high above the line and curls deter-
minedly below (though the same scribe inconsistently uses a different form of *s* in a few instances). Though we are clearly moving
away from the romanesque, we are far from having arrived at the
gothic, and the letters are virtually unclubbed. The abundance of
abbreviations suggest that the scribe may have had experience in a
chancery, and this seems even more likely when we note in line 10
of the manuscript text the form of *de* with the *e* astraddle the as-
cender--a typical chancery trick. But honesty forces us to face
the fact that the other three instances of *de* are written in the
usual way.

If we are correct in accepting a date roughly towards the end
of the twelfth century, the inference is that we have before us not
a copy of the original, but a copy of a copy of the original. Otherwise, it would be difficult to envisage a late twelfth-century copy
being made directly on the original letter delivered to Sherborne
around 1131. We could, of course, imagine that a monk of Rievaulx
copied the text on the course of a visit to Sherborne; or that a
monk of Sherborne brought the original to Rievaulx for copying. But
this is far-fetched indeed. Far less imagination is needed to surmise that when the colony of Cistercian founders of Rievaulx **arrived**
in 1132,[16] they brought with them, in a packet of other letters meant
for distribution to various parts of England (including Waverley and
Tintern, neither very far from Sherborne) a letter addressed to the
abbot and community of Sherborne Abbey. Though written, to all ap-
pearances, in somewhat **vague** and general terms, the Sherborn letter
touched at least obliquely on the strained relations between monks
of the standard observance and Cistercian radicals. It was just as
well, then, that a copy of the letter be kept at Rievaulx for future
reference. I suggest, then, that our scribe filled up part of a
blank folio of his manuscript, using as his model a copy of the letter made decades earlier, and probably removed from the abbot's *registrum* as no longer serving any useful purpose. Still, a letter by
so holy an old-timer as one of the founders of Cîteaux was interesting if only as a curio. Why not use it, then, to fill up an empty
space of some stray folio?

Since norms vary so much from editor to editor, I shall follow
my own preferences in my own transcription. I shall extend abbreviations and suspensions, and I shall use modern punctuation. But
I prefer to follow the scribe for matters of spelling and capitali-
zation (in most instances, non-capitalization). One further con-
cession to current *praxis:* I shall adopt the standard letter-format,
and even type in caps the initial word of the body of the text. Since
a photocopy of the text transcribed has been provided, the reader can
easily control the **transcription** except in one instance towards the
last part of the text, where the ink from the reverse side has worked
its way through so as to render at least one word conjectural.

CAMBRIDGE, **Jesus** College Library, Ms 34 (Q.B. 17), f. 108v, from
Rievaulx, late 12th century.

     T. uenerabili abbati scireburnie et Congregationi sibi a deo
commisse, frater Stephanus, cistertiensis Ecclesie seruus: christum
3   cum dilectione timere, et cum timore diligere.

     EPISTOLARE offitium est alloqui absentes quasi presentes, et
coniungere per caritatis contubernium quos interualla locorum ab
6   inuicem decludunt. Vnde quia os nostrum et caro nostra estis, commoneo uos ut me pauca scribentem patienter sufferatis.*a* Ego monachus
uester fui, et in baculo meo mare transiui, ut in me omnium uestrum
9   minimo, nullius momenti apud uos, dominus diuitias misericordie sue
demonstraret, et uos ad emulandum me prouocaret. Vas enim uacuum velut
uiuus fons, sicut uoluit, impleuit, ut uos qui meliores sanctissima
12   parentela eratis, religionem fortiter tenere, et de domino presumere
auderetis. Nunc enim qui solus de terra mea et pauper egressus sum,
diues et cum quadraginta turbis uiam universe carnis letus ingredior,
15   securus expectans denarium operariis fideliter in uinea laborantibus*b*
repromissum. Vnde uestram cohortor dilectionem, ut bonam famam que
de uobis ad nos usque manauit profectui uirtutum applicare satagatis;
18   ut de bono in melius proficientes, et uere religioni firmiter inheren-
tes, castitatem, humilitatem (?), studiis parsimonie cum caritate inseruientes corde et corpore usque ad mortem tenere non desistatis, ut
21   deum deorum uidere mereamini. Amen.

---

a sufferatis *1st hand correction, above line, of* erudiatis *b* laborantibus *1st hand correction (with expunction-dot) of* larborantibus

II. COMMENTARY

1. T. uenerabili abbati scireburnie: 'T.' for *T[hurstino]* or
T[hurstano] or some other form of the name of **Thurstan**, first abbot
of Sherborne Abbey in Dorset. **Sherborne's** importance as a monastic
and ecclesiastical establishment antedated Thurstan by many centuries. When the west Saxon see of Dorchester was divided around 705,
Sherborne was made the seat of a bishopric comprised of the counties
of Wilts, Dorset, Berks, Somerset, Devon, and Cornwall. Later **terri-**
torial divisions eventually left Sherborne with no more than the
county of Dorset. Secular canons staffed the cathedral church until 998, when King Ethelred gave **Bishop** Wulsin a charter authorizing
the replacement of the canons by a community of monks living *secun-*
dum institutionem sancti patris Benedicti,[17] and designating the
bishop as *abbas et pater* of the monastic community. As in the case
of other monastic cathedrals the acting head of the community was
the prior. In 1076 the see of Sherborne was translated to Old Sarum or Salisbury, in alleged conformity with the ordinance of the
Council of London of the preceding year, which decreed that bishops'
sees be removed from 'obscure places' to towns of the greatest note
in their dioceses.[18] It is true that William of Malmesbury expressed astonishment that Sherborne, being so tiny a place--*viculus*, he
calls it--could have perdured for so many centuries as seat of a
bishopric,[19] but he also describes Old Sarum as more of a castle
than a town.[20] At any rate, after 1076, the office of prior continued at Sherborne until sometime around 1122, when Roger of Caen,
Bishop of Salisbury, separated the office of bishop from the office
of abbot. Sherborne was erected into an independent abbey, and
Thurstan (around 1122 to around 1142) was blessed as its **first** abbot.[21] There can be no reasonable doubt as to the identification
of 'T., Abbot of Sherborne.'

1-2. et Congregationi sibi a deo commisse: 'and to the Congregation entrusted to his care by God.' This is specifically Holy
Rule language. Pick up any concordance of the Holy Rule, and look
at the entries under *congregatio*. Clearly, this is one of Saint
Benedict's terms of predilection for his community, the 'flock'
(grex) that has been brought together *(con-)*. More precise Rule-
resonance results, however, from the juxtaposition of *Congregegatio*
sibi and *commissa*. Only a reader unfamiliar with the Holy Rule will
fail to catch an echo of Saint Benedict's *non solum detrimenta GRE-*
GIS SIBI COMMISSI non patiatur (c. 2,32)   Abbas non conturbet
GREGEM SIBI COMMISSUM (c. 63, 2). With the very opening words,
then, Saint Stephen strikes a 'benedictine' note that will be sustained throughout the course of the entire letter.

We note, too, that this is a community letter addressed, not
to Abbot Thurstan only, but to Abbot Thurstan together with his
community.

2. *frater Stephanus, cistertiensis Ecclesie servus:*   'Brother
Stephen, servant of the church at Cîteaux.'   No room here even to
touch on the twelfth-century understanding of the monastery as a
local church, as the Church present in and through a given monastic
community!   It was standard usage for the Fathers, however, to refer, not to the monastery of Clairvaux or the abbey of Cîteaux, but
to the *church* at Clairvaux (or of Clairvaux), to the *church* at Cîteaux.   And the role of 'Brother Stephen,' relative to the church
at Cîteaux, is the role of servant, *servus*.   Elsewhere, in his *monitum* to the early Cistercian hymnal, he refers to himself as the
minister of the New Monastery, *Frater Stephanus Novi Monasterii
MINISTER.*[22]   At the time of writing, Saint Stephen is still in office, otherwise he would hardly style himself *servus*.   Since he renounced his abbatial office in 1132, this gives us a convenient *ter-
minus ante quem* for dating the letter.[23]

2-3. *Christum cum dilectione timere, et cum timore diligere:*
'Fear Christ, but with love; and love him, but with fear.'   Possibly
timere would be better rendered by 'reverence'; but the terms as
combined in this greeting are clearly meant to express something of
a paradox, and the intent of the author is probably better served
if we use 'love' and 'fear'--terms at first blush irreconciliable
with each other.   For a moment we have the impression that the phrase
must have been excerpted from the Holy Rule, and we think straight-
way of chapter 72.   But though all the terms are present, they are
present in different combinations.   We are dealing with a traditional *topos*: the dialectic between love and fear that provides the dynamism of the monk's ascent of the degrees of humility in chapter 7
of the Rule.   But rather than situate this salutation in the
context of the Rule as exegeted with the help of Cassian's three
kinds of 'fear' or Saint Augustine's 'chaste love,' we shall here
simply note that Saint Stephen introduces into his greeting-formula
a theme important for our understanding of the final lines of his
letter.   We might note in passing, too, that the object of our love-
fear, fear-love, is not simply 'God', but specifically Christ.

4-6. *Epistolare offitium est alloqui absentes quasi presentes,
et coniungere per caritatis contubernium quos interualla locorum ab
inuicem secludunt.*   'The function of a letter is to address those
absent as though they were present, and to bring together through
a union of charity those separated by long distances.'   The opening
formula is a splendid one, and has a Ciceronian air.   I suspect that
if I knew more than I do about the classical epistolary literary
genre, I would be able to point to a half-dozen variations on this
particular introductory formula. I am more interested, however, in the
content of the **phrase**.   If you find the translation too toned down
from the Latin original, you are probably right.   The vocabulary is

a bit 'intense'; but it is an insoluble **problem**, when working with
mediaeval texts, to judge just how 'used up' an originally colorful
word has become after centuries of general usage. *Coniungere* can
be strong: to join, to unite in a nuptial bond; and *contubernium*
originally meant a **tent**-fellowship. At its strongest, then, the
phrase means that a letter ought to bring together in close communion, and under the roof of charity, people separated from one another by geographical distance. *Contubernium* can also mean 'kinship',
people living together as one family in the same tent. From Cîteaux
to Sherborne, then, is quite a distance; but Saint Stephen meant
this letter to bring sender and receivers together in the family-
bond of a love unhindered by limitations imposed by geography. The
theme seems to have been a constant with **Saint** Stephen. In his own
words, the **purpose** of the *Carta caritatis* was to provide the bond
of charity by means of which monks 'scattered in body throughout
abbeys in diverse parts of the world, should be indissolubly joined
together in spirit,' *monachi . . . per abbatias in diversis mundi
partibus corporibus divisi animis indissolubiter conglutinarentur.*24
This is even more 'intense' diction than in the letter to Abbot Thurstan and brethren (especially since 'joined together' stands
for 'glued together,' 'cemented together'); but the greater intens-
ity is here justified by the closer communion among brethren of the
same family within the *ordo monasticus* at large.

    6. Vnde quia os nostrum et caro nostra estis: 'And so, because
you are our bone and our flesh . . .' The biblical point of reference is not the 'bone of my bone and flesh of my flesh' *(os ex ossi-
bus meis, et caro de carne mea)* of Genesis 2:23, but rather **Laban's**
joyful recognition of his nephew, 'Who, when he heard that Jacob
his sister's son was come, ran forth to meet him; and embracing him,
and heartily kissing him, brought him into his house. And when he
had heard the causes of his journey, he answered: Thou art my bone
and my flesh': *Os meum es et caro mea* (Gen 29: 13-14). Since the
Jacob-story is to supply a yet more explicit point of reference
just a few words later in the letter, we can be **fairly** certain that
the 'our bone and our flesh' comes from this recognition-scene where
Laban and the **pilgrim** Jacob celebrate the family kinship.

    6-7. commoneo uos ut me pauca scribentem patienter sufferatis:
'I admonish you to bear patiently with me as I write these few words.'
This line has a 'feel' of biblical diction, and even without a preliminary glance at a concordance we can turn to 2 Corinthians 11:19
on the strength of *sufferatis* (which the scribe first wrote as *erudiatis).* We remember that the pauline text about suffering fools
gladly introduces his extraordinary account of his apostolic ministry; and here, in our own letter, this sentence introduces Stephen's
own summary of his *curriculum vitae*. Contextually, the phrases are

concordant. But when we look at the actual Latin text, points of
verbal resemblance--the choice of words and the word order--are
practically nil: *Libenter enim suffertis insipientes.* . .Perhaps
it is the earlier verse one of the same chapter that we are re-
minded of, 'Would to God you could bear with some little of my folly; but do bear with me.' Unfortunately, the Vulgate text fails
to bear us out: *Utinam sustineretis modicum quid insipientiae meae,
sed et supportate me.* Instead of 'I admonish *(commoneo)*, we find
'Would to God' *(utinam)*; instead of 'some little of my folly' *(modicum quid insipientiae meae)*, '[bear patiently with] me as I write
these few words [or things].' As for the *sufferatis,* this appears
(in a different grammatical form) in verse nineteen, but with *libenter* for its adverbial modifier, rather than *patienter*. There
is, however, another possible pauline point of reference. In Acts
26, Paul gives King Agrippa an account of his life, conversion, and
calling. He begins by saying how happy he is to be able to address
his defense to someone who knows 'both customs and questions that
are among the Jews.' He then summarizes his life-work and experience, introducing all this with the remark: 'Wherefore I beseech
thee to hear me patiently' (Acts 26:2), *Propter quod obsecro, patienter me audias.* The context is *ad rem:* Paul is about to make
his *apologia* before one who knows both customs and questions that
are among the Jews; Stephen is about to make a similar *apologia*
addressed to a community well aware of the customs and questions
that are among monks.

Whether he is writing in 1131 or a bit earlier, it is a time
when tempers of monastics are flaring high, and controversy over
customs and questions that are among monks is the order of the
day.[25] Relations between communities of *status quo*-minded Benedictines and communities of Cistercian radicals are not always remarkable for their cordiality. The wide circulation of the Abbot
of Clairvaux's *Apologia* has added fuel to the flame; and in some
quarters, the conflagration has reached the proportions of a forest fire out of control. To make matters worse, it is precisely
at this period that the English invasion of the White Monks begins.
First comes Waverley, in Surrey, and the diocese of Winchester, in
1128. Waverley had been founded in 1120 as a Benedictine house;
but in 1128 it turned Cistercian and entered the filiation of Cîteaux, with l'Aumône as its mother-house. Tintern comes next, in
1131. Located in Monmouthshire on the banks of the Wye, it too is
a foundation of l'Aumône, and therefore has the abbot of Cîteaux
--a certain Stephen Harding, formerly of Devonshire--as head of its
filiation. If we look at a map of monastic southern England, we
shall find Sherborne roughly equidistant from Waverley on the right
and Tintern on the left; and though these are not precisely next
door neighbors of Sherborne, they are uncomfortably close. I,
myself, am quite sure that, had I been a monk of Sherborne Abbey

at the time, I would not have viewed these incursions of a foreign
monastic body into my own monastic neighborhood without real concern. My emotional response would have been further heightened by
my realization that this enormously successful new observance that
was about to turn England into Cistercian territory had had among
its founders, and now had as its leader, a monk who had abandoned
my own community in circumstances which were not particularly edifying. Stephen had been a monk of Sherborne, and he is explicit
about it:

> *7-8 Ego monachus uester fui:* 'I was your own monk.' Stephen's
youthful departure from Sherborne has always been a source of embar-
rassment for his biographers. The only account of it came from the
pen of William of Malmesbury, who can hardly be accused of anti-
cistercian or anti-Stephen prejudice. Quite the contrary, William
has nothing but praise for his compatriot monastic reformer. Yet
it is the sympathetic William who candidly tells us that the first
stage of Stephen's monastic odyssey terminated with his apostasy
from Sherborne.

> He had been a monk from childhood; but when then the
> pruriency of the world began casting its allurements
> on the youngster, he came to loathe those [monkish]
> weeds, and so struck out first for Scotland, then for
> France . . .26

In his wonderfully informative article, 'Saint Etienne Harding
mieux connu,'27 Fr Jean-Baptiste Van Damme, developping ideas proposed by Charles Oursel in a conference given in 1962,28 situates
Stephen's departure from Sherborne in a rather different context.
The Hardings were an important family in the area. Stephen's uncle
or grandfather, Elnod, had been steward to King Harold. But after
the Battle of Hastings, Elnod played the turn-coat and rose high in
the service of the Norman invader, William the Conqueror. In 1069
we find him suppressing rebellions in Dorset, Somerset, and Devon.
Elnod the Quisling was so hated in this region that--so the hypothesis goes--the entire Harding family became *personae non gratae*
in Devonshire. Because of the political turmoil, then, the young
Harding boy, who had been an **oblate** at Sherborne from an early age,
was constrained to cross the Channel by way of Scotland, the preferred route of English expatriates at this troubled period of history. The **hypothesis** is fascinating. If I personally hesitate in
accepting it, I do so because Stephen, upon leaving Sherborne for
family and political reasons, did not head for another monastic
community, but spent a number of years getting his education in a
non-monastic milieu on the **Continent**. Whether Stephen was still
an oblate when he left Sherborne, or whether he was a professed

monk, he was enough a member of the community to be able to write
in his old age, *Ego monachus vester fui*, 'I was your own monk.'
And again, whether he left Sherborne simply because the call of
the world was too strong to be gainsaid, or because his presence
had become a problem for himself and for the community by reason
of his politically compromised family, his departure from Sherborne was surely not attended by happy memories. We are, of course,
in the realm of pure hypothesis the moment we **disclaim** the probative
value of William of Malmesbury's account of Stephen's inglorious departure. If I am going to hypothesize, I think I should try to do
so in a way that would take account of both William's rapportage and
the recently proposed exile-with-honor interpretation. Since I have
known more than one monk who has left his community because of as-
pirations to a higher form of spiritual life, but who has somehow
failed ‹to reach his destination because of involvements along the
way, I would have no problem in envisaging the situation in this
way: A youngster in his mid-teens, raised from childhood in the
monastery, and now a bit restless, like any normal adolescent, is
constrained to leave his community because of difficulties occasioned by family connections. Since the problem would be the same
for Stephen in almost any English monastery after 1066, he must per-
force find his new monastic home on the Continent. He proceeds thi-
ther by the preferred escape route, Scotland. But before eventually finding a new monastic home, he cannot resist the opportunity of
seeing a bit more of life **outside** the cloister. In point of fact,
we find him in something of a university milieu. William states
specifically that he spent some years at his studies in France, and
that he finally went on pilgrimage to Rome in the company of a fellow student, who was a cleric.[29] The *Vita Sancti Petri, Prioris
Iuliacensis Puellarum Monasterii, et Monachi Molismensis*,[30] is devoted to this fellow student, himself another Englishman by the name
of Peter. It has them strike up a close **friendship** in Burgundy,
where Stephen, still a young man--but a young man of the utmost
moral probity *(continentissimae vitae)*--, is at his studies.[31] It
would seem that Stephen, upon leaving England, had betaken himself
to a region where the current Anglo-Norman fray posed less immediate personal **danger** for him. Quite possibly, then, the 'allure-
ments of the world' to which our Stephen succumbed temporarily were
less the brawling pleasures of the tavern than the heady joys of
dialectics. I shall **return** to this discussion later. Here it suf-
fices to insist that he thought of himself as having once been a
monk of Sherborne, and that he expected his former brethren to recognize the fact that, Yes, he had once been a monk of theirs; and
that between Sherborne and Molesme he had tarried an unconscionably
long time on the way, seizing the occasion to further his mastery
of the liberal arts.

8. et in baculo meo mare transivi: 'And with my staff I passed over the sea.' This is only a slight adaptation of Genesis 32:10b: *In baculo meo transivi Iordanem istum.* What makes this brief phrase exciting is the context to which it refers us. Once again we have a text from the Jacob-story. It immediately precedes the episode of Jacob's night-long wrestling with a mysterious 'man', and is part of the prayer Jacob addresses to God in his anguish over his coming encounter with his alienated brother, Essau. He had left his home and his indignant brother under the most painful circumstances; he had sojourned and prospered mightily in a distant land, and now he was returning in the company of his wives and children. 'Deliver me from the hand of my brother Essau,' prays Jacob, 'for I am greatly afraid of him: lest perhaps he come, and kill the mother with the children' (Genesis 32:11). Is Saint Stephen suggesting by his use of this biblical text that just as Jacob, a *persona non grata,* had once crossed the Jordan on his way to foreign parts, so also he, Stephen, had once **crossed** the sea on his way to foreign parts, a *persona non grata?* That he was now returning, so to speak, in the company of his family acquired across the sea (Tintern and Waverley, with foundation-plans for Rievaulx already laid)? And that he wanted to be sure that his brethren of former times would not be hostile to the family begotten by the former exile?

8-10. ut in me omnium uestrum minimo, nullius momenti apud uos, dominus diuitias misericordie sue demonstraret, et uos ad emulandum me prouocaret: '. . . so that in me, the least of all of you, and of no importance whatever when I was with you, the Lord might show forth the riches of his mercy, and **provoke** you to emulation of me.' The several pauline allusions discernible here are not accidentally juxtaposed; they are brought together in a contextual unity which has to be meditated upon to be appreciated. *In me omnium vestrum minimo,* 'in me, the least of all of you,' has two possible points of reference. In Ephesians 3:8, Paul expresses his wonderment that, 'To me, the least of all the saints *(mihi omnium Sanctorum minimo),* is given this grace, to preach among the Gentiles the unsearchable riches of Christ.' The immediate context is the justification of Paul's very special apostolate. He is not a maverick apostle; he is not the leader of a **splinter** group; he has a special mission to bring into the Church a whole category of Gentiles deemed by some as ineligible for salvation. 1 Corinthians 15:9 provides us with a similar context: *Ego enim sum minimus apostolorum,* 'For I am the least of the apostles . . . .' The risen Lord had appeared to Cephas, then to the Eleven . . . and last of all to Paul, as to one born out of due time, unworthy, by reason of his persecution of the Church, to be called an apostle. For all that, it was Paul who labored more abundantly than all the others; and it was Paul who was the privileged herald of the Gospel for the Gentile world.

Ut . . . Dominus divitias misericordiae suae demonstraret: 'so that . . . the Lord might show forth the riches of his mercy.' Here there is no doubt about the *locus biblicus*, Romans 9:23 *ut ostenderet divitias gloriae.* We may as well discuss at the same time the next phrase, *et vos ad aemulandum me provocaret*, which is a re-working of Romans 11:14, *si quomodo ad aemulandum provocem carnem meam*, 'if, by any means, I may provoke to emulation them who are my flesh.' Paul's discussion begins, at the start of chapter nine, with his love and concern for the Jews; but he shows that God's election is free and not confined to one nation only. For even the Gentiles are to receive God's mercy and show forth the riches of his glory. It is not without significance, perhaps, that where Saint Paul speaks of 'riches of his *glory*, Saint Stephen, paraphrasing freely, speaks of 'riches of his *mercy.*' ('What do you seek? a novice is asked, and he replies, the mercy of God and of the Order . . . .') At any rate, against the Romans context, the thought of the former monk of Sherborne becomes unmistakably clear. If Stephen, for reasons still not entirely known, had dissociated himself from the community at Sherborne and from their impressive tradition, it was to the end that a new monastic family might enter into the fulness of the great tradition. That God would choose so unlikely an agent as Stephen, and that his election would be operative outside the mainstream of the standard observance exemplified at Sherborne and elsewhere—all this is yet another instance of how God reveals the riches of his mercy in the most unexpected ways. Further, the **rise** of a new and **prodigiously** successful reform was not without positive meaning for the community at Sherborne. For just as the fulfillment of God's promises in the midst of the gentile world was meant to make Israel emulous, and so lead to the consummation of God's plan of salvation for Jew **and** Gentile alike, so also the astonishing vitality and spread of the Cistercian communities was meant, not just for Cîteaux, **but** for other communities of traditional observance; for these were now being encouraged, by the way God was working with the White Monks, to live to the full their own monastic ideals.

It would be nonsensical to press the analogy too far. All Saint Stephen does is to weave together with utter freedom, but with consummate artistry, pauline fragments helpful for our grasping of the real meaning of the **phenomenon** of Cîteaux for the *ordo monasticus* at large; and helpful, too, for insuring positive rapports between the community of Sherborne and their Cistercian neighbors.

9-10. Vas enim uacuum uiuus fons, sicut uoluit, impleuit.

'For, living fountain that he is, he filled the empty vessel: for
so he willed.' The vessel-theme might make us think that we are
still with Saint Paul in chapter nine of Romans, in the passage
about vessels of wrath, vessels of mercy, and about the utter gra-
tuitousness of God's election. But the point of reference is much
more interesting in that the passage is one unlikely to come spontaneously to mind. We turn to Jeremiah 14:2, where the word of the
Lord comes to Jeremiah concerning the words of the drought, and:

> The great ones sent their inferiors to the water: they
> come to draw, they found no water, they carried back
> their vessels empty . . . .

The Bible abounds in references to vessels; but this is the only
one, so far as I know, where *vasa* is juxtaposed to *vacua: Maiores
miserunt minores suos ad aquam: venerunt ad hauriendum, non in-
venerunt aquam, reportaverunt VASA sua VACUA*. If the *maiores -
minores* has a familiar ring, it may be because of Saint Stephen's
reference to himself in the preceding line: *omnium vestrum MINIMO,
nullius momenti apud vos* . . . . Stephen is the *minor*, indeed,
the *minimus*, sent by the 'great ones,' the community of Sherborne,
to draw water for a Judea plunged in mourning, for a Jerusalem whose
cry is gone up. According to the Prophet, the 'inferior' finds no
water and has to carry back his vessel empty; 'and for the destruc-
tion of the land, because there came no rain upon the earth, the
husbandmen were confounded, they covered their heads.' In the case
of Stephen, all this has been reversed. The 'inferior,' the least
of all, has been sent by his betters to look for water; and amid
the reeds and marshland of Cîteaux, God has not only filled his
empty vessels, but filled them with himself, the living Water. The
'words of the drought' have been reversed; those who are the least
of all are carrying back, not empty vessels, but vessels filled with
living waters. Stephen must have pondered long and hard over Saint
Jerome's exegesis of these words of drought. That he was familiar
with the commentary *In Hieremiam Prophetam* is quite certain; for it
was at his request during his visit to Flanders in 1124 that Osbert,
the scribe of Saint-Vaast d'Arras, wrote a copy of the *expositio*,
including a note about the visit and the request on folio 103 verso
of the manuscript.[32] As Saint Jerome sees it, it was 'the *maiores*
who ought to have gone to draw the water; but they send the *iuniores*,
who lack the grey hairs of wisdom. So they come to the wells, but
find no water such as, Scripture tell us, the patriarchs once found.
So the *iuniores* carry their vessels back empty: not because there
was no water, but because they could not find it.'[33] But if God
filled the empty vessel that was Stephen, it was because of no wisdom on Stephen's part, but simply because this is what God so willed:
sicut voluit. The verb *velle* occurs in Scripture hundreds of times;

but only twice, I think, in close connection with a *sicut*.   'And
that which thou sowest, thou sowest not the body that shall be,'
we read in 1 Corinthians 15:37; 'but bare grain, as of wheat, or
of some of the rest. But God giveth it a body as he will'--*sicut
vult*. There is, then, no proportion between Stephen's poverty and
the living waters that have sprung up through him. But here the
tense of the verb is 'wrong,' and the context not quite natural.
If we turn back a page to chapter twelve, verse 18, however, we
find a *sicut voluit* in a context that rings true. Saint Paul is
discoursing on the diversity of spiritual gifts and on the duty of
the members of the mystical body mutually to cherish one another.
'But now God hath set the members every one of them in the body *as
it hath pleased him*'--*sicut voluit*. So there are diversities of
graces, but the same Spirit; and there are diversities of minis-
tries, but the same Lord; and if God's choice has fallen on Stephen
for a special grace, for a special ministry in the body of Christ,
it is simply because this is 'as it hath pleased him'--*sicut voluit*.

   *11-13. ut uos qui meliores sanctissima parentela eratis, reli-
gionem fortiter tenere, et de domino presumere auderetis:* ' . . .
so that you, who were so much better by reason of the holiness of
your family-line, would have the courage to hold fast and strong
to monastic observance, and to presume on the Lord.' Sherborne had,
indeed, as aristocratic a blood-line in holiness as could be found
in any abbey of the realm: Saint Aldhelm, founder of the place, and
the first Englishman who wrote in Latin (or so they say--and a fright-
fully convoluted Latin it was); Saint Wulsin, 'loved by Saint Duns-
tan like a son with pure affection,' and one of the champions of the
monastic restoration in late tenth-century England; Saint Alfwold,
who had died as late as 1058, and whose abstemiousness and devotion
to Saint Cuthbert were legendary. Sherborne, then, had a family
history stretching back for centuries; Cîteaux's genealogy went back
as far as yesterday. And yet, says Stephen, without the slightest
trace of pride, the House of Sherborne can take courage from what
God has wrought with the peasants of Cîteaux, to hold fast to monastic literature), and to dare to presume on the Lord. *De Domino praesumere*. This is a bold aphorism, but a biblical one. It comes from
a book little quoted by monastic authors, the book of Judith (6:15).
The context is remarkable. Achior, captain of all the children of
Ammon, earns the wrath of Holofernes for stating that, 'If there be
no offence of this people [the children of Israel] in the sight of
their God, we cannot resist them, because their God will defend
them: and we shall be a reproach to the whole earth' (5:25). En-
raged, Holofernes sends Achior to Bethulia, there to be slain with
the Israelites. Achior tells them the tale of their imminent des-
truction, and all the people fall upon their faces, adoring the
Lord, and all of them together, mourning and weeping, pour out

their prayers with one accord to the Lord, saying: 'O Lord God of heaven and earth, behold their pride, and look on our low condition, and have regard to the face of thy saints, and shew that thou forsakest not *them that presume on thee*, and that thou humblest them that presume of themselves, and glory in their own strength . . .' (6:15). I must, however, confess that I have touched up the Douai version I love so much. The Vulgate text reads, at the critical point, *non derelinquis PRAESUMENTES DE TE, et praesumentes de se et de sua virtute gloriantes humilias.* The word 'presuming' is used twice: God does not abandon those who presume on him, but he humbles those who presume on themselves. The cautious translator lacked the hardihood to use so strong an expression as 'presuming on God,' so he toned it down: 'thou forsakest not them that *trust* on thee.' I should add, however, that Saint Stephen's *de Domino praesumere* was familiar to him chiefly through liturgical usage. The text formed part of the verse to the responsory, *Adonai, Domine Deus magne et mirabilis*, chanted in autumn at the Night Office during the period when the books of Tobit, Judith, and Esther were featured in the liturgical readings.[34] Objection: This particular responsory is conspicuous by its absence in the early 'Stephen Harding Breviary' edited by Dom Kassian Lauterer, O.Cist. (but not yet commercially available). Reply: This responsory may not have entered the Cistercian books, but Saint Stephen had been singing it for at least twenty years at Molesme before the foundation of the New Monastery in 1098. In the only extant manuscript of a Molesme breviary (Troyes, Bibliotheque municipale, ms 807, from the mid-twelfth century) you will find it on folio 74 verso.

13. Nunc enim qui solus de terra mea et pauper egressus sum: 'For now I, who was all alone when I went forth from my country, and poor . . . .' We easily catch the allusion to the Lord's command to Abram: 'Go forth out of thy country, and from thy kindred, and out of thy father's house, and come into the land which I shall shew thee,' *Egredere de terra tua* . . . (Gen 12:1).

14. dives et cum quadraginta turbis viam uniuerse carnis letus ingredior: 'am entering upon the way of all flesh, happy, rich, and with forty bands . . . .' Biblical and liturgical allusions accumulate and are inextricably interwoven here. Actually, the word *pauper* has to be included here from the preceding phrase to which it is grammatically attached. Starting with *pauper*, then, and combining with it *dives* and *laetus ingredior*, we have the key-words of a text which occurs several times in the Cistercian Mass and Office for St Martin of Tours (November 11): *Martinus Abrahae sinu laetus excipitur; Martinus hic pauper et modicus caelum dives ingreditur, hymnis caelestibus honoratur*, 'Happy, Martin is received into Abraham's bosom. Martin, who here was poor and lowly, enters heaven rich, and is honored with heavenly **hymns**.' The text occurs in this form as the antiphon for None and also as the body of the eleventh Night Office responsory. A truncated form of the text serves for the Mass Alleluia; but since the omitted words include *laetus*, which figures in Saint Stephen's phrase, I take it that the Saint's point of reference was either the antiphon or the responsory. The text itself ultimately derives from Sulpicius Severus' *Epistola 3 ad Bassulam*.[35] And what a wonderfully Cistercian note this reference to St Martin gives! In his characteristically perceptive article on 'Saint Martin dans l'hagiographie monastique du moyen âge,'[36] Fr Jean Leclercq gives a survey of the pertinent texts in chronological arrangement, showing that even in monastic circles St Martin was presented in the first **instance** as worker of mighty miracles—until the advent of the Cistercians. For them, St Martin is above all the *pauper et modicus* monk-bishop, who personifies, as a good monk should, all the beatitudes. In its own way, this single **fragment** from Saint Stephen's letter is as eloquent as the Saint Martin sermon preached by Saint Bernard before the abbots assembled in chapter at Cîteaux —one of his longest sermons.[37] Again, who could possibly read the *fioretti*-like vignettes about Saint Stephen in the *Exordium magnum*,[38] without instinctively thinking of Saint Martin, with all his poverty of spirit and unpretentiousness?

While clearly modelling himself on the Saint Martin antiphon (or responsory), Saint Stephen obviously cannot write *CAELUM laetus ingredior*. So he substitutes instead a phrase familiar to us all, *viam universae carnis*, 'the way of all flesh.' The expression is apparently derived from Joshua 23:14, or from 1 Kings 2:2, the former dealing with the final testament of Joshua, who had succeeded in bringing the Chosen People into the Promised Land, and the latter dealing with the final testament of the dying King David to his son and heir, Solomon. But the reference is only indirect, for the Vulgate reading in either instance is *ingredior viam universae TERRAE*. The fact is, however, that long before Saint Stephen's time, the variation, 'way of all flesh,' had become as much as a stock-phrase in Latin as it is in English.[39] It is symptomatic, perhaps, that although the translator of the Douai version kept to the Latin in his version of Joshua 23:14 ('I am going into the way of all the earth'), traditional usage got the better of him in the case of 1 Kings 2:2 ('I am going the way of all flesh'). I hope that someone will one day trace the history of this expression, which features in so many funeral inscriptions, and is used as a synonym for dying in so many hagiographical accounts. Even though the expression had become an overworked *cliché* by Saint Stephen's time, and enjoyed an existence independent of its biblical *locus*, I still prefer to relate Saint Stephen's use of the expression to the biblical context of the stalwart old and moribund leader giving us his final spiritual testament.

Four words remain: *et cum quadraginta turbis:* 'and with forty
bands'-- or 'throngs' or 'troops' or what have you. The Jacob-
story is still present to Saint Stephen. And, almost surely, the
scribe has miscopied the **important** word, giving us *turbis* instead
of *turmis*. I have left the text uncorrected, however, since *turba*
renders approximately the same sense. The context is, once again,
Jacob's return to his original home. His family, servants, and
retainers form a sizable entourage; and so he divides them into two
'companies,' saying 'If Esau come to one company and destroy it,
the other company that is left shall escape' (Gen 32:8); '. . .with
my staff I passed over this Jordan; and now I return with two companies' (Gen 32:10). The Latin word corresponding to 'companies'
is *turmae*. Stephen's family, however, has grown **hugely,** and is now
divided into no less than forty *turmae,* that is to say, daughter-
or grand-daughter houses. In an earlier paragraph I have already
alluded to the importance of this number in determining the date of
the letter. Here let me remark only in passing that we must be cautious when speaking of a particular house as the twelfth in the order of foundation, or the twenty-seventh, or the fortieth. The
chronology of foundation of the **early** houses is often tangled; and
we have to take into account houses that had only an ephemeral existence. Finally, I am not sure that C. H. Talbot is quite accurate
in referring to Neuberg, founded in 1131, as the fortieth abbey
founded.[40] It is true that Janauschek lists Neuberg under the Roman
numeral XL.[41] But Cîteaux itself counts as I. According to this
reckoning, La-Bussière, founded also in 1131, by Cîteaux, and quite
close to the mother-house in the (present-day) diocese of Dijon,
would be the fortieth foundation to derive, directly or indirectly,
from Cîteaux.[42] Of course, Saint Stephen could possibly be including Cîteaux itself among the *turmae,* in which case Neuberg would be
the fortieth 'company,' but only the thirty-ninth foundation.

*15-16. securus expectans denarium operariis fideliter in uinea
laborantibus repromissum:* '. . . looking forward with confidence to
the *denarius* promised to the laborers who work faithfully in the
vineyard.' We are already familiar with Saint Stephen's use of the
parable of the workers in the vineyard (Mt 20:1-16) in the Prologue
to the *Exordium parvum.*[43] In the Prologue, however, Saint Stephen
is combining **the** biblical text with allusions to Saint Gregory the
Great's homily on that same pericope assigned to Septuagesima Sunday.[44] Here Saint Stephen combines his workers-in-the-vineyard
material with an allusion to another liturgical text that is so
lightly touched upon that I hesitate to draw attention to it. But
I will. The first two words of the phrase under study, *securus expectans,* point at least vaguely in the direction of the classical
collect for the Vigil of Christmas. Let me insist that the verbal
connection is tenuous; and I am not suggesting that, in Saint Stephen's

mind, this particular allusion was consciously thought out. Further, if you feel an *a priori* discomforture at a Christmas formula providing a nuance to an eschatological theme, you would do well to look at the formula in question, which I here transcribe as it appears in the earliest extant **Cistercian** sacramentary:

> Deus qui nos redemtionis nostre annua **expectatione**
> letificas, presta ut unigenitum tuum quem redemptorem
> leti suscipimus, uenientem quoque iudicem securi uidea-
> mus: dominum nostrum ihesum christum filium tuum, qui
> tecum.[45]

This formula from the *Hadrianum* may be a Christmas formula, but its major theme is that of the Second Coming and of judgment. In the cadence of the first clause, *expectatione laetificas,* the word *expectatione* provides some of the syllables needed for the *cursus velox* cadence; and in the climactic termination of the third clause, *securi videamus,* the word *securi* occurs in an equally emphatic position, as part of the *cursus trispondaicus* ending. In the prayer, then, the three word-groups that tend to stick in one's mind are: *expectatione laetificas - laeti suscipimus - securi videamus.* I suggest, then, that as Stephen directs his gaze towards his fast approaching face-to-face encounter with the Master of the vineyard, a distant, barely perceptible resonance of the Christmas Vigil collect is evoked in his subconscious memory. But, once again, the association I am suggesting is so tenuous that I in no way wish to insist on it.

16. Vnde uestram cohortor dilectionem: 'And so I exhort your love . . . .' The expression strikes us as a bit odd; but it is simply a conventional epistolary form of address to be found in Augustine, Jerome, Gregory the Great, and still others, as a glance at the corresponding entry in Albert Blaise's *Dictionnaire Latin-Français des Auteurs Chrétiens* will show.[46]

16-17. ut bonam famam que de uobis ad nos usque manauit profectui uirtutum applicare satagatis: 'to strive to make the good repute you have, and which has reached from you even as far as us, the occasion for [further] progress in virtues . . . .' I am skating on thin ice, and am far from being sure I understand the structure of this sentence. C. H. Talbot, in his own transcription of the letter, suggested that the scribe mistakenly wrote *profectui* instead of *profectu;*[47] but I do not find this 'correction' particularly helpful in construing the phrase. Taking the elements in their logical order, the sequence seems (to me) to be: Saint Stephen urges you 'to strive' *(ut . . . satagatis)* 'to apply' (or some related word: *applicare)* 'the good repute' *(bonam famam,*

direct object of *applicare)* 'to progress' *(profectui,* indirect object
of *applicare).* If we fill in the modifiers now, the *bona fama,* the
good repute,' is described as a repute 'which has reached, or--more
literally--flowed' *(quae . . . manauit)* 'from you as far as even us'
(de uobis ad nos usque). The use of *de* instead of *ex* or *a* will make
the classical scholar squirm, but Saint Stephen is here in good company, for even Ambrose, Jerome, and Augustine sometimes follow late
Latin usage with respect to *de.*[48] Rather more idiosyncratic is the
final position of the adverb *usque* in the expression '[even] to us,'
ad nos usque. So far as I can determine, then, Saint Stephen seems
to be exhorting his Sherborne brethren to make the good renown they
enjoy the starting point for still further progress in virtue. "People speak well of you; we hear about you even here in Burgundy. But
do not rest on your laurels. Make your excellent reputation serve
as a spring-board for soaring still higher in your progress in the
life of virtue.' If it strikes us as a bit extraordinary that the
fame of Sherborne Abbey as a school of sanctity was being talked
about as far away as Burgundy, we are doubtless justified in feeling
a certain reserve. But all Saint Stephen says is that the good repute of the brethren has reached 'even as far as us,' that is to say,
even as far as Cîteaux. And it is easy to see how, given the fact
that by 1131 there were two monasteries of White Monks in regions not
far from Dorsetshire, and that both these abbeys were in the filiation of Cîteaux. Long-term preparation for these foundations and
their actual execution, must have given Saint Stephen numerous occasions of hearing a but of news about his old monastery of boyhood
days, about the translation of the bishop's seat to Old Sarum not
long after his own departure, and about the still recent separation
between the office of bishop and the office of abbot.

    18. ut de bono in melius proficientes: '. . . so that, progres-
sing from what is good to what is better . . . .' This has the 'feel'
of an implicit citation, but so far I have had no luck in tracking it
down. Should someone ever identify the source, I am prone to believe that the text will either be part of a **commentary** on Psalm 83:
8, or else will use this psalm-verse in a prominent way. 'They shall
go from virtue to virtue: the God of gods shall be seen in Sion,'
Ibunt de virtute in virtutem, videbitur Deus deorum in Sion. The
last part of the verse is used for the finale of the last line of
the letter; and the theme of section we are now studying is *profec-
tus virtutum.* I think almost automatically of Cassian's Conference
Eleven, where Abba Chaeremon discourses in his initial conference
about perfection, *De perfectione.* Especially pertinent is Chapter
12, on the various degrees of perfection, *De diversitate perfection-
um;* and it is in this section, as a matter of fact, that we find
Psalm 83:8 quoted.[49] But the entire conference is structured on
the dialectic between fear and love, between *timor* and *caritas.*

It deals with the journey of the monk from craven fear to the perfect love that casts out all fear, from a state of slavery to the
state of the adoption of sons, in which the progress is from one
perfection to another, *de virtute in virtutem, et de perfectione
ad aliam perfectionem.* Augustine's treatment of the same progress
in his *Enarratio* devoted to Psalm 83 is especially fine. He gives
a special twist to verse eight, however, by using a translation
that has us going from 'virtues' in the plural to 'virtue' in the
singular, from the virtues whose *raison d'être* is bound up with the
present ephemeral order of things, to that virtue which alone abides
forever. And what is that virtue? The virtue of contemplating.
Contemplating what? *Apparebit Deus deorum in Sion:* we shall contemplate Christ when he appears in all his glory; and this is that
virtue to which all others are directed.[50]

     18. *et uere religioni firmiter inherentes:* '. . . and cleaving
firmly to true monastic observance . . . .' Most of us will doubtless tend to equate *religio* with 'spirituality' or devotion or some
related and deeply interior reality. 'Monastic observance' can by
no means be separated from what is 'deeply interior'; but it takes
in everything. It is simply the monastic way of life, with all the
practices associated with it. It includes the satisfaction made by
the monk who stumbles on a word in choir as well as the interior
humility, reverence, and love that give the outward ritual gesture
its true meaning. Translators, failing to understand the technical
meaning the term has in mediaeval monastic literature, can easily
confuse the meaning of a text. Thus, when we read in the mini-
customary of the abbey of the Paraclete, *Religionis erat de cultu
terrarum et labore proprio vivere, si possemus,*[51] we would be wrong
if we were to translate it as, 'It pertains to the virtue of religion
to make our living from farming and our own work, and we would if we
could.' Rather, 'Earning our living from farming and our own work
is part of monastic observance, and we would do so if we could.'
Saint Stephen, then, is exhorting the Sherbornites simply to hold
fast to an authentic monastic observance. He specifies at least
some of the constitutent elements of this observance in the phrase
which follows--a phrase which has evidently been partially mutilat-
ed by a nodding scribe:

     19-20. *castitatem, humilitatem, studiis parsimonie cum cari-
tate inseruientes corde et corpore usque ad mortem tenere non desistas:* '. . . you may never cease to observe chastity [and] humility, submitting [yourselves] to the zealous practice of frugality together with charity even unto death . . . .' The Latin, as
I have already suggested, has become snarled; and I realize that
the translation has done little to unsnarl it. Perhaps it will
help to go through the phrase, as before, in logical order, begin-

ning with the verb that **governs** the whole convoluted period. *Tenere non desistas:* 'you may not cease to observe (or hold to).' The only possible object of *tenere* is a word or words in the accusative case; and here we have two such words in immediate succession: *castitatem humilitatem*. For the latter word, I have to take the word of C. H. Talbot and D. L. Bethell, for **on** my microfilm and enlarged photo, all I can see for the last part of the word is a dark blob caused by ink seepage from the reverse side. But if the Talbot-Bethell reading is correct, then either there is an *et* or *-que* missing for 'chastity' and 'humility,' or else these two virtues should be followed by yet a third: *castitatem, humilitatem, et obedientiam,* or something **similar.** This gives us the essential of the phrase, that is to say, the main verb with its infinitive ('may you not cease to observe') **and** the object ('chastity-humility'); all the other elements are modifiers of one kind or another, of which there are three: (1) submitting yourselves (or some related word) to the zealous practice (literally, 'zealous practices') of frugality (or parsimony) along with charity; (2) in heart and in body; (3) even unto death. Having divided, I am not sure we have conquered, but at least the main articulations of the period are a bit **clearer.** We are dealing with typical Rule-talk--with apparently one exception. *Studiis parsimoniae . . . inservientes* (note that *inservire* usually takes the dative rather than the accusative, which is why I have construed this participle with *studiis* rather than with *castitatem-humilitatem).* The closest the vocabulary of the Holy Rule comes to *parsimonia* is in the phrases *servata in omnibus parcitate* (c. 39:10) and *non usque ad satietatem bibamus, sed parcius* (c. 40:6). I have translated the word as 'frugality' rather than as 'parsimony,' since the latter term so often smacks of 'stinginess' in ordinary usage. Given Saint Stephen's known passion for poverty, one might expcet him to have urged the brethren of Sherborne to a zealous practice of evangelical poverty. **Instead** he uses a word that carries with it practically no resonance of the Holy Rule. I suggest, however, that in the choice of this one word, Saint Stephen reveals himself in all his gentle thoughtfulness and delicacy of feeling. 'Poverty' would be, perhaps, an unrealistic ideal in a cathedral-community structures and life-style much affected by the very nature of an episcopal minister. And though things may have changed somewhat since the separation of bishop's seat from abbey, we have no indication that much of a re-**orientation** did take place. 'Poverty' was a word that could cause hurt in such a context; a word that might suggest that Stephen was urging them to the same poverty that shone with such radiant simplicity and quiet splendor at Cîteaux. Poverty at **Sherborne?** To urge it would have been un-realistic, perhaps unkind. So we read, 'giving yourselves to the zealous practice of *frugality';* and always, of course, *cum caritate.* We all know what austerity can become, where there is no

charity. *Corde et corpore* is also the language of the Rule, though
it occasionally occurs outside the Rule (St Gregory sometimes uses
the expression). In our present context, we think instinctively of
the twelfth degree of humility in chapter seven, where the humility
of the monk is 'not only in his heart,' *non solum corde,* but naturally and spontaneously finds expression, no matter where he is and what
he is doing, outwardly, 'in his very body.' *Usque ad mortem* is also
from the Rule, towards the very end of the Prologue, where we are ex-
horted to persevere in the monastery in God's teaching 'even unto
death.' But before we can grasp the depth of what this means, we
must turn again to the chapter on humility, chapter seven, and find
in the third degree of humility the paradigm of all humility, of all
obedience, of all monastic observance: the Lord himself, who was obedient *usque ad mortem.* These three words were found, too, in the
promise of obedience made by all twelfth-century Benedictine and Cistercian monks in connection with the rite of monastic profession:
'Father, I promise you obedience according to the Rule of Saint Benedict, even unto death.' Which brings us to the final phrase of the
letter, the phrase towards which all the preceding has been leading
us--

    20-21 ut deum deorum uidere mereamini. Amen. '. . . that you
may see the God of gods. Amen.' We end then, with a fragment from
Psalm 83:8 that for Saint Stephen and for the monastic tradition he
represents stands for the goal of all ascetic striving, of all monastic observance, the face-to-face vision of God for all eternity.
Those of us long familiar with the psalm-verse may wonder why Saint
Stephen failed to include the two words of the Latin text, *in Sion.*
But read over the final clause a few times and try inserting *in Sion*
(which, according to Cistercian usage at the time would have had the
accent on the final syllable of the Hebrew indeclinable *Sión*). No
matter where you put it, the music and the strength of this final
phrase turn flabby.

*   *   *

    If this, then, is a sample of Saint Stephen's correspondence,
we can rightly weep all the more bitterly over the total disappear-
ance of his *registrum* of letters. One of the most striking features
of his literary style is his use of implicit citations from Bible
and liturgy. Not once does he quote a text word for word. He has
interiorized the texts and made them so much his own that he spontaneously, and obviously without forethought, rephrases them according to the exigencies of the music of the line and the nuance to be
brought out. More remarkable, perhaps, is the sure instinct he
seems to have for drawing his subtle allusions from contextually
significant *loci.* Not once does he draw an apt expression from a

biblical context foreign to the substance of the thought he is ex-
pressing. Indeed, the full meaning of his thought becomes all the
richer when we replace this word or that in the context of the passage from which it has been borrowed. On the strength of this one
brief letter, **copied** hastily and written inelegantly on a stray empty folio of a Rievaulx manuscript, we can recognize in Saint Stephen
a genius at the art of conveying more, hugely more, than the words
taken singly could possibly **convey**. Despite the tangled state of
the final part of the text, we can feel too a musicality of expression that in no way depends on his consistent and conscious appli-
cation of the rules of the rhythmic *cursus*. There is magic in a
line like *Vas enim vacuum vivus Fons, sicut voluit, implevit*. There
is an accumulation of no less than three *ut*-clauses from line 16 to
the end: bad style, surely; but we have only to read the text aloud
(snarled though line 19 is), and let ourselves be carried along by
the momentum of the **rhythm** to realize that the thrust of the ideas
leading to that final *Amen* is paralleled by a musical phrase that
soars to the same point of arrival and fulfillment.

What really overwhelms me is the gentle courtesy and delicacy
of feeling of this simple, profound, and noble man. Sherborne
territory was being invaded by a new and foreign breed of monks.
More colonies were soon to follow. The perpetrator of this great
White Plague was none other than a former monk of Sherborne Abbey,
a monk who had left the community in not particularly pleasant circumstances. Moreover, profound differences in the concrete living
out of monastic ideals had already led to such a pitch of animos-
ity on the Continent that certain irate communities did not baulk
at recourse to violence. Had you or I had to write a letter of re-
assurance to the brethren of Sherborne, asking for tolerance and
understanding as our colonies of monks gained a foothold across the
Channel, how would we have expressed ourselves? Not once **does** Saint
Stephen use an offensive word, a blunt expression. Not once does he
disparage the Sherborne observance in his joy at what God **has** wrought
through him. His letter is a sustained celebration of gratitude in
which he invites his brethren to take heart and to live to the full
their own monastic observance.

One particular point. I raise again the question of Saint
Stephen's **alleged** 'apostasy' from Sherborne. In the light of the
letter we have been studying, I have considerable difficulty in accepting at face value William of Malmesbury's presentation of Ste-
pehn's break with Sherborne in terms of a temporary succumbing to
the wiles of the world. Had Stephen been an apostate in any such
sense, his letter would have been couched in quite different terms:
'I was your monk. Yet, blind and sinner that I was, I threw off
the sacred garb to wallow in the cess-pool and the mire, till the
change of God's right hand etc., etc., etc.' Had this sort of
thing really been Stephen's experience, his celebration of his own

poverty and God's wholly gratuitous mercy would have been quite
the same; his point of reference, however, would not have been the
Jacob-story, but the parable of the Prodigal Son or some other biblical figure of a **converted** sinner. Instead, **Stephen** has cast himself in the role of an errant pilgrim, exiled because of family
troubles, but the founder of a new family: in brief, Stephen is
Jacob. At this point, then, the hypothesis that **Stephen**'s departure
ture from Sherborne was occasioned by his dangerous family connection seems rather attractive.

But if Stephen's problematic leave-taking involved no true
abandonment of his monastery for unworthy reasons, why does his
great admirer, William of Malmesbury, state the contrary? I honestly do not know, at least not with any degree of certainty. I
rather incline to think, however, that William included so disedi-
fying an episode in his pen-portrait of the English hero as monk
reformer because he was convinced that it was true. And since so
many details in his wonderful description of early Cîteaux are details such as only an eye-witness could record, the tale of Stephen's
apostasy was doubtless told William by the great 'apostate' himself.
'So you were a monk of Sherborne before coming to Molesme?' 'Indeed
I was.' 'But why did you leave?' Long pause--after all, we could
hardly expect Stephen, even forty years after the **event**, to volunteer the information that his quisling uncle's local unpopularity
had made his own presence at Sherborne not only embarrassing but
dangerous for himself and for the community. At last, a quiet smile,
and--'Why did I leave? Oh, it was the world, the flesh, and the devil.' And he would not have been all that wrong. After all, he had
tarried long enough in France to finish the equivalent of college
studies before finally, *tandem aliquando*, finding his way to a monastery in **politically** neutral territory. His years spent in the
guise of a cleric in a university milieu meant a foreswearing of
his monastic identity at least temporarily; and there **must** have
been times when the confused but earnest young man had all but decided to remain in the world. He may not have been an apostate
when he left England for Scotland and then for France. But what
was he during the years in Burgundy when he passed himself off as
a young cleric pursuing his course of higher studies? 'Why did I
leave? Oh, the world was just too strong for me. . . .'

All of this is no more than a **hypothesis** spun out, possibly,
with too much imagination and in no way demonstrable. Still, this
is the one hypothesis which, so far as I know, brings into harmony
the data drawn from William of Malmesbury, from the *Vita* of Peter
of Jully, and from recent investigations into Stephen's family connections in the immediate aftermath of 1066. It is this hypothesis, too, which seems best to accord with Stephen's remarkable letter to Abbot Thurstan and Community.

It now remains to string together the revised fragments of the translation used in the preceding notes, and to conclude by offering a rough attempt at a translation.

III.   DRAFT OF A TRANSLATION

To the venerable abbot of Sherborne, Thurstan, and to the congregation God has entrusted to his care, from Brother **Stephen**, servant of the church of Cîteaux. Fear Christ, but with love; and love him, but with fear.

The function of a letter is to address the absent as though they were present, and to bring together through their fellowship of charity those still kept apart by long distances. And so, because you are our bone and our flesh, I **admonish** you to bear with me patiently as I write you **these** few lines.

I was a monk of yours, and with my staff I passed over and beyond the sea so that in me, the very least of all of you and of no importance whatever when I was with you, the Lord might **show** forth the riches of his mercy and provoke you to emulation of me. For, living Fountain that he is, he filled the **empty** vessel: for so he willed; that you, who were so much better for the holiness of your family-line, would have the courage to hold fast and strong to monastic **observance**, would dare to presume on the Lord.

For now I, who was all alone when I went forth from my country, and poor, am entering upon the way of all flesh, happy, rich, and with forty companies, looking forward with all confidence to the *denarius* promised those laborers who toil faithfully in the vineyard.

And so I appeal to your love: make every effort to turn the good repute you have, and which has reached from you **even** as far as us, into the occasion for yet further progress in virtue; so that, moving forward from what is good to what is better, and cleaving resolutely to a **truly** monastic way of life, you may never interrupt your observance of chastity and humility, giving yourselves to the zealous practice of frugality--but not forgetting charity! --in heart and in body, even unto death: that so you may come to gaze at last upon the God of gods. Amen.

Gethsemani Abbey

NOTES

1. For a brief history of the archives of Cîteaux, with abundant
    bibliographical references, see Abbé J. Marilier, *Chartes et
    documents concernant l'abbaye de Cîteaux 1098-1182*. Biblio-
    theca Cisterciensis 1 (Rome: Editiones Cistercienses, 1961)
    pp. 1-22, but with special reference to pp. 2-5.
2. Frequently edited, as in Mabillon, *Opera Sancti Bernardi* (ed.
    of 1719), 1, p. xii; PL **166**:1375-1376; Marilier, p. 56, Docu-
    ment 32. The best edition is that by Charles **Oursel**, *Mini-
    atures cisterciennes (1109-1134)* (Macon: Protat Frères, 1960),
    unpaginated introductory loose folio.
3. Also frequently edited, but not without inaccuracies, as in
    P. Blanchard, 'Un monument primitif de la règle cistercienne'
    in *R Bén* 31 (1914) 35-44; Othon Ducourneau, *Les origines cis-
    terciennes*, p. 106, note 3 [=*Revue Mabillon* 23 [1933] p. 102
    note 1]; S. Marosszéki, *Les origines du chant cistercien* in
    ASOC 8 (1952) 9 (particularly inaccurate **transcription**); C.
    Waddell, 'The Origin and Early Evolution of the Cistercian
    Antiphonary. Relfections on Two Cistercian Chant Reforms' in
    M. B. Pennington, ed., *The Cistercian Spirit: A Symposium in
    Honor of Thomas Merton*. Cistercian Studies Series 3 (1970)
    p. 206, but with discussion and bibliographical references,
    pp. 204-206; finally, Marilier, p. 55, **Document** 31.
4. SBOp 7:133-134 and 7:14-141 for Letters 45 and 49 respectively;
    PL 182:149B and 157B.
5. Fr Hugh Talbot, 'An Unpublished Letter of St Stephen' in *Collec-
    tanea O.C.R.* 2 (1936) 66-69.
6. Talbot, p. 66.
7. L. Janauschek, *Originum Cisterciensium*, I (Vienna: A. Hölder,
    187-) p. 18.
8. Talbot, p. 6.
9. Ibid.
10. Pp. 349-350. Mr Bethell had attended school at Sherborne, in
    the same location where Saint Stephen had learned the first
    elements of reading and writing more than eight-hundred and
    fifty years earlier.
11. Marilier, p. 91, Document 88.
12. Ibid.
13. *Collectanea O.C.R.* 25 (1963) 404.
14. This information was communicated to me in a personal letter
    dated 22 January 1962, from the Assistant Librarian of Jesus
    College Library, Isobel Keith.
15. Talbot, P. 66; Bethell, p. 350.
16. The traditional foundation date is 1132; but preparations for
    the foundation would have involved a number of Cistercians in
    cross-channel travelling for a considerable period prior to the

official foundation date.

17. The material on Sherborne Abbey is particularly rich in W.
Dugdale, *Monasticon Anglicanum*, 1 (London, edition of 1817),
pp. 331-341. King Ethelred's charter and Saint Wulsin's charter are both reproduced in full, p. 337, Nums. II and III.

18. All recent authors I have seen give the translation date as
1075, so I write under correction. But Dugdale, whom I here
follow, gives the date of the London Council as 1075, and assigns the implementation of the decision, in the case of Bishop
Hereman, to 1076. See Dugdale, I, p. 333.

19. *De gestis pontificum Anglorum*, Lib. II, De Episcopis Schire-
burnensibus, Salisburiensibus, Wiltunensibus: 'Schireburnia
est viculus, nec habitantium frequentia, nec positionis gratia
suavis, in quo mirandum, et pene pudendum sedem episcopalem
per tot durasse saecula.' PL 179:1533C.

20. Ibid.: '. . . tribunal suum transtulit (Hermannus) a Schireburnia Salesberiam, quod est vice civitatis castellum locatum
in edito. . . .' PL 179:1538C.

21. Dugdale, I, p. 334. The author gives Thurstan as the first
known abbot of Sherborne, but wrongly presupposes that between
1075 and 1122 other abbots had preceded and resided at Sherborne.
During this period the abbot of the place remained the bishop,
presumably in residence at Old Sarum; and the chief function-
ary at the abbey was the claustral Prior who, for most (but
not all) practical purposes functioned as would an abbot.

22. See Note 3, above, for references to the *monitum*.

23. On the chronology of the first abbots, see Marilier, p. 26; but
for a more detailed presentation, see the same author's article,
'Catalogue des abbés de Cîteaux pour le XIIe siècle' in *Cister-
cienser-Chronik* 55 (1948) 1-11.

24. J. de la Croix Bouton and J.-B. Van Damme, edd., *Les plus anciens textes de Cîteaux*. Cîteaux: Commentarii Cistercienses,
Studia et Documenta 2 (Achel, Belgium: 1974), p. 89. Translation by Bede K. Lackner, taken from Louis Lekai, *The Cistercians. Ideals and Reality* (Kent State University, Ohio: Kent
State University Press, 1977) p. 462.

25. The literature about the feud between Citeaux and Cluny is extensive. For a fairly recent treatment of the topic, with a
helpful survey of the more serious scholarly contributions to
the discussion, see A. H. Bredero, 'Cluny et Cîteaux au XIIe
siècle: les origines de la controverse' in *Studi Medievali*
12 (1971) 135-175.

26. *De gestis regum Anglorum*, Lib. IV, n. 334: 'A puero Scireburniae
monachus; sed cum adolescentem saeculi urtica sollicitaret, pan-
nos illos perosus, primo Scotiam, mox Franciam contendit.'
PL 179:1287AB.

27. *Cîteaux: Commentarii Cistercienses* 14 (1963) 307–313.

28. Published as a pamphlet, Charles Oursel, *Saint-Etienne Harding,
     abbé de Cîteaux* (Dijon: Bernigaud et Privat, 1962).

29. *De gestis regum*, ibid.: 'Ibi [France] aliquot annis litteris
     liberalibus exercitus, divini amoris stimulos accepit: namque
     cum pueriles ineptias robustior aetas excluderet, Romam, cum
     consorte studiorum clerico, profectus est.' PL 179:1287B.

30. PL 185:1257–1270. The pertinent texts about Saint Stephen
     Harding are found in c. II, col. 1259B–D.

31. '. . . Burgundiae partes subintrans, quemdam continentissimae
     vitae reperit adolescentem, natione Anglicum, Stephanum nomine
     qui eodem desiderio ductus quo et Petrus, in hanc se contuler-
     at regionem; cuius vitam, et mores videns, et approbans Petrus,
     sese ei coniunxit familiarem et socium.' PL 185:1259B.

32. Reproduced in Marilier, p. 84, Document 75.

33. *In Hieremiam*, III, xxvii: 'Maiores quoque, qui deberent ipsi
     pergere ad hauriendas aquas, mittunt iuniores, in quibus cani
     non sunt sapientiae, et idcirco veniunt ad puteos et non in-
     veniunt aquas, quas patriarchas invenisse narrat historia.
     Reportant vasa sua vacua, iuniores videlicet, non quo aquae
     non fuerint, sed quo illi invenire non potuerint.' CCL 74:
     137, 6–11.

34. Text and manuscript information in R.-J. Hesbert, *Corpus Anti-
     phonalium Officii*. Rerum Ecclesiasticarum Documenta. Series
     Maior: Fontes 10 (Rome:Herder 1970) 4, p. 11, under n. 6043.

35. *Epistola III Ad Bassulam socrum suam:* 'Martinus Abrahae sinu
     laetus excipitur; Martinus hic pauper et modicus, coelum
     dives ingreditur . . .' PL 20:184C.

36. In *Studia Anselmiana* 46 (1961) 175–187.

37. SBOp 5, 399–412; PL 183:489–500.

38. Ed. B. Griesser, *Exordium magnum cisterciense*. Series Scrip-
     torum S. Ordinis Cisterciensis 2 (Rome: Editiones Cistercienses,
     1961), Distinctio I, cc. 21–28 and c. 31, pp. 74–86 and pp. 88–
     89. Parallel texts in PL 185:1012–1016 and col. 1013, but with
     a different chapter-numbering.

39. Unfortunately, by at least the seventeenth century the expres-
     sion had taken on a new twist in English. Samuel Butler (1835–
     1902) has immortalized the term as the title of his posthumous
     novel (1903), which reflects the Anglo-Saxon obsession with
     the sex-taboo.

40. Talbot, p. 67.

41. Janauschek, p. 18.

42. Ibid., p. 19.

43. Bouton and Van Damme, *Les plus anciens*, p. 54.

44. *Homilia in Evangelia*, Lib. I, Hom. 19, in PL 76:1153–1159.
     The pertinent texts are found in n. 3, cols. 1155–1156.

45. **Paris, Bibliothèque** nationale, ms latin 2300, f. 10r (pre-1147).
46. Turnhout, Editions Brepols S.A.: 1954, p. 273, under the word *dilectio* towards the end.
47. Talbot, 69.
48. Blaise, *Dictionnaire*, p. 238: 'dans la latinité postérieure, *de* s'emploie avec n'importe quel verbe et tend à remplace *a*, *ex.*'
49. E. Pichery, ed., *Conférences VIII-XVII*. Sources chrétiennes 54 (1958) pp. 113-115.
50. N. 11 in the *Enarratio in Psalm 83*--the divisions being the same in all accessible editions of the *Enarrationes*.
51. PL 178:314D-315A.

ANTHROPOLOGY AND SANCTITY IN THE *VITA PRIMA BERNARDI I*

Richard M. Peterson

William of St Thierry (c. 1085-1148) has contributed a number
of beautiful and important writings to the literature of twelfth-
century **monastic** theology. The discovery of William's theological
significance is a twentieth century **phenomenon**,[1] one not yet ex-
hausted. Ironically, one of his best known works--Book One of the
composite *Vita Prima Bernardi*[2]--has been assigned little theological value. This is perhaps explained by the tendency of historians
to approach the *Vita* either as a source of biographical information or as a piece of medieval hagiography conforming to the forms
and intentions of that genre.[3] It is the thesis of this paper that
William's contribution to the *Vita prima Bernardi* is an integral
part of his theological legacy. William perceived in Bernard an
embodiment of christian faith, and was determined to record that
perception.[4] By so doing, William laid out his understanding of
holiness. It is the purpose of this paper to unfold that understanding as found in the *Vita,* and to indicate the anthropology
which underlies it, and so to demonstrate the theological significance of the *Vita prima Bernardi I.*

Bernard the Monk

The *Vita prima Bernardi I* must be understood in its monastic
context. It is written by a monk about a monk, two of the most
important monks in the monastic ferment of the twelfth century.
Bernard was, in William's eyes, the ideal monk[5] and the quintes-
sential representative of the cistercian reform.[6] This monastic
quality is stamped **on** every detail of the *Vita;* the holiness por-
trayed is the holiness of the monk.
As William relates it, Bernard's life from the beginning was
ordered toward monastic perfection. Bernard's parents, people of
rank, each lived according to a rule of life taken from Scripture.
Bernard's father, Tescelin, a soldier of the nobility, took as his
rule John the Baptist's instruction to soldiers (Lk 3:14). Bernard's mother Aleth, by **far** the more important figure in William's
account, lived according to the rule of life given by Paul to the
women of Ephesus (Eph 5:21-33).[7] **In light of the cistercian con-**
cern with fidelity to the *Rule* and life of St Benedict[8]--one of
the major points of contention between Cluny and Cîteaux--this
attribution of a rule to each of Bernard's parents is significant.
Moreover, William reports that, because Aleth's six sons and one
daughter entered religious life, it was said of them that they
were begotten by God.[9] And, after consecrating each child to God,

Aleth would allow no one else to suckle them, as if **her goodness**
--manifest in her imitation of the life of a hermit or monk--was
in some manner poured into their nature with her milk.[10] As her
children grew, Aleth fed them a plain diet suited to the hermitage,
raising them as though they were to go directly there from her
home.[11]

   Bernard's holiness, then, was instilled in him by his mother,
to be perfected by his life at Clairvaux. Bernard's youth is passed over with relative brevity, as a transition from the 'monastery'
which was Aleth's home to Bernard's entry into the Cistercians.
William points out that by merit of his education and natural attributes, which led even married women to lose all discretion, Bernard had many prospects in the world, and his brothers encouraged
him to advance his study of letters. Bernard, however, saw in such
ambitions only vanity and was compelled instead by the **conviction**
that true perfection was to be found in leaving the world, and by
the memory of his mother who seemed to him to be reproaching him
for considering worldly ambitions.[12]

   In particular, Bernard was attracted to the cistercian reform.
The reasons William gives for this attraction are important: Bernard's soul was **truly** seeking God; he thought that among the Cis-
tercians he would be able to be hidden from the sight of men (Ps
31:22); most importantly, he sought to escape the pride he could
have taken in his lineage, his keen mind, or his reputation for
sanctity.[13] Bernard was drawn to the Cistercians because he would
be hidden from a world which apparently offered him praise, and so
would be free to look away from himself towards God.[14] This desire
to look towards God, with its emphasis on the desire for God, de-
termines the monastic quality of perfection as William perceived
it in Bernard.

   One final aspect of the monastic context of the *Vita* may be
observed. William places Bernard in a tradition of perfection
hearkening back to the Fathers of the Desert, a common theme in
twelfth century monasticism.[15] William claims that the first-
fruits of Bernard's youth were given to resuscitating the ancient
fervor for monastic life.[16] Reflecting on his first visit with
Bernard at Clairvaux, William speaks of the men of his day who
were following anew the path of their fathers, the Egyptian monks.[17]
To return to the life of the first monks by the strict observance
of the benedictine *Rule* was the intent of the cistercian reform,
to which Bernard, at least in William's mind, was the greatest
witness.

Bernard the Saint

What, then, is the essence of monastic holiness? The key to
opening William's understanding of holiness is the relationship he
envisions between nature and grace. He sees in Bernard no conflict
between nature and grace (*Natura quoque in eo non dissentiebat a
gratia*).[18] Grace complimented and enlivened Bernard's natural
strength of mind (*anima*), enabling him to contemplate the things
of God, so that his mind was placed under and served his spirit
(*spiritus*).[19] Further, Bernard was said by William to have regarded his body, which by the gift of grace and the subsequent support
of nature did not oppose his spirit, as a tool of his spirit in its
service of God.[20] A hierarchy therefore emerges: the body (*corpus*)
and the mind (*anima*) serve the spirit (*spiritus*), which in its turn
serves God.[21] William's understanding of holiness is determined by
this anthropology. By 'nature' William refers to the powers which
are proper to man, his body, mind, and spirit. The saint is one
whose natural powers, by cooperating with the working of grace, have
been restored to their right anthropological order.[22] The monastic
life is, in William's mind, the best way toward this end, and so
holiness is above all a monastic attribute. And it is as a means
toward this anthropological order, as an effort to move toward grace
by moving away from the world, that the monk's life in general and
the life of the saint in particular consists of asceticism and prayer.[23]

William devotes much attention to this dimension of Bernard's
life. William writes that from his early days, as if by nature,
Bernard practised in things of the world the mortification which
was to characterize his perfection in future years.[24] To overcome
carnalis concupiscentia he was reputed to have plunged into a pool
of cold water and stayed in it up to his neck until, *per virtutem
gratiae cooperantis,* his lust was cooled along with his blood.[25]
As a monk Bernard prayed standing until his knees and feet would
not hold him, wore a hair shirt until it was discovered by the
other monks, and ate only bread and milk or broth.[26] Bernard's
disregard for sleep was, in William's judgment, beyond description
or human endurance.[27]

To the modern mind this all appears rather excessive, a charge
apparently made even in Bernard's day.[28] Yet, Bernard's intent, as
William portrays it, must not be overlooked. William reveals this
intent in his account of the words with which the abbot Bernard
greeted his novices. He told them to leave their bodies outside,
meaning the inclinations and desires of the flesh which hold one
back from the spiritual service of God.[29] Bernard was intent on
removing himself from all things that impinged on his mind through
his senses by mortifying the very senses which stirred worldly desires.[30]

Bernard's asceticism was not, however, merely a matter of
deadening the senses in order to provide the spirit unobstructed
sensitivity to God. It was also a product of that very sensitivity
of spirit. William notes that what the senses perceive means nothing if the mind (*memoria*) ignores their reactions.[31] By the continual mortification of his senses Bernard was able to turn his
spirit to God until, so taken up was his mind in spiritual things,
it had almost ceased to respond to his senses.[32] By the end of
Bernard's novitiate, William tells us, he was so immersed in things
of God that he could not say if the novices' scriptorium had a
vaulted ceiling, or how many windows there were in the sanctuary
of the church.[33] With time Bernard learned to work with full awareness of what he was doing while his mind (*memoria*) was completely
united to his spirit in the enjoyment of God.[34]

Unfortunately, Bernard had not only mortified his senses but
ruined his health. William explains that the fasts and vigils
which Bernard undertook as a novice and which became an habitual
part of his subsequent routine, had broken his health, affecting
above all his digestion.[35] Bernard's friend and protector, William,
Bishop of Champeaux, had Bernard placed under his obedience for one
year in the hopes of restoring his health, but at the end of the
year Bernard returned to his former austerity.[36]

William was preoccupied with this problem. He clearly intended to present Bernard as the ideal monk and embodiment of holiness.
Yet the exemplar was marred by a chronic self-inflicted illness;
he was, when ill, *homo imbecillus et languidus*.[37] Moreover, some
of Bernard's novices apparently wished to follow him in his excess-
es. William includes a curious and singular story about a group
of fervent novices who thought that anything which sustained their
bodies was a detriment to their souls. This is an echo of the
young Bernard as William portrays him. These novices took pleasure in their mortification and complained when Bernard addressed
himself to considerations of the body.[38] They took their complaint,
not to Bernard, but to William of Champeaux, who answered that to
refuse the gifts of God is to rebel against God's grace, which makes
the gifts of nature fit for man.[39] William of St Thierry indicates
that Bernard accused himself of sacrilege, because his indiscreet
fervor rendered his body incapable of the service to God and men
which it was properly intended for.[40]

Nevertheless, William softens this critical picture of Bernard.
He argues that Bernard's life, offered as a model to be imitated,
could not have lacked the example of frugal self-control (*frugalis
continentiae exemplo*), Bernard's practice of which stands as an
example of fervor.[41] Further, he suggests that Bernard's illness
may have been part of God's plan to humble the great and powerful
of this world, and challenges those who might criticize Bernard by
affirming that he had already been justified by God, who did so

many marvelous things in and through him.[42] Bernard's arrival at
Cîteaux in 1113 is seen by William as the most important instance
of God's activity in and through Bernard. Bernard's intent in entering Cîteaux was to die to the hearts and memories of men, like
a discarded vase (*vas*). But, writes William, God's disposition
was to prepare Bernard as an implement (*vas*) to build up and extend
the monastic life of Cîteaux, and to carry God's name before kings
and peoples.[43] And, William continues, so great was the power giv-
en Bernard's words by the Holy Spirit that hardly any affection
could hold out against it: when Bernard started to preach, mothers
hid their sons, wives detained their husbands, friends were averted
by friends.[44] Today we smile at this often-cited story of women
and friends grabbing their loved ones and scattering to closets
and barns, but William in this passage gives a vibrant expression
of the power of Bernard's preaching, in which William discerned
the working of God.[45]

William expressed the cooperation of nature and grace in Bernard in one other, more subtle, way. Consistently throughout the
Vita, William uses scriptural allusions and images. Given the primary and integral role of Scripture in monastic life and thought,[46]
the reader would expect to find such reliance on Scripture in William's *Vita*. Bernard himself was immersed in Scripture. He studied letters as a child to enable him to enter into the Bible, where
God is known.[47] It was a New Testament reading, Philippians 1:6,
which confirmed Bernard in his plan to enter Cîteaux.[48] William
comments that, like the Fathers, Bernard drank eagerly at the fountain of Scripture until he was filled with the same Spirit who inspired its writers.[49] It may be argued, however, that William goes
further; that he sees Bernard conforming to scriptural types and
therefore being formed according to a supernatural order revealed
in the records of God's revelation.[50] To the monastic mind, steep-
ed in Scripture, the perfect life was one that conformed to the
accounts found in Scripture, above all to the example of Christ.
Further, the types presented in Scripture are realized again on
earth in the life of the saint, and it is in this way too that
grace works to perfect nature.

William's account of the saint comes to full flower in his
picture of Bernard's prayer. As we have said, the goal of Bernard's
ascetical efforts was not mortification itself, but the subsequent
freedom of the mind and spirit to turn away from things of the
senses and toward the things of God. And this Bernard achieved,
as both William's account and Bernard's own writings attest. William uses two themes common to the monastic imagination to describe
the quality of Bernard's life of prayer: the solitary life and the
vita angelica.[51] From his youngest days, we are told, Bernard
loved to be alone away from the turbulent life of the world, so
that he could give himself to thought.[52] The maturation of this

interior life took place in the **solitude** of the monastery.[53] Yet
by solitude, William understood not an eremitic life. He points
out Bernard's desire to participate fully in the common life, main-
taining that true solitude is something of the heart.[54] It is precisely this inner solitude of the heart, in which the saint is alone
with God, that the stabilizing influence of the *Rule* followed in silence and unity of purpose is meant to establish.[55] William **identi-**
fies Bernard's experience of God with the delights of paradise.[56]
So great was Bernard's experience of God that he lived an angelic
life on earth (*vitam angelicam gerens in terris vixit*), receiving
graces given only to those who are specially chosen to dwell in
God's house.[57]

Conclusion

The *Vita prima Bernardi I* gives the theologian a rich presentation of the meaning of holiness, a presentation whose success is
due precisely to the fact that it is developed around a single example of the life of faith and the desire for God. For William,
the nature of holiness is determined by the nature of man. Man's
natural powers, the elements of his existence, are ordered toward
God in a hierarchy of service. The body is to serve the mind,
which serves the spirit, which is meant to be turned toward God as
the source of life and delight. The fact of human existence, however, is that the hierarchy tends to be reversed so that man's intended nature is disrupted. The body tends to dominate, drawing
the rational man away from his spiritual nature into the realm of
the senses.

William is clear on one point: only grace can finally restore
man to order. The role of the believer is to move toward grace,
to open himself to the reality of God by turning away from his en-
slavement to the sense-world. And, William would insist, the sur-
est way to achieve this is the monastic life; it must be admitted
that in William's mind holiness was pre-eminently a monastic attribute.[58] Holiness outside the monastery, exemplified by Bernard's
mother, imitates monastic life. William was not, however, blind to
the dangers of monastic asceticism. He pictures in Bernard the
consequence of a desire for spiritual perfection which outstrips
the strength of the body. The efforts of even the holiest man can
misfire; only grace is sure.

Ultimately it is not in terms of the **efforts** of the man, but
by rather poetic efforts to express the working of grace that William speaks of holiness. Even the disruption of man's proper order
through an overzealous mortification of the senses can become the
place where God works in man. William struggles to communicate
the mystery of God's reality in the life of men, capturing it in
fleeting ways, no one of which is **satisfactory**. God works in and

through the saint; the saint is formed according to the revealed
types of Scripture; he dwells with God in the solitude of his
heart and knows in life the joys of the angels who see God's face.
With such images William attempts to capture the essence of holiness, which finally rests in the mysterious presence of the reality
of God in the lives of men. Bernard serves as a witness to the
honor and glory of God shining in the world, as a locus of God's
presence. William captured this insight when he wrote of his **first**
visit to Clairvaux that, upon entering Bernard's hut, he was filled
with the awe he felt on approaching the altar of God.[59] The life of
the saint is sacramental--through it God's reality is focused within the world--and it is this quality which William tried to communicate in the *Vita prima Bernardi I.*

Marquette University

NOTES

1. The most important study of William's life and thought is Jean
   Marie Déchanet, *William of St Thierry. The Man and his Work*,
   trans. R. Strachan, CS 10 (1972). See also A. Adam, *Guillaume de
   Saint-Thierry, sa vie et ses oeuvres* (Bourg, 1923); Etienne
   Gilson, *The Mystical Theology of Saint Bernard*, trans. A. H.
   C. Downs (New York: Sheed and Ward, 1940) pp. 198-214. For a
   survey of other modern studies and editions of William's work,
   see Déchanet, pp. 152-164. An illuminating example of how William's importance to the christian tradition was 'lost' is
   found in Déchanet's introduction to the English translation
   of *The Golden Epistle. A Letter to the Brethren at Mont Dieu*
   by William of St Thierry, trans. T. Berkeley, OCSO, CF 12 (1976)
   pp. ix-xiii.

2. The *Vita prima Bernardi I* may have been begun by William as
   early as 1145, probably after completion of *The Golden Epistle*;
   his death in 1148 brought it to an incomplete close. Book One
   of the *Vita* therefore covers Bernard's life to around 1130.
   The friendship of William and Bernard, who first met in 1118
   (*Vita I*, 7, 33-34; PL 185:246C-247C), encompassed most of their
   monastic lives, but William also acknowledges his **debt** to other
   'reliable' sources for the accounts included in the *Vita (Vita I,
   Praefatio*; PL 185:225C-226A), a common feature of medieval
   hagiography. Although the *Vita* conforms to the general conven-
   tions of the medieval *vita* genre, it has come from the hand of
   a theologian who sustains his theological activity as he writes
   the Life of a saint.

   The standard text of the *Vita prima Bernardi* is Mabillon's
   edition reprinted in PL 185: 225-267. An English edition, marred
   by unexplained omissions, has been offered by C. Webb and A.
   Walker, *St Bernard of Clairvaux* (Westminster, **Maryland**: The
   Newman Press, 1960). References to the *Vita I* provide chapter
   and **paragraph** according to Mabillon's numbering, and location
   within PL 185. English translations of the *Vita I* are my own.

3. In this paper, I do not intend to enter the discussion regarding the historical value of the *Vita*, nor to examine in detail
   its hagiographical elements. For examples of the discussion
   of the historical credibility of the work, see Déchanet, pp.
   106-107, and **Gilson**, p. 253, who argue for its historical value,
   and Jean Leclercq, *Nouveau visage de Bernard de Clairvaux. Ap-
   proaches psycho-historiques* (Paris: Cerf, 1976) pp. 11-34, who
   argues for caution and presents an intriguing 'psycho-historical'
   approach to the historical content of the *Vita*. On the hagiographical **context** of the *Vita*, see Jean Leclercq, *The Love of
   Learning and the Desire for God: A Study of Monastic Culture*,
   rev. ed., trans. Catharine Misrahi (New York: Fordham University

     Press, 1974) pp. 199-206.

4. *Vita I, Praefatio;* PL 185:225C.

5. Déchanet, p. 106.

6. Patrick Ryan, OCSO, 'The Witness of William of St Thierry to
    the Spirit and Aims of the Early Cistercians,' *The Cistercian
    Spirit: A Symposium,* ed. M. Basil Pennington, OCSO, CS 3 (1970)
    p. 225. See *Vita I,* 8, 38 (PL 185:249C). It is worth noting
    that in many respects the *Vita prima Bernardi I* serves as an
    apology for the cistercian life. The debate, at times acrimoni-
    ous, between the various monastic observances must be kept in
    mind. For an example of this debate, in which William was in-
    timately involved, see St Bernard of Clairvaux, 'Cistercians
    and Cluniacs: St Bernard's Apologia to Abbot William,' trans.
    M. Casey, OCSO, *The Works of Bernard of Clairvaux, Vol. 1:
    Treatises I,* CF 1 (1970) pp. 3-69. For a classic effort to
    bring an ecclesiological order to the diversity of religious
    communities, see the *Libellus de diversis ordinibus et proffes-
    sionibus qui sunt in aecclesia,* ed. and trans. G. Constable
    and B. Smith (Oxford: Clarendon, 1972), written by a regular
    canon active at Liège, William of St Thierry's birthplace,
    about the middle of the twelfth century (Constable and Smith,
    pp. xv-xviii).

7. *Vita I,* 1, 1 (227A-B). On the place of Aleth in William's
    account, cf. Leclercq, *Nouveau visage,* pp. 17, 20-27.

8. See *Vita I,* 7, 35 (248B), where Clairvaux is compared to the
    cave where shepherds found St Benedict (Gregory the Great,
    Dialogues II, 1).

9. *Vita I,* 1, 1 (227C).

10. *Vita I,* 1, 1 (227C); 2, 5 (229D).

11. *Vita I,* 1, 1 (227C).

12. *Vita I,* 3, 6-9 (230B-232A). On Bernard's education at Châtillon-
    sur-Saone, see *Vita I,* 1, 3 (228B). Aleth appears again to the
    fourth son, Andrew, convincing him that he should join Bernard;
    Vita I, 3, 10 (232A-C). It is also the memory of Aleth which
    changes Bernard's sister Hombeline from a lady of wealth to
    one who, like her mother, lived the life of the hermit in the
    world until her husband freed her, according to the rites of
    the Church, to enter the convent at Jully-les-Nonnaines, found-
    ed by Bernard for the wives of men he had lured into the cister-
    cian order; *Vita I,* 6, 30 (244C-245B).

13. *Vita I,* 3, 8 (231C-D).

14. Note that the *Libellus de diversis ordinibus* discusses the Cis-
    tercians in 3, 22-29 (pp. 44-57) under the heading 'Monks who
    remove themselves far from man.' Cf. Introduction, p. xxiv.

15. *Golden Epistle* I, 1: '...the brethren of Mont Dieu introduce
    to our Western **darkness** and French cold the light of the East
    and that ancient fervor of Egypt for religious observance...'

Cf. Leclercq, *The Love of Learning*, p. 125; Gilson, pp. 15-20.

16. *Vita I*, 8, 42 (251C).

17. *Vita I*, 7, 34 (247C).

18. *Vita I*, 4, 21 (239A).

19. *Vita I*, 4, 21 (239A): 'Ad contemplanda quippe spirituali quae-
que seu divina, cum gratia spirituali, naturali quadam virtute
pollebat spiritualibus studiis, et in eis, quae ad Deum sunt,
sponte subditam spiritui et servientem....'

20. *Vita I*, 4, 21 (239B): 'etsi neglectum minus, sicut oportebat,
curaretur, ad serviendum spiritui in servitio Dei aptissimum
instrumentum. Sed cum caro in eo ex dono praevenientis gratiae,
et adjutorio subsequentis naturae, et usu bono spiritualis disciplinae vix jam aliquid concupiseret adversus spiritum, hoc
est, quod spiritum laederet....'

21. William uses both *anima* and *animus* to refer to man's rational
power. The feminine denotes the mind in as much as it looks
toward things of the senses. The masculine denotes the mind
which is formed by and serves the spirit. See *Golden Epistle*
I, 152; see also Bernard McGinn, 'Introduction,' *Three Treatises on Man*, Cistercian Fathers Series, 24 (Kalamazoo, Mich.:
Cistercian Publications, 1977) p. 37. William's use of the
feminine in this context is peculiar.
  The anthropological hierarchy, *corpus-anima/animus-
spiritus*, is drawn out with great subtlety and beauty in *The
Golden Epistle*.

22. It is curious that in the *Vita*, William does not go on to discuss explicitly the restoration of the *imago Dei*, a central
anthropological concept in his earlier work, 'The Nature of
the Body and Soul. Book Two: Physics of the Soul,' trans. B.
Clark, OCSO, *Three Treatises on Man*, pp. 125-152.

23. See, for example, *Golden Epistle II*, 251.

24. *Vita I*, 1, 3 (228B).

25. *Vita I*, 3, 6 (230C).

26. *Vita I*, 8, 39 (250A). It should be noted that Bernard's diet
was largely dictated by his ruined digestion. Wine and beer
were also available to the monks, but Bernard indulged rarely
and then sparingly.

27. *Vita I*, 4, 21 (239B).

28. *Vita I*, 8, 41 (251A-B).

29. *Vita I*, 4, 20 (238B). But see Leclercq, *Nouveau visage*, p. 28.
William saw the life of the senses as one which 'draws the soul
out of itself' and attaches it to material things by 'the strong
flue of love and habit,' so that the soul becomes alienated from
its spiritual nature and end; cf. *Golden Epistle* I, 46-47.

30. *Vita I*, 4, 20 (238B-C); cf. *Vita I*, 7, 33 (247A-B).

31. *Vita I*, 4, 20 (238D-239A). 'Memory for William is not simply
the faculty which remembers, rather it is that part of the soul

where all the knowledge coming into it from outside is gathered together and where all thoughts are elaborated'; *Golden Epistle* I, 120, fn. 36.

32. *Vita I*, 4, 20 (238C).

33. *Vita I*, 4, 20 (238D).

34. *Vita I*, 4, 23 (240C). On the 'unity of spirit' which is for William the summit of the mystical life, see *Golden Epistle* II, 256-257; 262-263; 275; 286-289.

35. *Vita I*, 4, 22 (239D-240A); 8, 39 (250A-C). But see Leclercq, *Nouveau visage*, pp. 27-30.

36. *Vita I*, 7, 32 (246B); 8, 38 (249C-D).

37. *Vita I*, 8, 38 (249D).

38. *Vita I*, 7, 36 (248C-D). In his earlier years as abbot Bernard was evidently quite demanding of his monks (*Vita I*, 6, 28; 243A-C), but was later noted as gentle, understanding, and concerned, an abbot who cared for the physical as well as spiritual welfare of his monks (*Vita I*, 8, 38; 249C).

39. *Vita I*, 7, 37 (248D-249B); cf. *Golden Epistle* I, 68; 74; 126-127.

40. *Vita I*, 8, 41 (251B). On the unique importance which William assigns the body, see McGinn, pp. 29-30.

41. *Vita I*, 8, 41 (251B).

42. *Vita I*, 8, 41 (251A).

43. *Vita I*, 4, 19 (238A). William uses the same terms to describe the choice made by Stephen Harding, Abbot of Cîteaux, to send Bernard as the founder and abbot of the community of Clairvaux; *Vita I*, 5, 25 (241C). Cf. *Vita I*, 3, 10 and 13 (232A-B and 234D).

44. *Vita I*, 3, 15 (235C); 6, 29 (244B).

45. The numerous miracle stories found in the *Vita* are to be understood in the same light, as a further way in which God works through and is revealed in the life of the saint. William drew almost all of the miracle accounts from Geoffrey of Auxerre's *Fragmenta de vita et miraculis S. Bernardi*, ed. R. Lechat, SJ, *Analecta Bollandiana* 50 (1932), 83-122. Of the 71 paragraphs in the *Vita*, 38 (1-4, 6-14, 17, 26-27, 29, 31-34, 43-46, 48-55, 58, 65-68) rely to some extent on Geoffrey's notes; of the 65 **paragraphs** in Lechat's edition, William uses 33 of the first 42 (excluding 13-15, 17, 27, 29, 32, 35-36). By recognizing that William did not write his own miracle accounts but used those of Geoffrey it is possible to distinguish *(but not separate)* the explicit theological activity of William from his function as hagiographer. This is not to suggest that William did not believe the historical verity of the miracle accounts, nor does it imply that they do not serve a theological purpose. In fact they do: they are used to further communicate the active presence of God in the saint.

46. Leclercq, *The Love of Learning*, Chapter 5, 'Sacred Learning,'
    pp. 87-109.
47. *Vita I*, 1, 3 (228C).
48. *Vita I*, 3, 13 (234C). This is a standard hagiographical de-
    vice, found, for example, in the *Vita Antonii* 2. It was, how-
    ever, also an authentic form of response to Scripture; see
  . Augustine, *Confessions* VIII, 12.
49. *Vita I*, 4, 24 (241B).
50. *Vita I*, 1, 2 (228A); 2, 5 (229C); 3, 13 (234D); 3, 15 (235D-
    236A); 4, 19 (238B); 5, 25 (241C-D); 8, 38 (249C).
51. The solitary life is among the principle themes of the Lives
    of the Desert Fathers and the early Western **monastic** *vitae*.
    On the *vita angelica*, see Leclercq, *The Love of Learning*, pp.
    73-76.
52. *Vita I*, 1, 3 (228B).
53. *Vita I*, 6, 28 (243A-B); 7, 35 (248B).
54. *Vita I*, 4, 23-24 (240B-241A).
55. *Vita I*, 3, 14 (235C); 7, 35 (248B); cf. *Golden Epistle* I, 29.
56. *Vita I*, 6, 27 (242D-243A); 7, 33 (246C).
57. *Vita I*, 4, 19 (237D-238A).
58. See *Golden Epistle* I, 15-16: 'For you have vowed not only all
    holiness but **the** perfection of all holiness and the utmost
    limit of all consummation.' Cf. I, 25-26.
59. *Vita I*, 7, 33 (246D).

EARLY CITEAUX AND THE CARE OF SOULS

Bede K. Lackner O. Cist.

    Whether the White Monks offered priestly ministrations to
laymen living outside the monastic enclosure is a question of obvious importance for today's Cistercian intent on discovering his
roots, but it is also of interest to the modern historian aware of the
studies of Berlière, Leclercq, Georg Schreiber and Philipp Hofmeister,
which explore the thoughts of the Black Monks in some detail, but say
rather little about this subject of fundamental importance.[1]
    The *cura animarum* was, of course, not a new problem facing the
Cistercian pioneers; they did not have to devise original--Cister-
cian--answers but could simply draw from a rich monastic tradition,
the teachings and example of St Benedict, and from papal and conci-
liar legislation dating back to the Council of Chalcedon (451), all
of which offered abundant resources and guidelines from which they
could formulate their principles on their ideals. This became
necessary because the clericalization of the monastic order had
just then begun its victorious **course,** and because the Order incorporated already existing monasteries, (eventually) admitted
flourishing convents, became aware of the Church's missionary needs,
or heard arguments advanced by monastic champions advocating **the**
ordination of monks to the priesthood. Of course, one cannot possibly review the **whole** range of this vast material within the limits
of a brief paper, but one may hope at least to make a start by tracing and defining its main points.
    As is well known, the Cistercian pioneers simply wished to fol-
low the teachings and example of St Benedict in every respect, as
they found them recorded in the Rule and the life (biography) of the
saint. The Rule bade them stay aloof from the doings of the world,
and to do all things within the monastery so that they would not be
compelled to go outside. It also insisted that the workshop where-
in the monk must practice the instruments of good works and execute
his other duties is the enclosure of the monastery. Since the Rule
did not talk about a *cura animarum* but made reference to the celebration of the mass in the community, priests were obviously needed
in Benedict's monasteries; but ordination to the priesthood or the
admission of ordained **candidates** into the monastery depended on
the abbot's judgment and, as a general rule, the priesthood always
yielded to the *monachatus*.[2]
    Faithful to their Master, the founders of Cîteaux established
their monasteries not in cities, castles, or villages, but in places
far removed from the traffic of men. In obedience to his Rule they
insisted that the proper dwelling place of the monk is the cloister
where he must **stay** day and night in the service of God. They even

refused to live in **buildings** outside the gate of the monastery.[3]
As monks possessing lands, they wished to live as well from
their own labor--physical labor, agriculture, and the produce of
their animals. Hence they refused serfs, but admitted laybrothers
with the local bishop's permission, and employed hired men not attached to the monastic community. Opposed to exemption, they upheld and submitted to the pastoral responsibilities of the bishop
of the diocese.[4] And since they found no mention of it in the
Rule or in the life of St Benedict, they decided to renounce all
un-earned incomes, explaining: 'Our very name [of monks] and the
constitution of our Order prohibit the possession of parish churches, altar revenues, burials, tithes from the labor of others, and
all incomes of the kind, as contrary to monastic purity.'[5] Implementing this principle, they further stated: 'We receive no outsider to confession or Holy Communion; nor do we grant burial to
any outsider unless he is a guest or one of our hired workers who
dies within the monastery. Also, we do not accept offerings from
outsiders during the conventual mass.' Finally, they explicitly
rejected the care of women since they did not find that women had
ever entered St Benedict's monastery.[6]
In addition to the Rule, the White Monks were certainly inspired by the reform decrees of the French local councils (1074-
1100) which had sought to implement the ideals of the gregorian
reformers. These councils had decreed that monks must observe
the Rule of St Benedict without any change. Accordingly, they were
not to pursue parish work, for this would mean usurping the rights
of the secular clergy. By the same token, parish churches situated
on monastic grounds were to be administered not by the monks but
by chaplains appointed by, and responsible to, the bishop, insofar
as the care of souls was concerned.[7]
Only one council (Nîmes, 1096) insisted on the monks' worthi-
ness of the priesthood and its exercise, but it qualified its definition by listing the example of St Augustine of Canterbury and St
Martin of Tours--both of whom were bishops--and by upholding St
Benedict's injunction that monks were not to involve themselves in
secular affairs. Subsequent councils (1100-1238) consistently pro-
hibited every ministration outside the monastery.[8]
Yet the White Monks needed and actually did have priests in
their midst to take care of the community's needs. St Robert himself was a priest, as the reference to his *capella* and the **Exordium
Parvum** indicates.[9] He and his successors received the shepherd's
staff from the local bishop, who conferred on them the care of
souls. Accordingly the early legislation of the Order called the
abbot a *shepherd*, defined his office as 'pastoral care' for the
'salvation of souls,'[10] and ordered the removal of unworthy, negli-
gent, or incorrigible abbots from their pastoral responsibility.[11]
In later years the general chapters would suspend deliquent abbots

a divinis.

The first cistercian statues contain a number of provisions concerning the oratory, the altar, priestly vestments and the books and vessels needed for the sacrifice of the mass and the celebration of the liturgy. Additional definitions dealt with the chalice, communion reed, vessels, cruets, priestly vestments and altar furnishings. Finally, the White Monks were told to have the same missal, Gospel book, epistolary, book of collects, gradual, antiphonary, hymnary and calendar in every monastery and new foundation.[12]

The future of the New Monastery, uncertain at first, was assured when St Bernard entered the novitiate of Cîteaux with thirty fellow 'converts,' among them laymen powerful in the world and many literate and noble clerics. Later, as abbot of Clairvaux, Bernard continued to attract, in part through his rousing sermons, many other clerics (whom Bernard Lucet has sought to identify).[13] Obviously, the early Cistercians gave no preference to these priests in their community, nor did they specify or limit their number within a given monastery as their Carthusian contemporaries had done.[14]

To determine the number of priests found in early cistercian monasteries, one must **consult** the *Ecclesiastica Officia*, the **customary** of the Order, which describes and regulates in considerable detail such priestly functions as the celebration of the mass and the administration of the sacraments. Several priests were needed to celebrate the daily conventual mass, the periodic morrow mass, the so-called private masses, the devotional masses and, eventually, the masses prescribed by the general chapters.

The *Ecclesiastica Officia* associate **priestly** functions with a number of monastic officials, above all the abbot. The **cantor** anointed and brought Communion to the sick. The cellerar ministered to the spiritual needs of the laybrothers. Certain duties were assigned to the prior, the subprior, or the sacristan, in the event they were priests. Whether the novice master was a priest cannot be deduced from the fact that he heard the *confessiones* of his charges, for the expression could also refer to the chapter of faults.[15] Finally, when at a much later date the Cistercians admitted convents of women into the Order, the Fathers Immediate were given permission to hear the nuns' confession.

In spite of the **presence** of priests, St Bernard (who hardly ever abstained from the celebration of the mass) insisted that a clear distinction must be made between the monastic and the clerical vocation, irrespective of **a monk's** ordination to the priesthood. The cleric, he argued, received a special vocation from God which no monk can claim or exercise on his own. As a servant of the altar, the cleric administers baptism, buries the dead, visits the sick, blesses marriages, instructs the ignorant, corrects the errant, excommunicates the proud, **absolves** the fallen,

and reconciles the penitent. He is appointed and sent by the
bishop; he performs a public ministry. **In charge of many, he is
also responsible for many and must,** therefore, share, distribute,
instruct, and minister. In all these multitudinous concerns he
will be exposed to many **dangers,** especially when called upon to
make visits and to undergo journeys. Finally, as the servant of
the altar, he rightfully lives from the altar, not from the labor
of his hands.

Monks, on the other hand, did not receive such a calling from
God. They stay in the house of God, in the monastery, which is
their inclosed paradise, while the outside world is a jail to them.
Their vocation is to delight God and to delight in God within this
paradise. Segregated from the world, they lead a hidden life,
knowing that their vocation in the **Church** is not to speak but to
keep silent. Being unlearned and ignorant, they will listen rather than preach. As St Jerome had expressed it, their business is
not to teach but to weep. They will teach by the example of their
silence.

Monks have not been given a direct pastoral responsibility
over outsiders; rather, every monk must rule himself and work out
his own salvation. He must seek personal **perfection;** in this he
will succeed only if he does not dissipate his resources, but devotes all his efforts to the attainment of his goal, for perfection consists in fullness. Faithful to the teaching of the saints,
the monk must cultivate not the external man, but the interior man;
he must rely on prayer rather than on activity, and **realize** that
God is more easily and more securely reached through prayer than
through human words and arguments.

Bernard rejects the view that the ministry is legitimate because it is an exercise of love which seeks not its own. He reasoned: Love must seek it proper object; the ministry, however, is not
the proper object for the monk, but that of the cleric and the canon.
Therefore, a monk who pursues the work of a cleric is a usurper. Also, if a monk should feel that he is **wasting** his love in the monas-
tery, that he should rather share it with his brothers and friends,
for he will take on their lifestyle and thus lose his soul without
having gained anyone else's. Nor is it proper for a monk to roam
about outside the monastery, because he will fall victim to all
kinds of vices. He must not even go to the aid of the earthly Jerusalem, but must seek instead the heavenly Jerusalem.[16]

Pope Eugene III, the cistercian pontiff, vigorously defended
the White Monks' vocation and their views about the ministry. He
called on his former confrères to adhere to the Rule which they
had professed and to cherish the legacy of their founding Fathers
who had left the world in total renunciation and hastened to the
desert. While others are busy in frequent ministrations, they
sit with Mary at the feet of Jesus. This is their vocation, this

is what they must do, even if men of the world should attempt to
lure them away from the quiet of contemplation and the silence of
the desert or entreat them to take charge of their souls. The
pope urged the White Monks to remain faithful to the institutes
of the Fathers and prefer to live in abjection in the house of
God rather than dwell in the tents of seculars.[17]

The cistercian monk Idung, author of the famous *Dialogus duorum monachorum,* argued from the teaching of St Paul and from the
canons of the Church that the office of the altar, being a special
vocation, required a special call from God. The cleric who offi-
ciates at the altar, celebrates mass, gives Communion and hears
confession, receives the care of those who live within his parish
from the local bishop. Similarly, the office of preaching, that
is, public preaching, is done only by those who are sent: by the
bishops and the diocesan priests in their diocese or **parishes**;
and by abbots charged with the care of souls in their own monasteries.

The monks, on the other hand, have left all things for God;
they are God's portion and God is their portion. Their vocation
is the divine service, as St Benedict in his great wisdom had
determined. They are rightly called monks because dwelling in
their monasteries they are brothers dwelling *in unum,* separated
from those living in the world. Their life is apostolic, because
they live the life of the Apostles. Following the Rule of St
Benedict, they insist that worthy candidates be chosen **for** the
priesthood and that priests seeking admission into the monastery
be received only if they prove steadfast.[18]

In spite of this, Idung warned: 'According to St Augustine,
'People say, a bad monk makes a good cleric.' But I [Idung] say,
it is very difficult for a good monk to become a cleric.'[19] To
the great Augustine the office of the altar was such a sublime
vocation that even those who led a very holy life, above all the
monks, could not really be considered worthy of it. This is why
the early monks refused ordination, at times through flight or
self-mutilation, or, if ordained--on occasions, against their
will--abstained from saying mass throughout their lives.

The monk who is worthy of ordination shall become a priest
only through coercion, Idung insisted. He deplored the 'attitude
of modern monks, **because all** of them, worthy or unworthy, want to
be ordained.' He criticized abbots who said that nobody is worthy
[of ordination] and yet, when the opportunity presented itself,
had almost all their monks ordained priests, without discrimination
or selection, challenging the Rule and the **canons** and making them
look foolish. As for the reason why yearning for the priesthood
so tickles modern monks that they want to be ordained to the priesthood whether they are worthy or not, Idung explained: 'Perhaps it
lies in the fact that they take pleasure in the honor attached to

the higher status, but never give a thought to its burdens and
dangers. Yet, it is improper to seek after the higher status
even if it is held with **propriety**. The monk who is worthy of ordination should become a priest only through coercion, while the
unsuited monk not even when coercion is applied, for he must not
ascend to such high status in violation of the Rule and the **canons**,
or by the false testimony of those who present him to the bishop
for ordination.'[20]

From this Idung concluded that the chapels of nuns must be administered by secular priests sent and commissioned by the local ordinary. The Cistercian Order forbade its abbots to engage in the
direction of nuns for the reason that this would be greatly detri-
mental to their soul. Moreover, the White Monks were frightened
by the prospect of taking over the affairs of many and also by
those all too frequent chats (*confabulationes*) which take place
at the windows of convents, involving even fervent abbots. Finally, it was contrary to the example of St Benedict who conversed with
his sister but once a year and then only on spiritual topics. The
Cistercians were contemplatives, not because they engage in **manual**
labor, but because they abstain from the ministry for the sake of
contemplation.[21]

Conrad of Eberbach devoted an entire chapter of his *Exordium
Magnum* to the topic 'How Dangerous it is to Seek Holy Orders.' To
prove his point he listed the plight of a recently deceased cistercian monk who in his carnal thinking had yearned for the diaconate.
Conrad repeated the apostle's warning that no one must aspire to
the priesthood except he who has been called by God, and therefore
condemned all those who endeavored to secure holy orders improperly,
by illicit or seemingly licit means. Monks should be mindful of
the numerous divine judgments which befell the latter and devote
themselves to vigils, fasts and prayers--that is, remain monks--
and thus save their souls.[22]

These teachings of the early Cistercians rested on the general
principles **outlined** by the very founders of the Order; the particu-
lars were enacted by the general chapters which sooner or later had
to deal also with the question of the *cura animarum*. Thus, an early
chapter legislated: 'Our abbots are forbidden to bless a nun, baptize an infant or hold an infant in baptism.'[23] In another instance
abbots were told not to celebrate mass while on a journey.[24] After
1154 the general chapters became more specific and hence more informative on the subject.

The chapter of 1154 decreed that anyone ordained after leaving
the Order will in case of his return forever lose the right to exercise the order he had received while outside; but he could dis-
charge the order he had received before leaving the monastery, if
the abbot so desired. Also, a fugitive ordained to the priesthood
was assigned the last place among the priests of the monastery and

told, when assisting at mass as a deacon, to wear the stole diagonal-
ly over one shoulder only, as is done by deacons.[25] In 1157 the
chapter added: 'No abbot shall cause a monk of our Order to be ordained without the consent of his own abbot.'[26] In 1189 the chapter
further legislated that monks who directly or indirectly, in person
or through others, importune their abbots to secure ordination,
were to have their request put aside for two years, unless in the
meantime, they were elected abbots. The chapters of 1191 and 1192
repeated the decision of 1189 while the chapters of 1192 and 1193
additionally explained that monks must not seek higher offices.[27]

At times the very opposite happened; some postulants concealed
the fact of their priesthood. According to Caesarius of Heisterbach, they did this out of humility, preferring as laybrothers the
status of shepherd to a life of studies and responsibilities over
others. Accordingly the general chapter of 1202 decided: 'A certain laybrother of Grandselve, who when entering the Order concealed the fact that he was a subdeacon when in fact he was one, and
then leaving his monastery went to **another** abbey where he was received as a subdeacon and subsequently promoted to the diaconate,
shall be dismissed from the Order and never rejoin it.'[28] In 1214
the Fathers decreed: 'Clerics in holy orders who [when presenting
themselves] are received among the laybrothers, shall be expelled as
soon as this fact is discovered by the abbot.'[29] The chapter of the
following year (1215) restated this decision, ordering the expulsion
of such culprits or their **relegation** to the tonsured *familiares*.[30]

Dealing with a related matter, the general chapter decided that
a monk of Perseigne who had run away from his monastery and celebrated mass though he was only a subdeacon could be readmitted if
he should request it, but might not go on to higher orders. Moreover, he was to do penance for seven years (fasting on bread and
water on Fridays) and thereafter function **only as a** subdeacon.[31] In
1221 the chapter even ordered that fugitive Cistercians who ventured
to say mass outside the monastery must, after their return, abstain
from celebrating mass, fast on bread and water, and be given the discipline once every Friday for as long a time as they had stayed in
the outside world; and it empowered the abbots to take further actions if they judged them to be necessary.[32]

The prohibition of the *cura animarum* obviously included the administration of baptism. Already in 1157 the chapter decreed that
abbots and monks must never baptize infants, except in the case of
imminent death when no parish priest was at hand.[33] It also stated
that while Saracens were not to be ransomed, they could be baptized
--presumably to enable them to join a monastery in some capacity,
since they were not under the jurisdiction of the local bishop.[34]
In 1185 the chapter condemned to three days *in levi culpa* abbots who
acted as sponsors of boys, while those who **actually** performed the
rite of baptism were given six days *in levi culpa,* one of them to

be on bread and water. Abbots guilty on both counts were to remain *extra stallum* for seven days. A monk accused of this trans-
gression received the same punishment if he acted with the permission of his abbot or prior; if he had proceeded on his own, he was
to fast on three additional days on bread and water. The chapter
insisted: 'As a general rule, all who have the temerity to do such
things must be severely punished, because it is a violation of the
sacred canons.'[35] The chapter of 1186 added a further reason: 'It
is an extremely grave matter and a violation of the institutions of
our Order if abbots take the liberty to administer baptism.' Therefore all who were guilty of such temerity during the previous year
were told to fast for seven days on bread and water, refrain from
celebrating mass until Christmas and remain outside their choir
stall for the same period of time. If an abbot should baptize in
the future, he must fast on every Friday on bread and water, remain *extra stallum* and not celebrate mass until the chapter granted him permission to do so. If a monk blessed the baptismal water
or acted as a sponsor, he was to be given a similar punishment.[36]
Implementing its decision, the chapter promptly proceeded against
the abbot of Stürzelbrunn, in whose abbey an infant had been baptized (and women allowed to enter) while he was at home. It also
made the abbot's councillors fast on a given Friday on bread and
water, because they assisted him in this matter.[37] In 1192 the
chapter absolved the abbot of Sept-Fons, whom it had similarly censured for **baptizing**, but told him to remain *extra stallum* until the
feast of Christmas, because he had failed to carry out in every detail the sentence imposed on him by the general chapter.[38] The
chapter's stand remained unchanged, for it reiterated the existing
legislation on baptizing infants and Saracens as late as 1215.[39]

     In the question of preaching outside the monastery, the chapter
of 1191 reprimanded the abbot of Aiguebelle, explaining that a monk
may not preach in the churches of laymen, for this is the responsibility of the local bishop.[40] In 1197 Durannus of Clairvaux was
transferred to another monastery of the Order to keep him from
preaching and defending his errors.[41] The next chapter (1198) even pro-
hibited preaching undertaken for the purpose of soliciting alms for
the construction of churches or similar projects, but allowed the collection of alms when no preaching was involved.[42] One year later
(1199) the chapter charged the abbot of Kamp to proceed against a
monk of Loccum who was said to be preaching to the heathens of the
area.[43] Branding monks or laybrothers who engaged in preaching
guilty of innovation and levity, the chapter of 1200 ordered abbots to transfer such culprits to another house where they were
to remain until it allowed them to return to their own monastery.[44]
Thus, in 1201, Rayner, a monk of St Peter de **Aquilis** in Portugal,
was dispatched to another house and told to return to his own monastery only when the general chapter gave him such permission, because he had been preaching and thus violated the laws and the good

name *(honestas)* of the Order.[45] In 1204 the chapter again prohib-
ited all preaching undertaken for the purpose of securing funds
and condemned abbots and officials who disregarded this injunction
to six days *in levi culpa* (two of them on bread and water) and the
community to a day of fasting on bread and water, and ordered that
the money thus collected be handed over to the general chapter.[46]
Accordingly, the chapter of 1212 reprimanded the abbot of Bonlieu
who had sent one of his monks on a preaching mission in order to
collect funds and charged two abbots to visit Bonlieu and settle
the matter with the authority of the general chapter. The same
chapter also condemned Peter, a monk of Preuilly who was preaching
against the Albigensians, and ordered his immediate recall. It
called monks engaged in outside preaching *fugitives* guilty of rash-
ness and usurpation, and decreed that neither Peter nor anyone else
should thereafter engage in such illegal preaching.[47] Even in 1233,
when the Cistercians received permission to preach to the monastic
familia on Sundays and feasts, the authorization remained optional
since it contained the proviso: 'if the abbot so wishes.'[48]

     As champions of monastic purity, the first Cistercians reject-
ed churches, altars, burials and tithes which they judged incompa-
tible with their institutes. Even in 1214 the general chapter still
refused the acceptance of parish churches and decreed that any abbot who violated this law would incur automatic deposition while
those who aided him with their counsel should be transferred to
another monastery of the Order.[49] In the following year (1215) it
specifically stated: 'By the authority of the general chapter it
is forbidden that anyone accept parish churches hereafter. If the
transgressor is an abbot, he shall be deposed at once and have no
recourse to any remedy; others shall be banished from their houses
with no prospect of returning.'[50] Much stronger language was used
by the chapter of 1234: 'The monks of our Order are strictly forbidden to administer, or serve in, parish churches, to accept the
care of souls or to be allowed to stay in them on any occasion for
any length of time. Should there be monks in any parish church,
they must be recalled immediately.'[51] In 1235 the chapter decreed:
'Monks who are in churches which belong to the Order shall be recalled in every instance by the Feast of the Purification of the
Blessed Virgin Mary. Neither they nor any other monk may hence-
forth serve or stay in them. Instead, monasteries which have such
parish churches shall cause them to be administered by *donati* or
by secular chaplains, in case there is a need for it.'[52] Abbeys
which had belonged to another order before joining the Cistercians
were told by the chapter of 1236 to have the chapels and churches
which they possessed before joining the Order administered by persons who customarily administer them.[53] This shows that the admission of such abbeys into the Order did not imply an acceptance of
the *cura animarum*. In all other cases the decision of 1235 was to

be followed.

The only exception, made by the same chapter (1236), involved the abbeys of Les Dunes and Ter Doest, which had churches and a considerable number of laybrothers on some islands inhabited by seculars. Since, in view of the stormy sea, the islands could not be reached without the great physical danger of capsizing and drowning, and since the absence of a priest would have endangered the spiritual welfare of the islanders, the abbots in question were given permission to keep three monks in these churches to administer the sacraments to the laybrothers and the other inhabitants;[54] but this regulation did not imply the establishment of a monastic parish.

In the question of imposing penances on seculars, the general chapter of 1191 reprimanded the abbot of Aiguebelle for disregarding the Order's prohibition.[55] The chapter of 1220, which allowed abbots to place monks at the service of Cistercian bishops, gave permission for such priests to hear **confessions** if they received the proper authorization, but ordered their immediate recall in case they displayed a secular conduct contrary to the *honestas Ordinis*.[56]

In imitation of St Benedict, the Cistercians also denied burial within their grounds to outsiders. While the *Exordium Parvum* made no exceptions from the general rule, the *Ecclesiastica Officia* allowed the burial of two *familiares* and their wives. In 1190 the general chapter insisted that no one else was to be buried in the monastery during the lifetime of these *familiares*, but that others could be considered if one or both had already been deceased.[57] A further consideration was shown to bishops, princes, and the secular founders of the monasteries, obviously in view of their close association with the community. But there were to be no other exceptions. Accordingly the same chapter (1190) reprimanded the abbot of **Quincy and placed** him *in levi culpa* **for** three days (during which he was to fast on bread and water) for granting burial *extra formam Ordinis*.[58] In like manner, the chapter of 1191 censured the abbot of Aiguebelle who had granted burial in the abbey's house in the city, and condemned him to six days *in levi culpa* (one of them on bread and water) and the penalty of remaining *extra stallum* for forty days.[59] In 1199 the abbot of Swineshead, who had buried his *advocatus* in the chapter room, was sentenced to six days *in levi culpa*, one of them on bread and water; the same censure was pronounced also against his councillors.[60] In 1213 the abbots of Valroi and Foucourmont were consigned to three days *in levi culpa*, one of them on bread and water, for burying a layman *contra formam Ordinis*.[61] Two years later (1215) the abbot of **Fontfroid,** who had given a **resting** place to the queen in his church, was sentenced to six days *in levi culpa* (two of them on bread and water) and to forty days *extra stallum*, while his community was told to abstain from wine on six consecutive Fridays.[62]

On principle, the White Monks outlawed every contact with
women and renounced all feminine work. Under no circumstances
were monks and laybrothers to live under the same roof with women.
Nor could women be guests in the granges or proceed beyond the gate
when visiting a monastery. Thus the White Monks would not serve as
chaplains in monasteries of cistercian nuns. Yet sometime between
1190 and 1210, the Order began to accept women's houses, perhaps
on higher orders or possibly to induce the nuns to return to a
cloistered life, as the chapter of 1213 seems to imply. But this
turn of events did not change the fundamental principles or the
character of the Order, for the nuns were to recruit chaplains
from the secular clergy and then give these chaplains a cistercian
formation. The chaplains began the noviciate, after which, giv-
en the cistercian habit, they made their profession, fully detailed by the chapter of 1254, in the presence of the abbess.[63] Already in 1220, and again in 1258, these chaplains were told to celebrate mass *secundum formam et consuetudinem Ordinis* or face a severe reprimand by the abbess.[64]

In time however, the Order allowed the Father Immediate to hear
the nuns' confessions (1237) or to delegate an upright and prudent
man to the purpose.[65] If monks stayed at a nuns' monastery for some
reason, the general chapter kept a watchful eye on them, as in 1246,
when it ordered the recall of a monk from the nuns of Camberona, to
which he was never to return because *male se habuit*.[66] It is also
a fact that, after 1220, the Order made repeated attempts to stop
the incorporation of nuns. In this it eventually succeeded, when
in 1251 Pope Innocent IV empowered the Order to disregard future
papal appeals soliciting the acceptance of nuns.[67]

The preceding facts and details have shown the White Monks'
success in keeping the ideals of their Founders unchanged for centuries. They were determined to uphold the institutes of the Order, the *honestas Ordinis*, the *rigor Ordinis*, the *libertas Ordinis*,
the *forma Ordinis*, as the decisions of the general chapters have
shown. Rejecting exemption, they also upheld the rights of the
local ordinary. While making some allowances, their general chapter condemned *curam regere animarum* even to the end of the fifteenth
century (1487)[68] and ordained as late as 1667 'that every permission
to go outside the monasteries on account of the care of souls must
be withdrawn.'[69]

Yet, the White Monks were not self-centered, less than apostolic, or·pastorally deficient on this account; many records imply the
exact opposite. Thus, the Cistercians made each abbot responsible
for the spiritual welfare of his monastery and, in the case of filiation or the attachment of houses of nuns, for his daughter house
as well; the same applied to the Fathers Immediate and the canonical
visitors of nuns. Their general chapters met to promote the salva-

tion of souls, while their Charter of Charity voiced a concern for
'all the children of holy Church.'[70] They ministered to their
guests: confrères, other monks, canons regular, bishops and papal
legates, the pope, or the king of France. These visitors were led
into the chapel and the chapter room, greeted with a blessing and
readings, allowed to assist in the liturgy, and given sacramental
ministrations in the case of illness or imminent death. Thus one
could speak of a guest-house apostolate. Moreover, they prayed for
the dead: for the recently deceased, for deceased confrères, parents, brothers and sisters, close relatives, for those buried in
the cemetery, for persons prescribed by the general chapter and for
all the faithful departed.[71] And their general chapter allowed the
administration of baptism *in articulo mortis*. Nor was preaching
unknown in the Order, as the example of St Bernard and the long
list of such great successors as Guerric of Igny, Isaac of Stella,
Odo of Morimond, Alan of Lille, Adam of Perseigne and Caesarius of
Heisterbach clearly proves. Finally, abbots and monks did accept
the episcopate out of obedience to their abbots, the general chapter, and the pope.

While the Order never changed its stand officially, it did
seemingly abandon its primitive ideals in isolated instances. Berlière listed the abbeys of Baudeloo, Les Dunes, Ter Doest, Saint,
Bernard-sur-l'Escaut, Aulne and Kamp in this connection, though
without offering specific details.[72] Already long before, the
congregation of Savigny had also done pastoral work prior to and
even after its admission into the Cistercian Order, but Pope Alexander III apparently revoked this privilege. Louis Lekai has listed additional instances, but, given his objectives, did not explain
the nature of this pastoral involvement.[73]

To obtain a balanced picture, one must obviously consider the
reasons given for these exceptions, for they are quite enlighten-
ing. First of all, it is not surprising that the Cistercians should
make provisions for their hired men and other such associates, because this did not involve the need to go outside the monastery.
Also, in some instances the Cistercians were approached by the popes
who called upon the Order for the pastoral assistance not of a monastery but of a qualified individual. Innocent III and Gregory IX
asked for such individual preachers, and the general chapter devis-
ed a way to satisfy the papal wishes without weakening the principles of the Order.[74] In many cases these requests dealt with the
frontier apostolate, in the Baltic, in Sicily, or in Spain, where
heathenism or Islam were prevalent. Some monasteries attracted
pilgrims because of a local shrine or relic, but even in these
cases--here San Galgano comes to mind--the general chapter (1234)
disapproved parish work and ordered the recall of monks involved
in it. Other causes could be attributed to economic hardship and
the ravages of war, as in the case of the Hussite Wars. In most

of these instances the exception involved individual monks, not
an entire abbey.

The only departure from the general rule occurred in Austria
where local conditions created particular needs. But if Zwettl
was given the right to install perpetual vicars in the abbey's
churches, it must be remembered that the pontiff in question was
the notorious Boniface IX and that all this occurred during the
Great Western Schism.

To the motives which guided the cistercian pioneers one must
add also the poverty ideal of the White Monks which caused them
to return to the *vita apostolica* and its simplicity and primitive-
ness. Cîteaux renounced the great estate and its appurtenances
and refused the establishment of monasteries in cities or towns.
A necessary consequence of this was the renunciation of the pastoral ministry which would have led to unwholesome entanglements
with the feudal world. This is why Cîteaux opposed the acquisi-
tion and possession of churches and chapels. This is why it refused tithes as an unjust usurpation of the rights of others, in this
case of the secular priest administering the parish church. This
is why it insisted that the traditional fourth part of the tithe
be given to the parish priest. The Cistercians gave to the parish
priest what was rightfully his. Thus, as Georg Schreiber observed
long ago,[75] cistercian monasticism, in its own way, considerably
influenced the emergence and growth of the parish system. And
this means that the Cistercians, who renounced the care of souls,
made great contributions to the establishment and growth of the
parish clergy and the diocesan institutions--a paradox of no mean
significance!

University of Texas in Arlington

NOTES

1. Ursmer Berlière, 'L'exercice du ministère paroissial par les
    moines dans le haut Moyen-Age,' *Revue Bénédictine* 39 (1927)
    227-250; idem, 'L'exercice du ministere paroissial par les
    moines du XIIe au XVIIIe siècle,' *Revue Bénédictine* 39 (1927)
    340-364; Georg Schreiber, 'Gregor VII, Cluny, Cîteaux, Prémon-
    tré zu Eigenkirche, Parochie, Seelsorge,' in *Gemeinschaften
    des Mittelalters* (Münster i.W. Regensberg, 1948) pp. 283ff.;
    Philipp Hofmeister, 'Mönchtum und Seelsorge bis zum 13. Jahr-
    hundert,' *Studien und Mitteilungen zur Geschichte des Bene-
    diktinerordens und seiner Zweige* 65 (1955) 209-273. See also
    Jean Leclercq, 'On Monastic Priesthood According to the Ancient
    Medieval Tradition,' *Studia Monastica* 3 (1961) 137-155 and idem,
    'The Priesthood for Monks,' *Monastic Studies* 3 (1965) 53-85.
2. *Regula Benedicti*, chs. 4, 66, 73. See also Hofmeister, p. 222,
    and Bernard Lucet, 'Les ordinations chez les Cisterciens. Té-
    moignage d'Eude Rigaud pour la Normandie,' *Analecta Sacri Or-
    dinis Cisterciensis* 10 (1954) 268.
3. *Instituta monachorum Cisterciensium de Molismo venientium*, in
    Joannes-B. Van Damme (ed.), *Documenta pro Cisterciensis Ordinis
    historiae ac juris studio* (Westmalle: Typis Ordinis, 1959) p.
    14. See also *Instituta Generalis Capituli apud Cistercium*, in
    'Cistercii Statuta Antiquissima,' *Analecta Sacri Ordinis Cis-
    terciensis* 4 (1948) 16f., 19.
4. *Instituta monachorum Cisterciensium*; Van Damme, p. 13.
5. *Exordium Cistercii cum Summa Cartae Caritatis et Capitulis*,
    23; Van Damme, p. 28.
6. Ibid., 24; Van Damme, p. 28. See also n. 17 and *Instituta
    monachorum Cisterciensium*; Van Damme, pp. 27 and 13.
7. Bede **Lackner**, *The Eleventh-Century Background of Cîteaux* (Cis-
    tercian Studies Series, 8; Washington, D.C.: Cistercian Publi-
    cations, 1972), pp. 113ff.
8. Ibid., p. 126f. See also Berlière, 'L'exercice du ministère
    paroissial par les moines du XIIe au XVIIIe siècle,' pp. 342,
    344 and Hofmeister, pp. 245, 247.
9. *Exordium Parvum*, 7; Van Damme, p. 9.
10. Ibid., 4, 9-10; Van Damme, pp. 7, 10.
11. *Carta Caritatis*, VIII (9); Van Damme, p. 18; *Exordium Cistercii*,
    V; Van Damme, p. 24f.
12. *Exordium Parvum*, 16; Van Damme, p. 14; *Exordium Cistercii*, IX-X,
    Van Damme, p. 26.
13. *Exordium Parvum*, 16; Van Damme, p. 15. See also Lucet, p.
    278f.
14. Gregor Müller, 'Die Cistercienser Ordenspriester,' *Cistercienser-
    Chronik* 21 (1909) 23. See also Lucet, p. 268.
15. Lucet, pp. 268-274, 276.

16. *Sancti Bernardi Opera*, ed. J. Leclercq and H. Rochais (Rome:
     Editiones Cistercienses, 1957-1977), I: 104, 167; II: 128, 170;
     V: 234-236, 239-241; VII: 34f., 235; VIII: 129, 320f., 374 and
     379. See also Leclercq, *Monastic Priesthood*, p. 148; Bede Lack-
     ner, 'The Monastic Life According to Saint Bernard,' *Studies in
     Medieval Cistercian History II*, ed. John R. Sommerfeldt (Cis-
     tercian Studies Series, 24; Kalamazoo, Michigan: Cistercian
     Publications, 1976) p. 59.

17. Bede Lackner, 'Friends and Critics of Early Cîteaux,' *Analecta
     Cisterciensia* 34 (1978) 18.

18. R. B. C. Huygens, 'Le moine Idung et ses deux ouvrages: "Argu-
     mentum super Quatuor Quaestionibus" et "Dialogus duorum mona-
     chorum"' (Spoleto: Centro Italiano di Studi Sull' Alto Medioevo,
     1972) pp. 461, 434, 406. See also Berlière, 'L'exercice du
     ministère paroissiale par les moines dans le haut Moyen-Age,'
     p. 248.

19. *Dialogus duorum monachorum* (ed. Huygens), p. 435.

20. Ibid., pp. 434-436, 463.

21. Ibid., p. 443.

22. *Exordium Magnum Cisterciense*, ed. Bruno **Griesser** (Series Scrip-
     torum S. Ordinis Cisterciensis, II; Rome: Editiones Cistercienses,
     1961) 284ff.

23. *Cistercii Statuta Antiquissima*, 29; Turk, p. 20.

24. Ibid., (59)XX; Turk, p. 24.

25. 1154:18; **Joseph** M. Canivez, *Statuta Capitulorum Generalium Or-
     dinis Cisterciensis ab anno 1116 ad annum 1786* (Louvain: Biblio-
     thèque de Revue d'Histoire Ecclésiastique, 1933-1941) vol. I,
     p. 57. See also 1154:27; Canivez, I, p. 58.

26. 1157:2; Canivez, I, p. 60.

27. 1189:25, 1191:69; 1192:14; Canivez, I, pp. 114, 144, 148. See
     also Lucet, p. 277.

28. 1202:14; Canivez, I, p. 277. See also Lucet, p. 279 and Müller,
     p. 23.

29. 1214:59; Canivez, I, p. 429.

30. 1215:62; Canivez, I, p. 448.

31. 1193:51; Canivez, I, p. 167. See also Müller, p. 24.

32. 1221:11; Canivez, II, p. 3. See also Müller, p. 27.

33. 1157:7; Canivez, I, p. 60.

34. 1157:49; Canivez, I. p. 66.

35. 1185:8; Canivez, I, p. 99.

36. **1186:5; Canivez, I, p. 103.**

37. 1190:74; Canivez, I, p. 132.

38. 1192:30; Canivez, I, p. 151.

39. 1215:10; Canivez, I, p. 436.

40. 1191:20; Canivez, I, p. 137f.

41. 1197:55; Canivez, I, p. 220.

42. 1198:3; Canivez, I, p. 224.

43. 1199:71; Canivez, I, p. 246.
44. 1200:12; Canivez, I, p. 251.
45. 1201:49; Canivez, I, p. 273.
46. 1204:14; Canivez, I, p. 298.
47. 1212:33, 50; Canivez I, pp. 386, 400.
48. 1233:7; Canivez, II, p. 112.
49. 1214:57; Canivez, I, p. 428.
50. 1215:63; Canivez, I, p. 448.
·51. 1234:1; Canivez, II, p. 126.
52. 1235:2; Canivez, II, p. 139.
53. 1236:3; Canivez, II, p. 153.
54. Ibid.
55. 1191:20; Canivez, I, p. 137f.
56. 1120:3; Canivez, I, p. 516f.
57. 1190:4; Canivez, I, p. 119.
58. 1190:59; Canivez, I, p. 129.
59. 1191:20; Canivez, I, p. 137f.
60. 1199:78; Canivez, I, p. 247.
61. 1213:28; 30; Canivez, I, p. 410.
62. 1213:3; 1215:31; 1254:5; Canivez, I, pp. 405, 441; II, p. 399f.
63. 1254:5; Canivez II, p. 399f. See also Lucet, p. 271.
64. 1258:18; Canivez, II, p. 441f.
65. 1231:6; 1233:12; 1237:7; 1241:6; Canivez, II, pp. 92, 113, 169, 231.
66. 1246:49; Canivez, II, p. 311.
67. Louis J. Lekai, *The Cistercians. Ideals and Reality* (Kent, Ohio: Kent State University Press, 1977) p. 352.
68. 1489:17; Canivez, V, p. 678.
69. 1667:52; Canivez, VII, p. 452.
70. *Prodesse enim illius omnibusque sancte ecclesie filiis cupientes;* Van Damme, p. 16.
71. Bruno Griesser, 'Die "Ecclesiastica Officia Cisterciensis Ordinis" des Cod. 1711 von Trient,' *Analecta Sacri Ordinis Cisterciensis,* 12 (1956) 257ff. See also Bede Lackner, 'Early Cistercian Life as described by the *Ecclesiastica Officia*' *Cistercian Ideals and Reality,* ed. John R. Sommerfeldt (Cistercian Studies Series, 60; Kalamazoo, Michigan: Cistercian Publications, 1978) 73.
72. Berlière, 'L'exercice du ministere paroissiale par les moines du XIIe au XVIIIe siècle,' p. 364.
73. *The Cistercians,* p. 386f.
74. Canivez, I, p. 223; 1213:52; Canivez, I, p. 414. See also Hofmeister, p. 269f.; Berlière, 'L'exercice du ministère paroissial par les moines du XIIe au XVIIIe siècle,' p. 364.
75. *Gemeinschaften des Mittelalters,* pp. 357, 359.

MATERNAL IMAGERY IN TWELFTH-CENTURY CISTERCIAN WRITING[1]

Caroline Walker Bynum

When the twelfth-century abbot Aelred of Rievaulx composed for his sister a *Rule for Recluses*, he proposed the following object of meditation:

> On your altar let it be enough for you to have a re-
> presentation of our Saviour hanging on the cross; that
> will bring before your mind his Passion for you to imi-
> tate, his outspread arms will invite you to embrace
> him, his naked breasts will feed you with the milk of
> sweetness to console you.[2]

And Aelred is by no means the only cistercian author to use maternal imagery to describe Jesus or God. Bernard of Clairvaux exhorts a fellow monk, 'If you feel the stings of temptation,...suck not so much the wounds as the breasts of the Crucified. He will be your mother, and you will be his son.'[3] Guerric of Igny comments: 'The Bridegroom...has breasts, lest he should be lacking any one of all the duties and titles of loving kindness,' and speaks of the Holy Spirit as milk poured out from Christ's own breasts into the apostles Peter and Paul, who, in turn, become nurses and mothers to individual christian souls.[4] William of St Thierry writes: 'Since that ever-lasting blessed union and the kiss of eternity are denied the Bride [the soul] on account of her human condition and weakness, she turns to your bosom [Christ's]; and not attaining to that mouth of yours, she puts her mouth to your breasts instead....'[5] I could give many other examples.[6] The question I would like to ask here is why this explicit and elaborate maternal imagery—imagery which modern trans-lators have **frequently** found offensive—was popular with twelfth-century Cistercians.[7]

I begin by pointing out certain explanations which I am not going to offer. First, I am not going to argue that the image of Jesus or God as mother is an exclusively or peculiarly 'cistercian' theme. It is more elaborate in some cistercian writers than it is in any non-cistercian writer from the eleventh or twelfth century except Anselm; and there are certain **aspects** of the form it takes in cistercian authors that express concerns particularly intense in cistercian spirituality. But it is by no means a theme limited to Cistercians.[8]

Second, I am not going to argue that the way in which mater-nal imagery is used in twelfth-century texts reflects either, on the one hand, a more positive view of women and motherhood in medi-eval society or, on the other hand, an increasing ambivalence about

or antagonism **toward** the family. Scholars have sometimes used imagery
taken from human relationships as an indication of society's attitude
toward those relationships.[9] We can see in the cistercian authors I
will be discussing occasional passages that suggest either a highly
sentimentalized view of actual mothering[10] or an intense hostility
toward biological **parents** which leads to an idea of God as substitute
mother.[11] But I am suspicious of an approach that isolates imagery from
its literary context and then **relates** the isolated image directly to
the world of institutions and social relations. The study of a particular religious **image** should begin with a consideration of the other images among which it occurs and the basic theological tenets it expresses.
When we look at the context within which maternal imagery appears in
twelfth-century texts, we discover that it tells us less about men's attitudes toward women than about their attitudes toward authority and
toward themselves.

Third, I am not going to argue that the theme of God as mother is
simply a repetition of an established **literary** tradition. It is true
that the image was not new in the twelfth century. In the Old Testament, God speaks of himself as a mother bearing the Israelites in his
bosom, conceiving them in his womb (Is 49:1, 15, Is 66:3). Although
such imagery is absent in the New Testament, Christ is described
(M 23:37) as a hen gathering her chicks under her wings. The contrast drawn in the Epistles between milk and meat as types of instruction (1 Cor 3:1-3; Heb 5:12; 1 P 2:2) seems to have suggested to later
writers that the apostles responsible for the Epistles, Peter and Paul,
provided milk for beginners and should therefore be seen as mothers.
Clement, Origen, the author of the **apocryphal** third-century Acts of
Peter, Irenaeus, John Chrysostom, and Augustine all describe God and
Christ as mother.[12] The theme of the church as (virgin) mother, popular throughout the centuries, suggested to twelfth-century authors an
association of instruction and pastoral responsibility with maternity
and nursing.[13] But the mere **existence** of earlier 'maternal' texts
does not explain why twelfth-century authors chose to borrow them.
And closer examination reveals that patristic and twelfth-century
authors used the theme to express very different concerns.

An **answer** to the question 'why do cistercian authors speak of
God as mother?' should begin with further exploration of the image
itself and of its context. Such exploration reveals three things.
'Mothering' imagery was extremely popular generally in the twelfth
century. The new interest in the Virgin concentrated on her
not as queen of heaven but as mother of the human Jesus and as the
second Eve, mother of us all.[14] More relevant to the theme of God
as mother is the fact that many male figures are, in twelfth-century
writing, referred to as mother, or described as nursing, conceiving,
and giving birth.[15] Male figures so described are invariably those
whom both twelfth-century and modern readers would recognize as authority figures: twelfth-century writers refer to prelates--abbots
and bishops--as 'mothers.' They also use maternal imagery to des-

cribe male figures from the Old or New Testament in their capacity
as leaders or teachers; two of the most powerful and elaborate uses
of maternal imagery in the high Middle Ages are the meditations of
Anselm and Guerric on Peter and Paul.[16] Twelfth-century authors not
only refer to a variety of male figures in 'feminine' adjectives,
they also link discussions of God as mother with discussions of authority figures, chiefly abbots or the apostles Peter and Paul.
Moreover, certain biblical passages, especially the hen gathering
her chicks under her wings (M 23:37) and the reference to the delights of the bridegroom's breasts in the Song of Songs (S 1:1-2),
are as likely to trigger in the minds of twelfth-century authors
references to the burdens of pastoral responsibility as to the motherhood of God. Let me give an example.

When Bernard of Clairvaux comments on Song of Songs 1:1-2, he
first explains it as referring to Christ. He then remarks (without
making any explicit connection between the ideas) that greedy prelates are 'devoid of maternal instinct,' but 'there is no pretense
about a true mother; the breasts she displays are full for the taking.'[17] When, a number of sermons later, Bernard returns to the
breasts of the bridegroom, he adds the exhortation: 'Learn, you who
rule the earth. Learn that you must be mothers to those in your
care, not masters.... Be gentle, avoid harshness, do not resort to
blows, expose your breasts, let your bosoms expand with milk not
swell with passion.'[18] In twelfth-century texts, therefore, references to mothering often occur as a way of describing a **figure** or
an institution (God, Christ, the abbot, Moses, the church) which
teaches or exercises authority; and in such passages, *mater* is usually quite explicitly a complement to *pater* or *magister* or *dominus*.
Furthermore, the tendency of certain twelfth-century cistercian authors to associate God's motherhood and the pastoral burdens of
clergy or abbots is in marked contrast to patristic authors, like
Clement of Alexandria, who do not connect Jesus' mothering with the
mothering of earthly men.[19]

The second general characteristic of maternal imagery in twelfth-
century cistercian writing is the consistency of the sexual stereotypes that lie behind it. Certain personality characteristics are
seen by these authors as female and certain others as male. Throughout twelfth-century sermons and treatises, gentleness, compassion,
tenderness, emotionality and love, nurturing and security are labeled
'female' or 'maternal'; authority, judgement, command, strictness,
and discipline are labeled 'male' or 'paternal'; instruction, fertil-
ity, and creativity are associated with both sexes (either as beget-
ting or as conceiving). Moreover, these stereotypes remain the same
whether they are evaluated as negative or positive. Thus to Adam of
Perseigne, the **maternal** and female is strong; to William of St Thierry
the female is a symbol of both weakness and penitence. Helinand of
Froidmont gives a complex and **repeated** explanation of *mulier* as related

to *molis* ('soft' in the sense of weak) and *malleus* ('hammer' in the
sense of scourge)--an explanation intended to interpret the tenderness of women in a very pejorative light.[20] Because these sexual
stereotypes are constant throughout the literature, it seems clear
that authors spoke of 'fathers' as 'nursing' or joined 'mother' to
'father' in order to add a specific dimension to their general conception of **leadership**, authority, and pastoral concern.

There is a third characteristic of maternal imagery in cistercian writing which contrasts with the use of such metaphors both by
Anselm a little earlier and by several writers of the thirteenth
and fourteenth centuries, especially Julian of Norwich.[21] Among
twelfth-century Cistercians, breasts and nurturing are more frequent
images than conceiving or giving birth. Where birth and the womb
are dominant metaphors, the mother is described as one who conceives
and carries the child in her womb, not as one who ejects the child
into the world, suffering pain and possibly death in order to give
life. Conceiving and giving birth, like suckling, are images primarily of return to, union with, or dependence upon God, not images
of Christ's sacrifice or of human alienation. References to God as
mother usually occur not in the context of castigation of sinners or
elaboration of the gulf between human and divine but rather as part
of a general picture of the believer as child or **beginner**, totally
dependent on a loving and **tender** God. Indeed descriptions of the
soul as nursing child are even more common in cistercian writing than
explicit references to the breasts of God: when the soul is described
as Christ's brother, **for** example, it is usually seen as a brother of
the nursing, not the adult Christ.[22] The metaphor of the womb of
God is only one among many physiological metaphors used to express
union. Guerric of Igny writes:

> He [Christ] is the cleft rock...do not fly only to him
> but into him.... For in his loving kindness and his com-
> passion he opened his side in order that the blood of
> the wound might give you life, the warmth of his body
> revive you, the breath of his heart flow into you....
> There you will lie hidden in safety.... There you will
> certainly not freeze, since in the bowels of Christ
> charity does not grow cold.[23]

Aelred of Rievaulx, in his explanation of the crucifixion, weaves
together what appear to be nursing and womb images:

> Then one of the soldiers opened his side with a lance and
> there came forth blood and water. Hasten, linger not,
> eat the honeycomb with your honey, drink your wine with
> your milk. The blood is changed into wine to gladden you,
> the water into milk to nourish you. From the rock streams

> have flowed for **you**, wounds have been made in his limbs,
> holes in the wall of his body, in which, like a dove, you
> may hide while you kiss them one by one.[24]

Isaac of Stella goes beyond images of souls drawn into the womb or
side or bowels of God to develop a theory of the mystical body
which claims that Christ himself is not complete until we are all
incorporated into him.[25] When maternal imagery is applied to prelates, in contrast, it is more apt to stress the pain of giving
birth. The point of the image in this context is to underline the
difficulties of being a good father-mother. Yet even in these references, the image most often expresses that tender and affective
bond between mother-abbot and child which prepares for the **similar**
bond between soul and God.[26]

The maternal imagery of twelfth-century cistercian treatises
can thus be seen as an expression of the theological optimism which
is a familiar characteristic of twelfth-century religious writing.[27]
However deep their grief at sin, these authors all assume that God
is approachable and forgiving. As Bernard puts it, a mother cannot
fail to love her child; sin is a tarnishing of what the child-soul
should be, a naughtiness; but the fundamental bond with mother-God
remains.[28] Moreover, such maternal imagery is yet another example
of the affectivity and interest in human relationships which many
recent scholars have seen as typical of the high Middle Ages.[29]
Close analysis of the mothering images themselves and of their context suggests, however, a more specific answer to the question 'why
do twelfth-century Cistercians speak of Jesus as mother?' All these
authors use maternal imagery to add something to authority figures
qua rulers or fathers; and the 'something' added is always nurturing, affectivity, and accessibility. The specific context in which
maternal imagery appears suggests not only that twelfth-century authors saw God, abbots, and prelates as rulers, but also that rule,
to them, was problematic--that it needed to be softened or comple-
mented by something else. These authors appear to have supplement-
ed their image of God with maternal metaphors because they needed
to supplement their image of authority with that for which the 'maternal' stood: emotion and nurture. To make this argument is not,
of course, to propose that their concept of God is merely a pro-
jection of their own psyches. It is to say that the language in
which they chose to speak of their relationship to God expressed
the particular ideals and problems of the religious life they lived.

The need to supplement authority with love as the motive behind much maternal imagery is perhaps clearest in the case of Bernard. As I demonstrated a moment ago, Bernard's mind frequently
leaps to the topic of pastoral responsibility when it finds maternal metaphors in the Bible; it leaps to maternal or feminine imagery when it must discuss rule or discipline (either human or divine).

Moreover, explicit claims to be 'mother' as well as 'father' and
'brother' to his monks form one of his favorite self-descriptions.[30]
Bernard reveals himself in his letters as a person who worried more
about whether he loved adequately than about whether he was loved;[31]
some of his need to supplement images of command with images of nurture may express his particular **psychological** make-up. But the concern to add affectivity to rule in descriptions of God, prelates,
and self occurs also in William of St Thierry, Guerric of Igny, Aelred of Rievaulx, Adam of Perseigne, and Isaac of Stella.[32] Aelred's
dying words to his own monks were: 'I love you...as earnestly as a
mother does her sons.'[33]

It appears to be no accident that every twelfth-century cistercian author in whose writings **maternal** imagery plays a prominent
role was himself an abbot (and in some cases a novice master as well).
Moreover, in several of these authors, the effort to **expand** or supplement the concept of rule occurs in conjunction with intense and
articulated ambivalence about their own exercise of leadership.
William of St Thierry several times expressed feelings of exhaus-
tion and a desire to leave his abbacy, a desire upon which he finally acted.[34] Bernard wished to renounce the cares of pastoral responsibility and return to contemplation, yet he issued violent re-
bukes to other abbots who acted upon such yearnings. His ambivalence
is at times acute enough to seem a self-hatred, an antagonism toward
the gift for administration and preaching which he knew he possessed.[35]
Even Aelred, who had a sunnier disposition than Bernard or William,
expressed differing views of the value of administration and pastoral
responsibility depending upon his audience. When writing for hermits
and recluses, at least, he speaks of such activities in pejorative
terms.[36] Furthermore, there are institutional indications that the
abbatial role was seen as a heavy burden in the twelfth century. We
know that a number of abbots resigned, Cistercians prominent among
them. By the **thirteenth** century many of the new orders began to move
toward election of abbots for a limited term rather than for life--
clearly a response to twelfth-century feelings that life-long rule
was too great a burden for both the abbot and his sons.[37]

The reasons for this anxiety about rule are complex. Ambivalence
about taking on pastoral care inside the monastery or outside it (often
expressed as a debate between the active and contemplative lives)
formed part of the monastic tradition. Some twelfth-century Cistercians, especially Aelred, began to make creative use of the traditional texts in a way that points toward a concept of one 'life'
which alternates between action and contemplation.[38] And, as I
have argued elsewhere,[39] almost every twelfth-century cistercian
writer struggled toward a concept of 'service' to neighbor that
defines service as largely affective. The anxiety of abbots about
their role is part of a far larger cistercian anxiety about the place
and meaning of 'love of neighbor' in the monastic life.

Moreover, as the institution of child oblates was rejected and a greater emphasis placed on adult choice and conversion, it is probable that more demands were put on abbots to offer spiritual guidance to sensitive souls who worried about the quality of their inner life. Aelred of Rievaulx, drawing on his own experience as novice master, writes of a novice who worried because his gift of tears has dried up upon entering the monastery.[40] Both Bernard and Adam of Perseigne speak of similarly delicate problems of spiritual direction.[41] It seems possible that adult or adolescent converts, whose **awareness** of having made a personal choice could be acute, needed fewer rules (or 'discipline') and more advice (or 'nurture') than the young children common in monastic houses a hundred years earlier. In any case, discussions of spiritual direction by cistercian authors indicate that twelfth-century abbots were in fact called upon to respond with qualities men of the period considered 'feminine.' The large number of resignations, the agonized musings of William and Bernard over the burdens of rule, the statement of even so temperate a man as Aelred that service of others is a fall--albeit a necessary fall--from repose with Christ[42] suggest that cistercian abbots sometimes felt taxed, even trapped, by the intense emotional response they considered to be a crucial part of the 'father-mother' role.

Against this background, the twelfth-century cistercian articulation **of a** new concept of authority (both the authority of God and the authority of the monastic superior) is not surprising, nor is it surprising that they used 'maternal' imagery to express this concept. The image of 'mother' stood consistently for nurture and unfailing love throughout the literature of the **period**; the image of 'women' stood generally, although not universally, for 'weakness.'[43] To speak of God, of apostles, bishops and popes, abbots and novice masters, and of oneself, as *mater et magister* or *mater et pater* expressed perfectly an ideal of discipline with affectivity. But the anxiety about rule which led twelfth-century authors to complement authority with nurture was not necessarily stilled by the new ideal; nurturing, like discipline, could be a burden. When twelfth-century monks described the emotionality they cultivated as 'effeminate,' they sometimes meant that they were weak beginners who would develop more masculine virtues as they grew toward God. Sometimes they saw their 'womanly' qualities as a sign of their rejection of the values of the world.[44] Real women they saw primarily as sexual temptation.[45] Thus 'maternal' images could have negative or at least ambiguous connotations despite their consistent denotation of unflagging love. It is possible that describing themselves as 'mothers' in their capacity as rulers was a good way for twelfth-century cistercian men to express the ambivalence they felt about the necessity to rule, even if (perhaps especially if) the rule included nurture and emotional response.

I realize that this argument leaves many questions unanswered.
It does not explain what in society or in the depths of the human
psyche led cloistered males to associate women with tenderness or
mothers with closeness. Nor does it say why affectivity became a
central value, authority a **central** problem, to twelfth-century Cistercians. To explain these facts would require a general essay on
twelfth-century religion and twelfth-century life. But I hope I
have been able, in this short paper, to show that religious imagery,
if studied in its literary context, can yield important and surprising information about the basic concerns of the **authors** who use it.
I hope also that I have answered a question which is not without interest to modern theologians as well as to medievalists: why did
twelfth-century authors, especially Cistercians, make frequent and
un-selfconscious use of an image of God as mother which is to twenti-
eth-century people an oddity, an affront, or a self-conscious **slogan**
of liberation?[46]

University of Washington

NOTES

1. This paper was given at the Seventh Cistercian Conference at
   Kalamazoo, Michigan, 5-8 May, 1977. I am grateful to the Grad-
   uate School of the University of Washington for a grant which
   made it possible for me to attend the conference. I am also
   grateful to Catherine Moony of the Harvard University Divinity
   School who checked some of the references for me. Much of the
   material here has appeared in different form in 'Jesus as Mother
   and Abbot as Mother: Some Themes in Twelfth-Century Cistercian
   Writing, *Harvard Theological Review* 70 3/4 (1977) 257-84.
2. Aelred of Rievaulx, *De institutione inclusarum*, in Aelred of
   Rievaulx, *Opera omnia*, I: *Opera ascetica*, ed. A. Hoste and C.
   H. Talbot, CC, CM 1 (Turnhout, 1971) c. 26, p. 658; tr. M. P.
   Macpherson in *The Works of Aelred of Rievaulx*, I: *Treatises
   and Pastoral Prayer*, CF 2 (1971) p. 73.
3. Bernard of Clairvaux, Letter 322: *Epistolae*, ed. J. Mabillon;
   PL 182:527.
4. Guerric of Igny, Second sermon for SS Peter and Paul, c. 2;
   Sermons, ed. John Morson and Hilary Costello, vol. 2, SCh 202²
   (Paris, 1973) pp. 384-386; tr. by the monks of Mount St Bernard
   abbey, in Guerric of Igny, *Liturgical Sermons*, CF 32:155.
5. William of St Thierry, *Exposé sur le Cantique des Cantiques*,
   c. 38, ed. J.-M. Déchanet, SCh 82 (Paris, 1962) pp. 122-124; tr.
   Columba Hart, *Exposition on the Song of Songs*, CS 6 (1970) p. 30.
6. See, for example, Bernard of Clairvaux, SC 9.5-10 and 10.1-4
   (SBOp 1:45-50); William of St Thierry, *Meditativae Orationes*,
   8 and 10; PL 180:230C and 236A; Guerric, Fourth sermon for Palm
   Sunday, *Sermons* 2:212-214; Aelred, *De institutione*, c. 31, *Opera*
   I:668; Gilbert of Hoyland, *Sermones in Canticum Salomonis*, sermon 5; PL 184:32C. Another well-known example is Anselm, prayer
   10 to St Paul, *Opera omnia*, ed. Schmitt, vol. III (Edinburgh,
   1946) pp. 33 and 39-41. Anselm may have influenced the Cistercians in this usage, especially Guerric: see André Cabassut,
   'Une dévotion médiévale peu connue: la dévotion à "Jésus Notre
   Mère,"' *Mélanges Marcel Viller, Revue d'ascétique et de mystique*
   25 (1949) 239; J. Lewicki, 'Anselme et les doctrines des Cister-
   ciens du XIIe siècle,' *Analecta Anselmiana* 2 (1970) 209-216;
   S. Vanni Rovighi, 'Notes sur l'influence de saint Anselme au
   XIIe siècle,' *Cahiers de civilisation médiévale* 8 (1965) 46-50.
7. The only scholars who have dealt with the question of maternal
   imagery for God in medieval writing are Cabassut, *RAM* 25:234-
   245, and Eleanor C. McLaughlin, '"Christ My Mother": Feminine
   Naming and Metaphor in Medieval Spirituality,' *Nashota Review*
   15 3 (1975) 228-248. Neither gives twelfth-century examples
   other than Bernard, and their analysis of the theme differs
   greatly from the one which follows.

8. For non-cistercian examples, see Hugh Lacerta, *Liber de doctrina vel liber sententiarum seu rationum beati viri Stephani primi patris religionis Grandmontis,* c. 10, CC, CM 8 (Turnhout, 1968) p. 14; *Ancrene Riwle: The English Text of the Cotton Nero A.XIV,* ed. Mabel Day, Early English Text Society 225 (London, 1952) p. 103; and n. 6 above. William of St Thierry was, of course, not a **Cistercian** for most of his life.

9. Elaine H. Pagels, 'What Became of God the Mother? Conflicting Images of God in Early Christianity,' *Signs: Journal of Women in Culture and Society* 2 (Winter, 1976) 293-303, and Giles Constable, 'Twelfth-Century Spirituality and the Late Middle Ages,' *Medieval and Renaissance Studies* 5, *Proceedings of the Southern Institute of Medieval and Renaissance Studies, Summer, 1969* (1971) 42 and 51.

10. See Bernard of Clairvaux, *Dil,* 7.17; SBOp 3:134; and Letters 258 and 300; PL 182:466A-467A and 502A-C. It is worth noting that twelfth-century saints' lives seem to have a strikingly positive view of maternal influence; see Mary M. McLaughlin, 'Survivors and Surrogates...,' *The History of Childhood,* ed. L. DeMause (New York, 1974) 115-118.

11. Bernard of Clairvaux, Letter 322; PL 182:527C-D, and Letter 104; PL 182:240A-C. Isaac of Stella, Sermon 29; *Sermons,* ed. A. Hoste and Gaston Salet, vol. 2; SCh 207 (Paris, 1974) p. 172 (cols. 1785C-D). David Herlihy has suggested that medieval religious movements are part of a general rebellion against the family: 'Alienation in Medieval Culture and Society,' *Alienation: Concept, Term, and Meanings,* ed. Frank Johnson (New York, 1973) 125-140; a similar approach is taken by Michael Goodich, 'Childhood and Adolescence among the Thirteenth-Century Saints,' *History of Childhood Quarterly* 1.3 (1974) 285-309. While the argument is attractive, it seems to me to oversimplify somewhat a complex phenomenon.

12. See the passages cited in Cabassut, *RAM* 25:237, and Pagels, *Signs* 2: 293-303. See also Irenaeus, *Adversus haereses,* 3.24.1; PG 7:966-967, and Augustine, *In Iohannis Evangelium Tractatus CXXIV,* chapters 15.7, 16.2, 18.1 and 21.1, CC 36 (Turnholt, 1954): pp. 153, 165, 179 and 212.

13. See J. A. Jungmann, 'The Defeat of Teutonic Arianism and the Revolution of Religious Culture in the Early Middle Ages,' *Pastoral Liturgy* (New York, 1962) 48-63.

14. See Hilda Graef, *Mary: A History of Doctrine and Devotion,* 2 vols. (London and New York, 1963) 1, especially pp. 210-264.

15. See, for example, Anselm, prayer 10 to St Paul, *Opera omnia,* 3:33 and 39-41. Bernard, *SC* 9.9 (SBOp 1:47), 10.2-3 (49-50), 12.2 and 4 (61 and 62-63), 23.2 and 7-8 (139-140 and 142-144), 29.6 (207), 41.5-6 (SBOp 2:31-32), 85.12 (315). Bernard, Letters 1, 71, 110, 146, 152, 201, 238 and 258; PL 182:76A-B,

183B-184A, 253, 303B-C, 312A, 369B-C, 429C-D, 466B-467A; see
also Suibert Gammersbach, 'Das Abtsbild in Cluny und bei Bern-
hard von Clairvaux,' *Cîteaux in de Nederlanden* 7 (1956) 85-101.
William of St Thierry, *Sur le Cantique*, c. 52, p. 144. Guerric
of Igny, Third Christmas Sermon, cc. 4-5, *Sermons* 1, ed. Morson,
Costello, SCh 166 (Paris 1970) 198, and second sermon for SS.
Peter and Paul, c. 2: *Sermons* 2:384-386. Aelred of Rievaulx,
De Jesu puero duodenni, c. 3.30; *Opera omnia*, 1:276. Adam of
Perseigne, Letters 2 and 4; *Correspondance d'Adam, abbé de
Perseigne (1188-1221)*, ed. J. Bouvet, Archives historiques du
Maine 13, fascicules 1-10 (Le Mans, 1951-1962) 19-23 and 30-32.
Isaac of Stella, Sermon 27; *Sermons* 2:150-152 (col. 1780D).
Helinand of Froidmont, sermon 14; PL 212: cols. 591-594.

16.   See references in n. 15 above.
17.   Bernard, *SC* 9.5-6 (SBOp 1:45-46), and 10.3 (49-50); tr. Kilian
      Walsh, CF 4:62-63.
18.   Bernard, *SC* 23.2 (SBOp 1:139-140); tr. Walsh, CF 4:27. See also
      SC 41.5-6 (SBOp 2:31-32).
19.   Cf. Clement of Alexandria, *Paedagogus*, 1.6, in *Clemens Alex-
      andrinus*, ed. O. Stählin, I (Leipzig, 1936), Die griechischen
      christlichen Schriftsteller der ersten drei Jahrhunderte 12:
      pp. 104-121; see also *ibid.*, 1.5, pp. 96-104.
20.   Adam, Letter 2; *Correspondance*, pp. 20-21; William, *Sur le
      Cantique*, c. 38, pp. 122-124, and c. 63, p. 162; Helinand, Ser-
      mon 20; PL 212:646-652, and *Epistola ad Galterum*; PL 212:753B.
      See also Bernard, *SC* 12.8-9 (SBOp 1:65-66).
21.   See E. McLaughlin, *Nashota Review*, 15.3 (1975) 228-248.
22.   See, for example, Adam of Perseigne, Letter 35; *Correspondence*,
      305-307 (cf. PL 211:602-603); Letter 45, p. 443 (cf. PL 624);
      letter 48; pp. 471-474 and 477 (cf. 635-636 and 638); letter
      53, p. 544 (cf. 606); letter 54, pp. 553-555; letter 64, pp.
      629-630 (cf. 651).
23.   Guerric, Fourth sermon for Palm Sunday, *Sermons* 2:212-214; tr.
      CF 32:77-78.
24.   Aelred, *De institutione*, c. 31; *Opera*, 1:671; tr. Macpherson,
      CF 2:90-91.
25.   Isaac, Sermon 14, *Sermons* 1:270-80 (cols. 1735B-1738A); Sermon
      34; 2:232-254 especially p. 234 (col. 1801A-B); and Sermon 42;
      PL 194:1829D; Sermon 51; PL 194:1862-1863A.
26.   I hope to discuss this third aspect of maternal imagery at
      greater length in another article.
27.   Robert Javelet, *Image et resemblance au douzième siècle de
      saint Anselme à Alain de Lille*, 2 vols. (Paris, 1967) I:451-
      461; R. W. Southern, *Medieval Humanism and Other Studies* (New
      York, 1970) 29-60; see also Colin Morris, *The Discovery of the
      Individual, 1050-1200* (New York, 1972).
28.   Bernard, *Dil* 7.17 (SBOp 3:134); *SC* 12.4 (SBOp 1:62-63), 23.2

(139-140), 26.6 (173); Letter 258; PL 182: 466A-467A, and Letter 300; PL 182:502A-C.

29. See n. 27 above.

30. Bernard, Letters 1, 71, 110, 146, 152, 201 and 258; PL 182: 76A-B, 183B-184A, 253, 303B-C, 312A, 369B-C, 466B-467A; and *SC* 29.6 (SBOp 1:207). See also Gammersbach, *Citeaux in de Nederlanden* 7, pp. 85-101, and Gervaise Dumeige, 'Bernard de Clairvaux, "Père et Mère" de ses moines,' *Études* 277 (June, 1953) 304-320.

31. We see this especially in Letter 85 (PL 182:206C-210A), Letter 87, (211-217), Letter 258 (466-467), and in Letter 73 (187-188), where Bernard says that loving ought to be difficult. Bernard's own ambivalence comes out clearly in Letter 72 (186D), where he admits that he is the father but refuses fatherly authority because, he says, he and all the monks are brothers.

32. See n. 15 above.

33. Walter Daniel, *The Life of Ailred of Rievaulx*, tr. F. M. Powicke, Medieval Classics (New York, 1950) 58.

34. William, *De natura et dignitate amoris*, c. 8; PL 184:393-395; *Meditativae Orationes*, 11; PL 180:237-242; and *Sur le Cantique*, c. 52, p. 144.

35. Bernard, **Letter** 87 (PL 182:211-217), and Letter 233 (420-421); *SC* 52 and 53 (SBOp 2:90-102).

36. Compare Aelred's tolerant view of the demands of administration in *De Jesu puero*, c. 3.31; *Opera* 1:277-278, with his harsh description of it as a 'dungheap' in his *De institutione*, c. 28; *Opera* 1:660-661.

37. Pierre Salmon, *The Abbot in Monastic Tradition: A Contribution to the History of the Office of Religious Superiors in the West*, tr. Claire Lavoie, CS14 (1972) 46-104, especially 95-97.

38. C. Dumont, 'L'equilibre humain de la vie cistercienne d'après le bienheureux Aelred de Rievaulx,' *Collectanea O.C.R.* 18 (1965) 177-189; A. Squire, 'Aelred of Rievaulx and the Monastic Tradition Concerning Action and Contemplation,' *The Downside Review* 72 (1954) 289-303; G. Constable, *Med. and Ren. Stud.* 5:40-45.

39. 'The Cistercian Sense of Community: An Aspect of Twelfth-Century Spirituality,' *Harvard Theological Review* 68.3/4 (1975).

40. Aelred, *De speculo caritatis*, 2.17; *Opera* 1:86-91. See Louis Bouyer, *The Cistercian Heritage*, tr. E. A. Livingstone (London-Westminster, Md., 1958) 139, and A. Squire, 'The Composition of the *Speculum caritatis*,' *Cîteaux: commentarii cistercienses* 14 (1963) 229-230.

41. Adam, Letter 23; pp. 162-177 (cf. PL 211:583-589); Bernard, *SC* 9.2 (SBOp 1:43).

42. Aelred, *De speculo* 3.37; *Opera* 1:153-156.

43. See nn. 20 and 28 above; Eleanor McLaughlin, 'Equality of Souls, Inequality of Sexes: Women in Medieval Theology,' in Rosemary

Ruether, ed., *Religion and Sexism: Images of Women in the Jewish and Christian Traditions* (New York, 1974) 213-266; Vern Bullough, 'Medieval Medical and Scientific Views of Women,' *Viator: Medieval and Renaissance Studies* 4 (1973) 485-501.

44. See, for example, Bernard, *SC* 12.8 and 9; SBOp 1:65 and 66.

45. M. McLaughlin in DeMause, *History of Childhood*, pp. 124-139; E. McLaughlin in Ruether, *Religion and Sexism*, pp. 213-266; Bullough, *Viator* 4, pp. 485-501; R. W. Southern, *Western Society and the Church in the Middle Ages*, The Pelican History of the Church 2 (Harmondsworth, England, 1970) 309-331.

46. On the theological implications, see E. McLaughlin, *Nashota Review* 15.3, pp. 228-248.

CAESAR OF HEISTERBACH AND THE CISTERCIANS
AS MEDIEVAL PEOPLE

Brian Patrick McGuire

The Cistercians make up an especially attractive group within medieval studies because they incorporate the mixture of idealism and practicality that characterizes medieval civilization and differentiates it from our own. There is no better way to introduce the High Middle Ages to the student than through the story of the founding of Cîteaux and the life of Bernard of Clairvaux. Here in concentrated form we find the expansion of Europe in the **twelfth** century: the inner spiritual dimension and the outer conquest of land and passion for building and organization.

Once we leave the clarity and brevity of the *Exordium parvum* and the *Vita prima Bernardi,* the very success of the Cistercian Order makes it difficult to grasp the movement as a whole. The hundreds of new foundations each have their own stories and, **though** there are similarities, the historian can get lost in a maze of local particularities. Moreover, the sources quickly divide between the narrative and the documentary. On the one hand we have a literature of edification; on the other the collections telling only of privileges and **properties**. The former say little or nothing about the material concerns of the monks, while the latter provide information solely about their material pursuits. Depending on the type of source we use, it is easy to end up with a one-sided picture of the monks.

It is difficult to reconcile saints with farmers. **Marx** and Freud have added to the challenge. How can medieval historians today come to terms with idealism? Most choose to concentrate on the economic side of the cistercian advance. The spiritual aspect has been left in the hands of modern monastic writers.[1] If we turn to one of the **main** early sources for cistercian ideals and attitudes, the *Exordium magnum cisterciense,* we find nothing that reflects a growing criticism of the Cistercians for their acquisitiveness.[2] But buried deep in one chapter, we hear how a cistercian abbot is told by a holy woman that one of the monks' faults is their desire to increase their lands.[3] The author, Conrad, mentions this accusation without any comment or defence. He is caught up in another of the woman's criticisms, that the monks give too much attention to elaborate forms of chant. In the *Exordium magnum* Conrad shows no awareness of what we might call the gap between the poverty and simplicity of life espoused in the *Exordium parvum* and the great holdings of many cistercian houses by the end of the twelfth century. Conrad is concerned with the content of interior, daily life in the monasteries, and especially the attentive singing of the

offices. Such matters are far more important to him than the economic functions of monasteries, clearly an affair for specialists
and thus outside the province of **edifying** stories.

The problem of silence in cistercian narrative sources concerning the contrast between early ideals and the Order's growing wealth
first became apparent to me when I studied the Danish monasteries.[4]
Here, because of the paucity of sources, we can say hardly anything
about how the late twelfth-century monks in **Esrum or** Soro looked at
their own substantial possessions compared with the poverty of the
first monks at Citeaux. My frustration with the Danish sources led
me to Carl Wilkes's monograph on Himmerod.[5] The sources for this
monastery are so abundant and so varied that Wilkes could look at
both economic and spiritual sides of existence. Wilkes's study is
grounded in the documentary **evidence** for Himmerod, but his work
takes on life because he can use the many stories in Caesar of
Heisterbach's *Dialogus miraculorum* that have to do with Himmerod.[6]

Thanks to Wilkes, I discovered the world of Caesar of Heisterbach, a **daughter** house of Himmerod first founded at Stromberg across
the Rhine from Bonn in 1189, but moved into the valley of St Peter
in 1191 (thus the medieval name: *Vallis Sancti Petri)*. Here is the
type of source that can tell us about the Cistercians as they had become a century after the Order's founding. Caesar gives us the inside story, the view of the Cistercians themselves, but he is confident and tolerant enough to allow criticism and dissent. He is aware
of what other people say about the monks and not afraid to report
their words and evaluate them. He is a subtle artist when it comes
to reproducing or reconstructing conversations. Daily life and people of all descriptions are a constant source of curiosity to him.
Thanks to his contacts all over northwestern Europe, he provides a
diversified picture of the Cistercians functioning in the midst of
medieval society.

Caesar's *Dialogus miraculorum*, with its skepticism about idealism, is a medieval source for our age. Caesar takes on life at
ground level, while he always is ready to ascend the spiritual
heights--or to go into the depths. He is interested in everyone
and everything, except perhaps the hapless peasants who usually are
his bad guys and nothing else. It would be dangerous to try to
glean from Caesar concrete facts, for he is careless and inconsistent. But if we keep away from this practice and instead look at
Caesar as a person telling us about other persons in medieval society, he becomes one of the most invaluable of all sources for the
early thirteenth century.

The Person of Caesar

With the biographical facts about Caesar of Heisterbach, we
run into difficulties, the usual conflict between our age's require-

ment of scientific exactitude and the medieval lack of interest in
precise and controllable facts. We know neither the date nor the
place of his birth. The German historian who has written the best
monograph on him summed up the evidence by saying that it is not
certain he was born in Cologne.[7] But a story from his boyhood which
Caesar himself dates to 1188 would put his birthdate at about 1180,
and it is clear that by 1188 he already was going to school at Cologne
(IV, 79, III, 19). His stories reveal an intimate knowledge of the
streets, parishes, churches, and clerics of Cologne at the end of the
twelfth century (IV, 74, 98). We can conclude that Caesar came from
a family that was well enough provided for that it could afford to
give him a clerical education, starting at the church of St Andrew
and ending at the cathedral, where Caesar heard the famed scholastic Rudolph, who had also taught at Paris (I, 32, 38. IV, 26).

Caesar mentions an aunt who purchased a little slave girl and
had her baptized (X, 44). The baptismal cloth was wetted and wrap-
ped around the boy Caesar when he was ill, and is supposed to have
cured him. The fact of slave ownership does not necessarily indicate that Caesar's family was rich, but it contributes to the evidence that it enjoyed comfortable financial standing. It is tempting to think that they were citizens of Cologne, but the only evidence for this is of a negative and indecisive kind. Caesar is very
much the outsider when it comes to his descriptions of nobles: they
are either strikingly bad or amazingly good. Their existence appears foreign and exotic to him, as the knight who made a dramatic
entrance at Himmerod by offering his armour on the altar of Mary.
For Caesar this is an appropriate way of *conversio,* a symbolic act
he seems to approve.[8] But it is perceived from a distance.

There is one boyhood story from Cologne which has not received
the attention it deserves. 'About the time when I was put into
school' *(positus fui ad literas),* Caesar says, there was a thief
put on the block in front of the Gate of Mars at Cologne (III, 19).
At the same gate there was a chapel, whose priest Eustace heard the
thief's confession. He also sent the thief his cup so he could have
something to **drink**. The citizens were so surprised at this act of
mercy that the judges are supposed to have concluded that the man
must have been innocent. Caesar says he heard the story from the
priest Eustace himself *(sicut mihi retulit idem sacerdos).* Already
here we find Caesar as an eager listener absorbing the remarkable
and edifying experiences of other men.

The 1188 episode likewise manifests a precocious child's anti-
cipation of later concerns. Caesar heard the sermon of Henry, Cardinal of Albano, the former Abbot of Clairvaux, in the cathedral of
Cologne, where Henry was preaching a crusade (IV, 79). This 'just
and holy man' **made** a great impression on the boy, as did the scene
in which 'I saw many there taking the cross.' Caesar mentions this
incident only in passing, in connection with a much more detailed

anecdote about a lay brother in the cardinal's company who warned
him against forgetting his cistercian origins.

Similarly, in telling of the life of Everhard, priest at the
church of St James in Cologne, Caesar volunteers information which
comes from his own experience (IV, 98). Everhard was taking the
Eucharist to a sick parishioner and ran into a donkey cart blocking
stratam altam (Hochgasse?).

Here Caesar says he himself often walked. In Cologne there
were many young men--some of them canons--whom Caesar knew and who
later became monks at Heisterbach. One of them, the notorious Theo-
bald, was totally given to drinking and dice, and Caesar often saw
him running naked through the streets of Cologne (IV, 6). The heads
of Cologne churches, whom Caesar calls *priores,* saw to it that Theo-
bald was accepted by Abbot Gevard for entrance at Heisterbach. This
anecdote was used by Kaufmann in his study of Caesar to show that
morals were loose in Cologne when Caesar was a boy.[9] Caesar himself has a much more sophisticated view of the sweet life of the
young male citizens of the town. He tells how once the priest Everhard was shocked by the confessions of these 'rich and soft young
men.' Everhard could not understand their carnal sins, but Caesar
states quite simply that such impulses 'commonly disturb delicate
vessels,' and he shows that Everhard himself had to learn that he
too could be subject to such temptations.[10]

Was Caesar one of these *iuvenes divites ac delicate*? We do not
know, but it is clear that his conversion to cistercian life was
not the result of any overwhelming experience of sin and repentance.
He tells how, on a journey to Cologne in 1198, he happened to be
travelling with Abbot Gevard of Heisterbach, who had been visiting
the cistercian nuns at Walberberg (I, 17). On the road Gevard did
what he could to convince Caesar to become a monk; the story that
did the trick was that of St Mary, St Ann and Mary Magdalen coming
at harvest time down from the mountains above Clairvaux to the monks
and fanning the sweat off their brows with the hems of their garments. Caesar says that he first had to fulfill a vow to visit the
shrine of Rocadamur in Southern France, but after three months, he
became a novice at Heisterbach.

This conversion has many elements worth considering carefully.
In the first place, there is nothing of the overwhelming change of
heart and the rejection of secular life with all its attractions
that characterizes many cistercian conversions, such as that of
Aelred of Rievaulx in Walter Daniel's biography.[11] Caesar is careful not to let his own person dominate his tales, but he makes it
clear that he came to Heisterbach not because he rejected his former life but because he felt strongly attracted by an order of men
so particularly favoured by Mary. The second point to note here
is that the story told to Caesar by Abbot Gevard can also be found
in the *Exordium magnum cisterciense,* but in this version Mary's

helpmates are Elizabeth and Mary Magdalen. **Also,** the three saints
enter the monastery itself instead of walking among the monks in
the fields.[12] The *Exordium magnum* version is thus much less striking than Caesar's, for his shows Mary doing the monks a personal
and **individual** favour. There is no doubt that Caesar knew the *Exordium magnum,* which was probably finished about a decade before
he started his *Dialogus miraculorum,* but he does not try to reconcile his own version of the story with the written one.

We will find this trait frequently in the course of the *Dialogus.* It becomes more and more clear that Caesar was not simply interested, as Conrad of Eberbach was, in collecting already existing written sources and rearranging them. Caesar's goal was to
pick up the **fragments** of conversation, the tales he had heard, the
experiences he had had, the whispered moments of intimacy with his
abbot.[13] Like Conrad, he wanted to edify and improve others, but
Caesar was interested in providing a brilliant, concise story instead of Conrad's long, tedious narration with rhetorical apostro-
phes and perorations. It is remarkable how two such different literary expressions could appear within the same milieu, the same
genre, and at almost the same time.

Caesar tried to transmit an oral culture and was not concerned
with most of the written manifestations of this culture, however
easily available they might have been to him.[14] The brevity of
his stories and the simplicity of his theology, which shows little
interest in deeper problems, are of course fitted for Caesar's audience, the novices of Heisterbach who are to be instructed. But
behind literary genre and moral goal, there emerges a monk who loves
listening to others and whose life was changed by a story.

The *Dialogus miraculorum* gives us many moments when Caesar allows us a glimpse into his life at Heisterbach. It is not known
exactly when he became novice master, but in this post we can see
him best.[15] A novice, for example, was tempted by the devil and
almost lost his faith (IV, 52). One day, as he stood in front of
the altar in the novices' choir, he looked at the image of Christ
on the cross. The figure began to speak to him: 'Why do you doubt?
Look at me. I am he who was born and suffered because of you.' The
crucified could only be seen from above the navel. Caesar was especially interested in this detail and asked the novice what this
might mean. He answered that this was so that 'I could think nothing improper about him [Christ], which might injure my modesty.'[16]
The meaning is clear, even if surprising: The nearly naked Christ
figure might be a source of scandal if it were alive in all its
fleshiness, so the **novice** was protected by being shown only the
upper body. Such an unexpected detail gives an element of credibility to the vision. We are experiencing something more than an
edifying **story** within the cistercian tradition: we are penetrat-
ing to the daily conversation of Caesar with the novices, his

encouragement of them, his awareness of their problems and weak-
nesses.

Even more striking and immediate is Caesar's story of Richwin,
who became cellarer at Heisterbach. As a young **novice** from Cologne,
he was doing quite well until a nun of the convent of St Cecilia began to try to convince him to leave the monastery.

> She dictated and wrote letters recalling him. In them
> she discussed his conversion, encouraged him to return,
> saying that she herself, her house and living, or any-
> thing she had, would be in his power so long as he lived,
> if he would return (IV, 94).

The very fact of a nun writing a letter to a novice shatters the
usual clichés about monastic isolation. Caesar reports that the
boy who brought the message was held off by Henry, the novice's
brother, but the resourceful **fellow** managed to find Richwin any-
way. 'As soon as he read it, his whole being was soon burning,
as if a javelin had been rammed into his heart.' This is the very
language of romantic love, but the antidote is monastic piety: Richwin was kept from leaving the monastery by the prayers and exhortation of the brothers. But Richwin also had to fight the battle,
even telling the devil one day that he could only get him out of
the monastery if he dragged him by his feet!

When it was all over and the victory was clear, Richwin must
have become something of a hero in Heisterbach. At any rate,
Caesar asked him one day if he was still bothered by thoughts a-
bout the nun. His answer was appropriate but also very vivid:
'Truly, brother, the temptations which then rent my heart, now
scarcely touch the outside of my clothes.' In this exchange we
find Caesar the novicemaster examining the hearts and minds of the
other monks, looking for the right impulses, and making no distinction between private emotions and public attitudes. In such a story
I think we get as far as we possibly can into the heart of the cistercian experience, this special mixture of sweet friendship among
men and brutal frankness in a rigid way of life.

Such stories, in which we see Caesar together with the other
monks at Heisterbach, indicate that he found a life there which
suited him. He could combine his intellectual training and youthful experiences in Cologne to get to know his novices as persons and
to train them in a mild and understanding way.[17] Soon after joining the monastery, he started writing biblical commentaries and sermons *(omelias morales)* for various feast days. His work became especially popular because he spiced the expositions of the biblical
texts with modern anecdotes and observations.[18] In about 1219, he
started writing the *Dialogus miraculorum*, at the **request**, he says
in his prologue, of Henry, abbot of **Heisterbach**, and Herman, abbot

of Heisterbach's new daughter house, Marienstatt.[19] The homily
form was put aside in favour of the anecdote but set in a theological context. Caesar had found his mode of expression.

The Dialogus miraculorum: *Form and Content*

The *Dialogus* cannot be dated precisely because there are so
many contradictions in it. In the tenth chapter of the second distinction, Caesar says that it is the twenty-second year since he
became a monk. If his conversion is dated to 1199, this puts the
time of writing at 1220. In the next chapter, he substantiates
this by saying that it is four years since the death of Innocent
III (1216). If we are to assume that Caesar wrote the twelve distinctions of the *Dialogus miraculorum* in the order we have them,
then we could assume that he started the first section in 1219.
But this thesis is undermined by the fact that in IV, 12, Caesar
mentions King Philip of France as a former king. Thus he would
be writing after Philip's death in 1223. This theory is compli-
cated by another reference to Philip in II, 33, where he is said
to be 'reigning today.' Because of this contradiction, Caesar's
editor, Strange, added the words 'the predecessor of the one' [who
today reigns], but this **solution** is hardly adequate. It is possible that the mention of Philip as 'then reigning' in the fourth
distinction was added later, but such an inconsistency makes it
impossible to think the book was written in the order in which we
have it.
Caesar gives us some help through a system of internal references by which he reminds the reader of stories he either has given
or else intends to provide later in the *Dialogus*. 'On this matter
I already have told (will tell) the story of N. monk of N. abbey,'
he will say, and in every case I have checked, Caesar does deliver
the goods. This means that he either went back after the work was
finished and added these cross-references, or else, in the course
of writing, he had a rough outline for the twelve distinctions'
content in chapters and then filled it out. I am inclined to accept the second possibility, for the references fit so well into
the course of the stories that they would appear to have been written together with the rest of the text instead of being added later.
The dialogue form between master and pupil, monk and novice, is
a well-known one in monastic literature. Anselm of Canterbury used
it, but Caesar's model seems to be the *Dialogus* of Gregory the Great.
Caesar says clearly he does not want to repeat the *exempla* there,
but the form is **similar** (VIII, 29). The organization of the work
into distinctions may have been taken from the *Exordium magnum
cisterciense,* but Caesar is more specific than Conrad in giving
specific titles for the various distinctions and thus dividing the
christian life into various areas: conversion to the Order, contri-

tion, confession, temptation, devils, simplicity, Mary, visions, Eucharist, miracles, the dying, the afterlife. As he says in his prologue, the first six distinctions 'pertain to merit,' the remaining 'to reward.'

Caesar does not merely collect a string of topical anecdotes within each distinction. He uses his stories to deal with various theological or pastoral problems. This side of his work has not been sufficiently noticed and deserves more careful study. About ten percent of the chapters in each distinction are given over to theoretical treatments of the subject at hand, and these chapters furnish bridges between different sets of examples. Occasionally Caesar allows himself to go off on a tangent, as in dealing with problems of predestination in the first distinction, but after a chapter or two he inevitably returns to the central subject matter. His structure within the distinction is sometimes completely logical, as in the fourth distinction, where the seven capital sins provide a natural division of the various types of temptation. But in the eighth distinction, Caesar is unable to divide up the various visions **according** to the stages of Christ's life because there are so few available that have to do with Christ's boyhood or his resurrection. At times he is tempted to borrow from Gregory's *Dialogue* or other collections of examples, but as he says to his novice, 'as it was promised, it is not permitted to speak to you except of new things, that is, things done in our times' (VIII, 29).[20]

Caesar is thus not interested in compiling written sources, and a preliminary count shows that only about four percent of his stories can be traced back solely to a written source. His fascination with the fresh, recent example naturally makes him much more valuable to us than Conrad of Eberbach, most of whose stories are taken directly from Herbert of Clairvaux and other Clairvaux writers.[21]

The *exemplum* form has a long tradition in christian and especially in monastic literature.[22] Caesar's work is a logical continuation of this effort, in which anecdotes instead of theological statements *(sententiae)* alone are used in instructing others. It is interesting that Caesar sets his work in a dialogue form at a time when this is going out of fashion in religious literature. In my initial reading of the *Dialogus*, I assumed that this was merely a literary device, of no special relevance to an understanding of Caesar. After all, he drops the dialogue later on in the *Librii VIII miraculorum*, and thus it seems as if his monastic readers were much more interested in the stories themselves for their own sake, and not in the give and take between master and novice.

But the novice in the *Dialogus* is by no means a **bloodless** creature who **nods** in affirmation at everything the monk says. He is an active participant, and at times the novice can challenge the monk, even confronting him with contradictions between statements in **earlier** work and in the *Dialogus*.[23] Most of the time, the novice's

role is limited to that of asking questions, but occasionally he
does volunteer information. Also he can demand further support for
a point of view.[24] Most remarkably, the novice is assumed to have
shared experiences at Heisterbach with the monk, who names recent
events when the novice was present or of which he knew.[25]

     There is no doubt that *monachus* is Caesar himself. As he tells
us in the prologue, his name is found in the first letters of the
twelve distinctions. *Novicius*, however, could be thought of as
merely an abstraction of the novices whom Caesar taught. But Alfons Hilka's study of the manuscript tradition of the *Dialogus mir-*
aculorum reveals a number of manuscripts in which the names *Caesar-*
ius and *Apollonius* replace *monachus* and *novicius*.[26] This is also
the case in some of the early printed editions of Caesar from Cologne in the fifteenth and sixteenth centuries.[27] It might be
thought that *Apollonius* goes back to some classical figure, but in
Paul Strait's helpful *Cologne in the Twelfth Century*, there appears
a Cleingedank family 'first recorded in Cologne in the last few decades of the twelfth century.'[28] One of their common names is Apollonius, 'not at all common in other families,' and it may well be
from this wealthy and expanding line in the Cologne patriciate that
Caesar's novice came. This can not be proven, but this odd name
in the *Dialogus* tradition does match the Cologne one. In view of
the fact that so many of Heisterbach's monks (including Caesar himself) came originally from Cologne, I think we may have found the
identity of Apollonius.[29] If this is the case and he was a real
person, then the dialogue form is more than a literary device. It
is based on the relationship between a novice master and one of his
novices. At the same time the work is meant for other novices and
presumably also for monks. Caesar acts as the teacher and trans-
mits his knowledge in an easily digestible manner through memorable
and striking stories.

     Many of the miracles in the *Dialogus* are of such a kind that
the word miracle has to be stretched to its limit. We find visions,
coincidences, prophecies, and only a few standard healings of soul
or body. Here Caesar is solidly grounded within cistercian tradition. The first writers of Bernard's life concentrated heavily on
his miraculous doings. Herbert of Clairvaux in the late 1170s and
early 1180s continued this tradition by collecting more recent stories.[30] After about 1190, Conrad of Eberbach reorganized Herbert's
stories in order to narrate the history of monasticism from the time
of the apostles to his own day, with emphasis on the Cistercians and
their miracles. Thus the *Dialogus miraculorum* can be seen as a meet-
ing place of three elements: the traditional *exemplum*, emanating
from Gregory the Great; the cistercian miracle story glorifying the
Order and its members, from the *Vita Prima* and the later literature
of Clairvaux; and finally the experiences and conversations of Caesar

himself, his meetings with innumerable monks, lay brothers, nuns, priests, and lay people.

Of these three traditions, by far the most important is the oral one. In recent years Bruno Griesser has shown how a number of stories in the *Dialogus* are taken from written sources, especially a Himmerod book of miracles.[31] This is something that Caesar himself indicates in a number of the relevant chapters, and in other cases where his anecdote matches one in the Himmerod source,[32] Caesar often refers to a Himmerod monk as his oral source. It seems that there is a great deal of overlapping in Caesar between written and oral sources, but normally he prefers the oral and does not try to check or collate it with the written source. Caesar is usually satisfied with repeating the story as it was told to him. In his prologue, he says quite plainly that if **anything** has happened in reality in a different manner from the way in which he has described it, then the fault is not his: it has to be ascribed to the people who have told him the story:

> *Testis est mihi Dominus, nec unum quidem capitulum in hoc Dialogo me finxisse. Quod si aliqua forte aliter sunt gesta, quam a me scripta, magis his **videtur** imputandum esse, a quibus mihi sunt relata.*

In a later work, Caesar emphasizes the great difference between *fabula* and *exemplum;* the first is a story without a moral, just a report, while the second has a lesson to it.[33] Caesar cared nothing about historical accuracy or literary antecedents. He saw his task as that of recounting, not researching. But it is precisely this attitude which makes him an invaluable source for the cistercian mentality. Huizinga once compared Froissart's mind to a photographic plate on which the impressions of the fourteenth century are recorded. Caesar is not like this because he is not writing a chronicle of events but is choosing suitable *exempla*. But Caesar's very selectiveness means that he is constructing a vision of the Cistercians and the Church in general, a pattern for good living and bad. Thus he reflects his sources instead of analyzing them, but at the same time his reflection is distorted into the shape of his own mind, a mind eminently worth our attention.

Caesar and the Cistercians: Views and Attitudes

Any understanding of Caesar's view of his Order and its place in the medieval church must be based on a comparison between him and his near-contemporary, **Conrad** of Eberbach. The author of the *Exordium magnum cisterciense* died in 1221, just when Caesar was in the midst of the *Dialogus*. Conrad ended as the abbot of a great cistercian house [up] the Rhine from Heisterbach and, like it, a

daughter of Clairvaux. Caesar certainly knew of the *Exordium*
but seems to have used it only in a limited manner. In comparing
the first chapter of the *Dialogus* with the chapters of the *Exordium* dealing with the founding of the Cistercian Order, we can begin
to understand Caesar's avoidance of this formidable work.[34]

Conrad was engaged in a polemic. He wanted to reassure everyone that the Order has a legitimate origin, that the departure of
monks from Molesme in 1098 happened in an acceptable manner and
had papal backing. Conrad complains of the assertion by German
Benedictines that the Cistercians started as apostates from their
rightful abbey. This defensive tone continues throughout the work
and **climaxes** in the final chapter of the sixth distinction, where
Conrad delivers an eloquent plea for the dignity and **spirituality**
of the cistercian way of life from its **beginnings** to his day. Conrad is **worried** about two dangers: external attacks and **internal
laxity**. The whole of the *Exordium magnum* can be looked upon as a
potent **reminder** of the past that should be an example for the un-
certain present and the endangered future.

The *Exordium magnum* is thus meant for both internal and external use. In that sense it is like the Cistercians' collections of
property deeds. It is there to remind them of what they have and
what they can lose if they are not careful in asserting their claims
against a suspicious and hostile world. The *Exordium magnum* looks
back in order to take stock and make the ideals clear to the monks
of the present day. This type of literature is common at the opening of the thirteenth century, when the monks, under the pressure
that finally released itself at the Fourth Lateran Council, had to
reconcile the **stories** of their foundations with contemporary attacks on their privileges and exemptions. We find, for example,
at Øm Abbey in Denmark, also a Clairvaux daughter, the writing of
an *Exordium* in this same period, 1207, in order to review 'the
truth of the foundation and the reverence of the founders.'[35]

Caesar had no such worries. His monastery's foundation story
is apparently very much cut and dried. He was writing after a time
of troubles in the Cologne diocese in the first decade of the century. This is over now, and the papal disputes with Frederick II
have not yet flared up. For the moment there is relative calm in
Germany. At the same time Heisterbach itself **has** just, in 1215,
founded a daughter house to the east, Marienstatt. Despite some
difficulties, the new foundation seems to be going fairly well.

In his chapter on the beginnings of the Cistercian Order, then
(I, 1), Caesar is not concerned about the old polemics. The German
Benedictines who plagued Conrad are of no interest to him. Caesar
retells the story of foundation in a **factual** manner, with names,
dates, and places, and he takes for granted the legitimacy of the
Order. He is more inclined to mention its organization than the
challenge from Molesme. On the whole he is far briefer: one

concise chapter instead of the ten in Conrad, who built on the original account in the *Exordium parvum* **and** added his own bitter remarks.

Here one might object that the audience of Caesar is completely different from that of Conrad. Caesar is writing for young, inexperienced novices who are supposed to be edified by what they read and are too tender to be dragged into polemics. Conrad's audience is the mature monk or cleric who knows that the Cistercians are under fire and needs to defend them. This is partly true. The beguiling simplicity of Caesar's description fits his audience well, but we should add that there are many other areas in which Caesar can be as sharp and acrimonious as Conrad, as in defending the Cistercians against the charge of greed. The different tone in the foundation accounts is not due just to the different audiences. It is the result of writers of vastly different mentalities. Conrad is out to impress, to convince, to persuade, and he does so by means of a flurry of rhetorical and stylistic devices that make a reading of the *Exordium magnum* a trying experience even for a trained latinist. There are many complex sentences in Conrad, often built on biblical language and images. Caesar can do the same, but he aims for a *stilus brevis et planus*. In one of his works he says that the monks had objected to his former set of homilies previsely because it was too long and subtle.[36]

Caesar can be direct and open,   because he wants to be understood immediately and because he is not particularly worried about the historical problems behind the Order's origins. He is willing to concede that many men join the Cistercians for the wrong reasons. But he asserts the hope that at some point in their lives, they will change their attitudes (I, 27). This happened to a Clairvaux prior who became a monk there in order to get an opportunity for stealing the altar's sacred vessels. Once he took on the monastic habit, this desire completely disappeared (I, 3). This particular story was told to Caesar by Godfred, a Heisterbach monk, when he was a novice together with Caesar. Godfred had been canon of St Andrew in Cologne, where Caesar had gone to school, and before that had himself gone to school at Rheims, together with a Philip who later **became** archbishop of Cologne (II, 16). Godfred must have been much older than Caesar when they entered Heisterbach. Godfred's story he had heard from a monk of Clairvaux, apparently before the Cologne canon entered Heisterbach. We find nothing **quite** like it in the *Exordium magnum:* the smudge on the Clairvaux prior's past would hardly have been a suitable contribution to the venerable Clairvaux tradition!

Caesar's willingness to use such a double-edged tale underlines the breadth of his approach: he is willing to admit that men can be evil, even men who join the Cistercians, so long as he can show how monastic life can improve them. He tells us that Godfred him-

self as a novice was tempted to leave **Heisterbach** (IV, 49). Towards
the end of his year of probation, he wanted to give up. The thought
of monastic discomforts, 'the **weight** of the clothes, the long vigils
and silences, heat in summer and cold in winter,' as well as 'regular fasting and the limited food available' was almost too much for
him. He told his fellow novice Caesar that he was thinking **of return-**
ing to the parish church of which he was pastor (and where, one as-
sumes, a vicar did all the work for him). There, even though the
church was badly located and probably did not provide a very fat living, he would try to do his best for the people. Or else he might
return to his prebend at St Andrew and 'choose in the cloister a
room for myself, where I shall live so much according to the Rule
that others may be edified by my example.' Caesar told **Godfred** this
was the devil's advice. One day when he was still in doubt and Caesar was sitting at his side, trying to console him, **Godfred** took a
book containing the Psalms, opened it, and looked for the **prophetic**
meaning of the first passage that met his eyes. Here, he said, he
could find out what the brothers of St Andrew would say about him
if he returned to their church. The passage in Psalm 68 (verse 13)
was hardly promising. Godfred understood immediately that on returning to Cologne, he would find that 'my fellow canons, when they
sit in the portico of the church, will speak against me, judging me,
and disputing of my salvation. At night when they sit at the fire
and are drinking, I shall be their song *(psalmus)*.' That was enough
for Godfred. He became a monk and soon afterwards died at Heisterbach.

I have recounted this **story** in detail because it tells so much
about Caesar at Heisterbach. For him, even as a novice, there was
no doubt that the cistercian life was superior to that of a parish
priest or a canon in a city church. The cistercian way of life with
all its rigidity is the best means of salvation (I, 33). But at the
same time Caesar is willing to show us how a cistercian novice could
be tempted, even on the eve of his monastic profession. He lets us
enter into the debate about the possibilities for a good life and
reconstructs the content and even the words of the conversation he
had with Godfred. All this is stylized and recounted as remembered
twenty years later. But there are still a freshness and directness
about it that point to a confidence in Caesar's own mind. The Cistercians are best, but it is clear that men have to find this out
for themselves. It takes time and many trials of soul, but the result is decided in advance.

Conrad of Eberbach conforms all his stories to a unitary goal:
the dignity and sublimity of the Cistercian Order. Caesar of Heisterbach uses his stories to show how different people can be and
yet how many can find a home with the Cistercians. He tells of the
knight who feared **joining the** Order because of lice in the monks'
garments (IV, 48), the novice who before his profession refused to

have his beard cut and had to be convinced by the prior in Himmerod, Herman (IV, 51), and of Reynard, the former scholastic of St
Andrew, whom Abbot Gevard dissuaded from returning to the world by
threatening in jest to cut off his feet (IV, 52). There is **much**
humour in the *Dialogus*. The smile of understanding, sympathy, and
even plain mirth has a place for Caesar. But at the same time he
tells many tales about monks who seek the gift of tears--and go to
holy women in order to obtain it.

The register of male emotions is much greater in Caesar than
it often is in the conventional narrative literature of our own
day. Caesar makes no distinction between what men feel and what
they are. Being a Cistercian means sharing in the sweetest bonds
of love and truth. Even though the ideology of cistercian superiority is the same as in Conrad, it is much more gently and subtly applied. Caesar's naïve self-confidence and natural trust in the Order's mission means that he can afford to present the charges of
the Cistercians' critics and even confirms some of them. This is
especially true of greed. Here the novice volunteers the information that many men accuse the Cistercians of this vice (IV, 57:
Saepe ordo noster a saecularibus de avaritia iudicatur). Caesar
answers that almost all monasteries today are burdened by debts
because of their obligations of hospitality and their care of the
poor. But even if he can excuse the officials of the Order for
'a great deal' *(tanto)*, he does not wish to explain away 'everything' *(toto)*. Often the needs of the abbeys make it necessary
for them 'to strive (after wealth) whether they like it or not.'[37]
This discussion is followed by ten chapters that give examples of
cistercian generosity--or the lack of it. Sometimes Caesar does
not give the names of abbeys, but he does mention Villers in Brabant, also a Clairvaux daughter (IV, 60). The monks there, in
hard times, decided to withdraw aid to the **poor** until the harvest,
but **the** same night this decision was made, a fishpond outside the
monastery spilled over its banks and flooded many workshops. This
altered the brothers' attitude. During a famine in 1197, Himmerod
continued to give food to the poor despite its own precarious situation. Eventually it was rewarded by a gift of 600 pounds of silver (IV, 66). Heisterbach did the same in 1197, and Abbot Gevard
found to his delight and edification that the small amount of
grain which the monastery had at its disposal seemed to be more
than enough for making **huge** loaves: a new miracle of multiplica-
tion (IV, 65). As the novice says elsewhere: *Antiqua nostris
temporibus renovantur miracula* (X, 2).

Caesar was aware that the coming of Cistercians to a new area
could be unwelcome to the local inhabitants because of the monks'
expansive policies (IV, 63). He even admits that Heisterbach itself was not welcome in 1189 because of the fear shared by peasants, knights, and even the Count of Berg (IV, 64). Caesar's

answer is clear. The abbey that deliberately works for the increase
of its possessions at the expense of its neighbours will be frus-
trated and grow even poorer (IV, 59), while the abbey that benefits
its neighbours and does not threaten them will ultimately obtain
their good will and even their land (IV, 61). Caesar insists that
every monastery must allow entrance to two brothers, *Date* and *Dabi-
tur*. They are always found together, and when they are present,
all goes well (IV, 68).

This aristocratic ethic of generosity, mingled with christian
charity, could only function at a time when the monks did not have
to fight to get enough to live on. At Heisterbach Abbot Henry, who
took office in about 1204 and continued apparently until about 1240,
was such a genius at administration and diplomacy that the monastery
reached its economic zenith while Caesar was writing the *Dialogus*.[38]
Thus experience seemed to confirm theory: **give** and you will be giv-
en. The Cistercians have a duty to provide for themselves, but they
can best do that by providing for others; then everything they need
will be given to them. It is a simplistic view of the world, but
in prosperous times, it can work.

The regime under which Caesar lived at Heisterbach seems to have
been relatively gentle by monastic standards, and yet in no way lax.
Monks, he insists, should have enough to eat. Otherwise they will
not be able to do their work properly (IV, 78, 79). He admits that
many of those who join later in life and who are used to more attractive foods have trouble in adapting. But here there are no com-
promises to be made. The rules are clear. Yet the limitation of
the diet to greens and herbs does not mean that **the** monks should
starve. Let them fill their stomachs, he insists: *oportet nos ex
eis* [vegetables] *sumere usque ad satietatem*.

Likewise Caesar accepts completely the strict sexual ban in
monastery life, but he is very open about the problems it creates.
Here perhaps we see him best of all as novice master, trying to com-
fort his listeners by showing them that even distinguished and holy
prelates could have difficulties in this area (IV, 97). He tells
his novice that he will **only** give examples showing victory over sexual temptations so that the novice will not lose heart (IV, 92).
Here there is self-censorship, for Caesar's *exempla* of other vices
show both successes and failures. But Caesar was by no means over-
concerned about the dangers of sex. Time and again he makes clear
that other offences, like **pride**, are much more serious (IV, 5). He
is aware that a single careless glance or a letter from a nun can
bring on years of religious crisis, temptation, and near-despair
for a monk (IV, 96), but he is confident that even the worst temptations can be overcome, as in the case of the young man in Himmerod who got rid of the devil simply by telling him, 'My confessor
orders you to stop tempting me' (IV, 95).

Such antidotes are of immediate use for the novices, and some

of the stories apparently deal in veiled form with the urge to mas-
turbate (IV 95, 96). There is a story of a Clairvaux monk who ex-
perienced spiritual castration in his sleep. Again we have an episode from Clairvaux which Caesar could have taken from the *Exordium
magnum*, but where variation in decisive details indicates that his
source was not the *Exordium* account itself but an oral cistercian
tradition.[39]

In a number of these anecdotes about lust, women are the ini-
tiators of the difficulty, so Caesar fits into the usual monastic
clichés about women. But Caesar himself had many and varied contacts
with women, especially nuns, but also holy women who lived in no particular order, as well as noble women. One of his collections of
sermons was written at the request of the abbess of Walberberg, Mar-
garet.[40] About four percent of the stories in the *Dialogus* Caesar
took from oral female sources. Thus it was not necessarily forbidden or shameful for a monk like Caesar to talk with women, as long
as they were of good reputation. Many of his stories show a lack of
the common prejudices against women. His sympathetic view deserves
more careful study.[41]

Here, as in so many areas, Caesar surprises us by his relative
tolerance and openness. In dealing with the question of illegitimate
birth, he flies in the face of legal attitudes and says he cannot see
how illegitimate sons can be held responsible for the misdeeds of
their parents (IV, 30). Caesar gives Christian, monk of Heisterbach,
as an example of an illegitimate son whose life in no way was marred
by the fact that his father was a clerk and canon of Bonn. We are
all born in sin, he says, all brought to grace through baptism, and
all are to be judged among the sons of glory who have lived a good
life and obtained final grace. Caesar is dealing with the spiritual
side of life and not the legal one, but his words underline an independence of mind. He sees a great variety of people in the world,
concedes their problems, faults, and different fates, and he refuses
to categorize them in any way that **does** not take into account their
own actions and merits.

Caesar is often helped in this tolerance by the fact that he
does not feel obliged to explain every event in the light of some
principle of **divine** justice. There are many incidents which he refuses to try to see in cosmic terms.[42] A prime example is suicide.
When a lay brother whom Caesar knew at **Heisterbach** drowned himself,
Caesar provided no explanation (IV, 41). Usually he can blame the
devil, but here he says: 'I don't know by what judgment of God he
[the brother] was made so depressed and weak....' The man was just
a hopeless case. Nothing could be done for him. When the brothers
asked him why he was despairing, he answered, 'I can't say my prayers
as I used to do, and so I fear **hell**.' Sick in the infirmary, he told
a visitor, 'I cannot fight against God any longer.' Shortly afterwards, he threw himself into the monastery's pond.

This story is one of many in Caesar that concern suicide (IV,
40-44). He must be one of the rare medieval informants about suicide in monastic communities, both male and female. Since it happens, he makes no attempt to suppress discussion of it. His attitude contrasts with that of the seventeenth-century collector of
cistercian literature, Tissier, who so greatly censored the *Dialogus
miraculorum* that Alfons Hilka had to conclude that his text was without worth.[43] Similarly one of Caesar's stories about a corrupt priest
who in confession took **payment** for sin was erased in the later Middle Ages from the Heisterbach manuscript itself.[44] The successors
of Caesar apparently found his frankness at times too bold.

We, of course, can be grateful for this frank loquacity, so long
as we remember that in most areas, Caesar is quite **orthodox** and con-
formist. He is as intolerant of Jews, usurers, and heretics as any
good monk should be. His tales about them do not have more than a
symbolic historical truth, as Walter Wakefield's analysis of Caesar's
account of the Albigensians has shown.[45] If we are to distinguish
between Caesar the open and informative narrator and Caesar the narrow orthodox monk, it might be useful to distinguish the stories he
got from distant exotic places from those that happen in the Cologne-
Rhine area where Caesar himself could talk to the people involved.
I would attach to the tales that happen at Heisterbach itself a high
degree of accuracy, while those from England, Toledo, Palestine, or
or Southern France came to Caesar by many intermediaries and were
clearly much mangled in the process.

In any case, Caesar is full of surprises. He accepts the world
around him and takes for granted the involvement of the Cistercians
in it. He is very much interested in the standards and practices of
life at the parish level (III, 41, 44-47, 52). His stories about
abuses of the sacrament of confession not only show his sense of the
superiority of cistercian life to that of the secular priest, who
neglects the laity. These many tales also **indicate a** genuine concern on Caesar's part for the maintenance of sacramental standards
--for the good of the laity as well as the honour of God. Caesar
is also critical when it comes to bishops who neglect their **spiritu-**
al duties and involve themselves solely in politics and war (II, 9,
28-29). In Caesar we find the **spirit** of parisian pastoral and moral
theology under Peter the Chanter and his circle. Many of Peter's
ideas became part of canon law at the Fourth Lateran Council, which
tried to involve the Cistercians in the reform of monasticism. According to the twelfth canon of that Council, the Cistercians as the
great self-organizers would in turn organize **other** Orders according
to their own pattern. Caesar reflects upon a well-established cistercian tradition of involvement in the fight against heresy, a cam-
paign led personally by the abbots of Cîteaux and Clairvaux. It was
not until the coming of the friars and the campaigns led by the north-
ern French nobility that the Midi finally had to surrender. Caesar

himself concedes in his famous account that heresy was still thriv-
ing in his time in southern France. Instead of trying to excuse
the failure, he simply admits it. The heretics at Toulouse, he says,
'to this day do not cease harassing and attacking the faithful.'

Many general histories of the Middle Ages, in treating the early
thirteenth century, deal at length with the foundation of the Domin-
icans and Franciscans while dismissing the Cistercians along with
other by now established orders as being too inward-looking and rur-
al to face the growing urban challenge. This is true, but only to
a point. Caesar is very much involved in urban culture, and his
monks seem to feel almost as much at home in Cologne as at Heisterbach. Caesar actually implicitly approves of the preaching of the
friars at Cologne.[46] He gives no hint that they will become rivals
of the Cistercians.

Caesar's confidence is also reflected in his refusal to bother
at length with reports about the approaching end of the world. He
says he has no clear information or answers. But his answer is a
passionate interest and involvement in the world of his day, primarily in its monastic life, but also to a great degree he is concerned with the structure of the Church, the conditions of the poor, and
the vicissitudes of politics.

The Cistercian Milieu in Caesar

Recruitment

Near the beginning of the first distinction, Caesar says that
it is very dangerous for young boys to join the Order (I, 3). He
cites John, archbishop of Trier, to the effect that boys or young
men who come to the monastery at too early an age end up either
being too tepid in their religious devotion or in leaving the Order. Without the experience of guilt for sin, they lack an accus-
ing conscience. So they take their own virtue for granted and easily succumb to temptation.

Cistercian recruitment policies did allow young novices to join
in certain cases, and Caesar has one story about the reception of
such a youth made acceptable by Mary herself (I, 20). Caesar thus
shows his awareness of the common argument that boys who are allowed
to remain in the world and get their education there can lose their
vocations. But ultimately Caesar banks on his own experience. He
would have been at the end of his teens when he joined Heisterbach,
perhaps slightly older. Most of the monks of Heisterbach whom he
mentions in the first distinction had first been priests or canons
at city churches, especially at Cologne. Indeed it seems as if
Heisterbach in Caesar's time was mainly composed of monks from the
churches of Cologne, Bonn, or Soest. These at least are the monks
about whose lives Caesar tells. The information he gives about

their former existences is of primary value in establishing the
type of people who became Cistercians in the early thirteenth century. The Order's monks in Bernard's time are often seen as coming
from noble families, but a century later the Rhineland Cistercians
seem to have drawn heavily on a bourgeois source: canons from city
churches.

Caesar admits that many men **joined** the Order to avoid poverty,
and he especially criticizes lay brothers for this practice (I, 27).
Here we get a taste of the non-idealistic motives that could inspire
conversion, including a **quotation** from a monk Caesar knew who told
him, 'If I had done well [in the world], I never would have come to
a monastery.' Some recruits came in their best clothing and accom-
panied by their relatives, while others for the sake of humility put
on rags (I, 36). This latter situation could sometimes lead to mis-
understandings; a rich young man asking for entrance could be mistaken for a tramp! Caesar here reveals that the Cistercians were
on their lookout for men who sought their way of life for the sake
of a full stomach. In a world where many must have gone hungry, the
plain vegetables and dark bread of Caesar's monks must have been ex-
travagantly attractive (IV, 79).

The fact that many men became Cistercians after they had reached
adulthood helps us understand better the surprising involvement of
Caesar in the world outside the monastery. For men who had lived
a number of years in a community of canons in the midst of a town,
who had heard lay people's confessions and had had to deal with their
problems, and who daily had seen women and perhaps discovered that
they took religion **far** more seriously than men, entrance into a cistercian monastery would have meant a more disciplined and isolated
life, but not necessarily one totally cut off from the secular world.
The requirements of travel for cistercian monks--visitation, General
Chapters, pursuit of legal disputes--meant that a number of Heisterbach officials was constantly dealing with the world. More importantly, the adult entrants had been formed in their youth **in** a non-
monastic world view, and this background meant a greater awareness
of individual differences in lay people and clerks. For monks **brought**
up from boyhood in the cloister, all seculars, including priests,
could be alike. But for a Cologne canon **who** came to Heisterbach, experience proved that the world outside the **cloister** was more than a
set of monastic clichés.

In Caesar's own case, we know of the lasting effect the dean of
St Andrew, Ensfrid, made on Caesar as a boy (VI, 5). Ensfrid was
the St Francis of Cologne, taking everything he had in order to give
to the poor, and even **acting** like a Robin Hood, stealing from his
own community. Caesar excuses Ensfrid by saying that some things
are permitted to saints which to others are not. Ensfrid, **for** Caesar, fulfills the ideal of the deeply religious man able to inte-
grate his personal piety with social **concerns**. In Caesar's more

critical but still deeply affectionate biography of the priest
Everhard, he emphasizes the sacramental care of the laity (IV, 98).
In these two men from Caesar's childhood we find important formative influences. Their concern for the laity, both in spiritual and
material matters, provides themes for many of Caesar's stories.

Geography

Caesar's world stretches from Ireland to India. In its midst
is the Rhine basin; at its very center the area around Heisterbach.
In the first four distinctions, out of one hundred-sixty stories
that can be placed in a well-defined geographical area, I find the
following distribution:

```
58 (36%) from Cologne-Bonn area (Heisterbach)
25 (16%) from Eifel (Himmerod)
21 (13%) from Brabant and Flanders (Villers, Aulne)
15 ( 9%) from other Rhine locations, including tributaries
             (Eberbach, Schönau, Altenberg, Camp)
 7 ( 5%) from Cîteaux and Clairvaux
14 ( 8%) from Paris and Northern France
 9 ( 6%) from Germany outside Rhine (Loccum, Riddagshausen)
 5 ( 3%) from Italy, Rome
 4 ( 3%) from fringe areas--Toledo, England, the East
 2 ( 1%) from Friesland and Holland
```

These figures would probably be confirmed by a review of the
other eight distinctions, but the first four are a good group because there Caesar is on the whole more precise in the background
information he gives than in later distinctions. Distinctions ten
to twelve, especially, present many stories without any specific
source information. The cistercian abbeys given in parentheses are
those of importance located inside the given areas, but not all the
stories set in the **regions** named take place in connection with cistercian houses. In the fourth distinction, for example, of twenty-
five stories from the central Rhine area fourteen are set at Heisterbach, while six take place in Cologne, **three** at villages near
Heisterbach (Obercassel and Königswinter), and the rest at other
Rhine villages. Similarly eleven out of sixteen Eifel stories are
set in Himmerod in the fourth distinction, while a number of others
happen in benedictine abbeys in the area. The high number of stories from Flanders and Brabant emphasizes the lively connection between Heisterbach and Villers and Aulne, all Clairvaux daughters,
and some exchange of personnel. Walter, abbot of Villers, is one
of Caesar's major sources, and many of his **stories** take place outside his own monastery and in various nearby towns, like Nivelles
or Lièges.

Sources

Caesar is not especially selective in his sources. He gives
us the impression that he gladly received information from where-
ever he could get it. But we should not imagine him as a folksy
monk inviting the peasant into his cell for a friendly chat. The
majority of his informants are other Cistercians, and the overwhelming majority of the non-cistercian stories come from clerical
and monastic **sources.** **Unfortunately,** Caesar is not consistent in
naming his sources. In the first and eighth distinctions, for example, he very carefully gives his informants, but in the second
and third and many of the later distinctions, he often leaves the
impression that he has heard a story which already by the time it
came to him had been depersonalized and **generalized,** emptied of
precise information. The following is a rough summary of source
distribution in the first four distinctions:

About 50% can be directly ascribed to cistercian
sources.

About 10% probably come from Cistercians, but in
these Caesar deliberately leaves out names, usually because the story is scandalous.

About 12% come from other priests and monks, about
equally divided between Benedictines, Premonstratensians
and Augustinians on the one hand, and miscellaneous canons,
parish priests, and scholastics (Caesar's term for the
teachers in various communities of canons) on the other.
But many of these are difficult to trace, for Caesar uses
a stock phrase, *quidam vir religiosus,* which indicates
that he is dealing with a man who has taken monastic vows.

About 4% come from written sources that easily can
be traced and there Caesar usually says that he got it
'by reading and not by hearing.'

About 4% come from women, mostly nuns, but also some
undifferentiated 'holy women,' some of whom Caesar calls
'Beguines.'

About 20% cannot be traced because of inadequate information.

Less than 1% (but still a few) come from laymen,
local knights, or *sculteti,* lesser judicial officials.

Even if the majority of sources are cistercian, a substantial
number of these were told to Caesar by men who had become monks but
were recalling indidents that happened before they joined the Order.
It is here that we get to know so much about Cologne in the late
twelfth century or about the disputes between Philip of Swabia and
Otto of Brunswick. Once again we see how substantial a part of the

life experience of many Cistercians came during years spent 'out in the world.' It is because of this that Caesar can take us into so many different milieux. The world of the cloister is the main setting, but Caesar does not hesitate to mention to the novice the dangers and temptations of the world outside. Likewise the novice is shown that many laymen and priests are good people.

Another noteworthy aspect of the cistercian informants is their broad geographical distribution. Here Caesar benefits from the practices of visitation and General Chapter. Several of the stories were brought back to Caesar by Abbot Henry from Cîteaux, while the visitations of Henry to houses in Friesland furnished interesting materials, as we find in the seventh distinction with an elaborate story about the wrath of Mary and natural catastrophes in that area. Sometimes abbots from German houses to the east or north stay at Heisterbach, perhaps on their way to the General Chapter. Here we can rightly imagine Caesar eagerly mining them for good tales. He does not limit himself to abbots, however: the humblest lay brother receives his full attention if he has a good story. In general we can see from the *Dialogus* what an important spiritual role the lay brothers could have in the monastery, regardless of their menial tasks and lack of education.

We can take the fourth distinction as representative and divide Caesar's informants:

> 58 Cistercians
> 9 theoretical chapters
> 6 undefined priests or religious persons
> 3 women
> 2 laymen
> 2 secular masters
> 2 Benedictines, 1 Augustinian, 2 Premonstratensians
> 1 canon (of St Severin in Cologne, from Caesar's youth)
> 1 written source

From cistercian sources, six come from lay brothers, four from Abbot Herman of Marienstatt, who also had been abbot at Heisterbach and Himmerod and who is one of the major sources for many of the visions related by Caesar. Abbot Henry of Heisterbach is responsible for seven stories, but many he had heard from other abbots and then told Caesar (apparently on his return from journeys). This way of studying Caesar of Heisterbach's *Dialogus miraculorum* obviously needs much more work, but the greatest surprise for me is that it has not previously been tried.[47] Caesar's information is on the surface and easily available. It merely requires patience in compiling and checking. But such an approach should not allow us to forget that Caesar is far more valuable for cistercian attitudes than for statistics. His keen interest in other people, lack of

concern in revealing unpleasant aspects of cistercian life, and desire to make theology digestible to novices--all these qualities
contribute to a work of primary importance for cultural history.
This has long been recognized, but Caesar has usually been plunder-
ed only for individual anecdotes in order to characterize various
areas of **church** life. He deserves to be perceived and appreciated
for his comprehensive view of monastic and secular life.

     Caesar is perhaps too naïve for historians, too obvious for
psychologists, and too simple for theologians. Everything is available on the surface of his work. But the *Dialogus miraculorum* is
much more than a collection of anecdotes. It is a carefully composed **manual** of instruction for cistercian novices, telling them
how they can become good monks. The lessons are provided through
the experiences of many lives, and it is here that Caesar's Cistercians begin to emerge as medieval people, with emotions and thoughts,
often contradictory but almost always stimulating and revealing to
us. Caesar's humanity enables him to appreciate the humanity of his
abbot, his fellow monks and his Cologne friends. But at the same
time he is united to them in a spiritual quest on which all are
agreed. The continuing [evidence] of miracles convinces the monks
that their choice of the Cistercian Order is right. In Eberbach,
Schönau, and Heisterbach, the traditions of Bernard and Clairvaux
live on.[48] In this world, all the details are important, for they
confirm the **message** of eternity. The miracle is grounded in everyday reality, and everyday reality gives rise to the miracle.

Copenhagen University

NOTES

1. See, for example, Jean Leclercq, *The Love of Learning and the Desire for God* (New York: Fordham, 1974), one of the central guides to medieval monasticism and its spirit.

2. Walter Map, *De nugis curialium* XXIV provides some of the sharpest criticisms. See David Knowles, 'The Critics of the Monks,' *The Monastic Order in England 940-1216* (Cambridge, 1966) 662-678.

3. *Exordium Magnum Cisterciense,* ed. Bruno Griesser, Series Scriptorum S. Ordinis Cisterciensis: (Rome, 1961), *Distinctio* V, chapter 20, pp. 335-6: 'Sciatis, domine pater, tria esse in ordine vestro, quae specialiter oculos summae maiestatis offendunt, multiplicatio agrorum, superfluitas aedificorum, atque lascivia vocorum.'

4. 'Property and Politics at Esrum Abbey, 1151-1251,' *Mediaeval Scandinavia* 6 (1973) 122-50. 'Patrons, privileges, property—Sorø Abbey's first half century,' *Kirkehistoriske Samlinger* (Copenhagen, 1974) 1-39.

5. *Die Zisterzienserabtei Himmerode im 12. und 13. Jahrhundert,* Beiträge zur Geschichte des alten Mönchtums und des Benediktinerordens, 12. (Münster in Westf., 1924).

6. I shall use the edition of Joseph Strange and cite from *distinctio* (in roman numerals) and *capitulum* (in arabic). Strange's edition was published (Cologne, Bonn, Brussels) in 1851 and reprinted in New Jersey, 1966. Professor Dr Fritz Wagner, Berlins Freie Universität, is at work on a new edition of the *Dialogus*. The Handschriftenabteilung at the Niedersächsische Staats- und Universitätsbibliothek, Göttingen, has been kind enough to send me photocopies of the notes Alfons Hilka made from 1912 until his death in 1939 on the manuscript tradition of the *Dialogus miraculorum*. These will be referred to as Göttingen, Hilka 135.

7. A. Kaufmann, *Caesarius von Heisterbach. Ein Beitrag zur Kulturgeschichte des 12. und 13. Jahrhundert* (Köln, 1862) p. 17. See also Fritz Wagner, 'Studien zu Caesarius von Heisterbach,' *Analecta Cisterciensia* 29 (1973) 79-95, esp. p. 79.

8. *Dial. Mir.* I, 37, pp. 45-46: 'Visum est ei congruum, ibi militiam deponere saecularem, ubi assumere proponebat militiam spiritualem.'

9. Kaufmann, p. 20.

10. IV, 98, pp. 266-67: 'Tempore quadragesimali cum civium filii, iuvenes divites ac delicati, confiterentur peccata sua, maxime carnis incentiva, quae fomentare solent multum cibaria delicata; quia tales minus in se experiebatur passiones, durius quandoque illos quam expediret arguit, dicens: Turpe est, quod homines Christiani motibus tam turpibus agitantur. Et scandalizavit

pusillos, aliquam illis ingerens desperationem. Sed iustus
et misericors Deus, qui Petrum ob gregis salutem cadere permis-
it, servum sibi dilectum flagello tentationis erudivit, ut
subditis sciret compati, passione corripuit consimili...Ex hoc
in se ipso didicit, quomodo aliis deberet mederi.'

11. Translated F. M. Powicke (London, 1950) 12-16.

12. *Ex. mag.* III, 13, p. 177.

13. See the prologue of the *Dialogus miraculorum:* 'Colligite fragmenta **ne** pereant' (Jn 6, 12).

14. Caesar seems to try to avoid reproducing accounts that already
are written down. See IV, 76 and 77, p. 178: 'Quod dicturus
sum, de sancto Bernardo gestum audivi, et quia nusquam scriptum
inveni, scripto mandare dignum duxi.' In the very beginning of
the prologue Caesar says: '...aliqua ex his *quae in ordine nos-
tro nostris temporibus* miraculose gesta sunt et quotidie fiunt,
recitarem noviciis, rogatus sum a quibusdam....'

15. Wagner (p. 81) says that Caesar became prior on Heisterbach.
His source is Henriquez, *Menologium Cist.* 25 Sept. I can find
nothing in Caesar's own works which substantiates this assertion, and thus it seems likely that if Caesar became prior at
all, this happened towards the end of his life.

16. IV, 52, p. 218: 'Interrogatus a me, si sciret quid hos signi-
ficaret, respondit: Dominus mihi contulit gratiam illam, ut
nihil impudicum, et quod laedere possit verecundiam meam, cogi-
tare possim de illo. Et ideo intellexi, quod tantum partes corporis sui superiores, non inferiores ostendere mihi dignatus
est.'

17. Like Anselm of Canterbury and a few other outstanding monastic
educators of the High Middle Ages, Caesar found physical punishment generally repulsive and counterproductive. See VI, 5, p.
353, where the dean of St Andrew interrupts the *scholasticus*
in the midst of a session of thrashing and upbraids him: 'Quid
agis, tyranne? Positus es, ut scholares doceas, non ut occidas.'

18. See Alfons Hilka, *Die Wundergeschichten des Caesarius von Heisterbach*, Publikationen der Geselleschaft für Rheinische Geschichts-
kunde XLIII, 1 (Bonn, 1933), especially Caesar's letter in which
he lists his own writings, pp. 3-7.

19. Wagner, p. 87.

20. VIII, 29, p. 104: 'Licet in Dialogo sancti Gregorii et in aliis
locis plura de his occurrant exempla, non tamen, quia ita promis-
sum est, tibi dicere licet nisi nova, id est nostris temporibus
gesta.'

21. On Conrad's behalf, it should be added that some of his stories
are taken from his own experience at Eberbach and have a freshness and vitality in their detail that his received and **reworked**
stories can lack. See for example, *Ex. mag.* V, 17, pp. 326-7,
the story of Conrad the knight and his visit to the monastery.

22. J.-Th. Welter, *L'Exemplum dans la littérature religieuse et
     didactique du Moyen Age* (Paris, 1927).
23. As in V, 5, where the novice demands why Caesar now has re-
     vealed the name of Herman of Marienstatt for visions of the
     devil, while before, in Caesar's homilies on the infancy of
     Christ, he had concealed the name of his source.
24. In V, 15, the novice objects against novices' being criticized
     for returning to the world when the Rule apparently leaves open
     the possibility.
25. I, 3, p. 10: [Monachus] Nostri fratrem nostrum, qui infra hunc
     mensem de grangia vicina deceptus a muliere recessit? Novicius:
     Optime. See also X, 16, p. 230, where the novice talks about
     the way vegetables taste to him now compared with earlier.
26. Göttingen Hilka 135, pp. 6, 7, 9, 11, 12. Most of these are
     fifteenth century manuscripts, but Louvain Univ. Bibl. G. 63v.64
     is from the thirteenth century, and belonged to the benedictine
     monastery of St James in Liège, an area from where many of Cae-
     sar's stories came, and where the sister monasteries of Villers
     and Aulne probably had copies of Caesar's works.
27. Göttingen, Hilka 135, p. 29. In the Cologne 1481 edition, the
     persons in the final six distinctions are called Caesarius and
     Apollonius, while in Cologne 1491 edition, these names are used
     in all twelve distinctions.
28. Gainesville, Florida, 1974, pp. 115-116.
29. In the first distinction there are eight instances of Cologne
     clerks who converted to the Cistercians. Four went to Heister-
     bach, while one, Godfred, was turned down there and had to seek
     entrance at Villers (ch. 35). One became abbot at Otterberg (38);
     another went to Altenkamp (22), and another to Himmerod (but later
     became an apostate, 14).
30. *PL* 185: 1273-1384. See also Bruno Griesser, 'Herbert von Clair-
     vaux und sein *Liber miraculorum*,' *Cistercienser Chronik* 54 (1947)
     1-39, 118-148.
31. 'Ein Himmeroder *Liber Miraculorum* und seine Beziehungen zu Cae-
     sarius von Heisterbach,' *Archiv für mittelrheinische Kirchen-
     geschichte* 4 (1952) 257-274.
32. XI, 3, p. 272: 'Duo haec capitula, sicut et quinque reliqua quae
     sequuntur, a quodam reperi notata, qui se ea quae dicta sunt vi-
     disse et audivisse commemorat; quae perire non sum passus. Habent
     praeterea plures testes, qui adhuc supersunt.'
33. Hilka, *Die Wundergeschichten* 1, p. 29; 'Quid enim tantum delec-
     tat et non edificat, fabula dici potest. Rumores regnorum, pro-
     vinciarum, et civitatum, in quibus nulla est utilitas, sed levi-
     tas et loquacitas, quis aliud nisi fabulaciones?'
34. For the following, see my article, 'Structure and Consciousness
     in the *Exordium Magnum Cisterciense:* The Clairvaux Cistercians
     after Bernard,' *Cahiers de l'Institut du Moyen-Age Grec et Latin*

(Copenhagen, 1979) 33-90.

35. See my *Conflict and Continuity at Øm Abbey. A Cistercian Experience in Medieval Denmark,* Museum Tusculanum, Opuscula graeco-latina (Copenhagen, 1976).

36. Hilka, p. 19 (the prologue to the Sunday Homilies): 'Et quia nonnulli fratrum causati sunt precedentes omelias **nimis** esse prolixas nimisque infirmis intellectibus subtiles, utrumque cavere curavi, stilo utens breviori atque planiori.'

37. The full passage IV, 57, p. 224: 'Quod illi avaritiam, hoc nos esse dicimus providentiam. Omnes enim hospites supervenientes, ex mandato regulae tenemur sicut Christum suscipere. Quibus si negaretur hospitalitas, quo modo ordinem iudicant de avaritia, tunc forte amplius eundem iudicarent de impietate et immisericordia. Pene nulla domus est ordinis, **quae** non sit obligata debitis, tum propter hospites et pauperes, tum propter eos, qui quotidie convertuntur, et sine scandalo repelli non possunt. Ut enim dispensatores nostros excusem, non de toto, sed de tanto, saepe hac **necessitate** oportet illos velint nolint avere.'

38. Ferdinand Schmitz, *Urkundenbuch der Abtei Heisterbach* (Bonn, 1908) 6-9.

39. IV, 97 in *Dial. mir.*; III, 15 in *Exordium magnum*. In the first the monk is known as Bernard, while in the second he is Peter of Toulouse. There may be two separate incidents, but I think not. Caesar is notoriously inconsistent with names, as when he dedicates a work of Lenten sermons to Everling, monk of Bloemkamp in Friesland (Hilka, p. 26), but in his list of works in a letter to Abbot Peter of Marienstatt (Hilka, p. 5), he says it was meant for Efferind, monk of **Klaarkamp**, also in Friesland, but a different monastery!

In both stories, the monk wakes up to think he has been physically castrated, but in Conrad's, the 'cleansing' is done by an angel and without pain, while in Caesar's, it happens in a much more traumatic way. Also Conrad's tale does not mention the monk's temptation to leave the monastic life.

40. Hilka, p. 10.

41. My student, Birgitte Thye, at Copenhagen University's Institute of History, is presently preparing a thesis on this subject.

42. As his interpretation of the vision of Simon: the immediate political implications are clarified, but as for the apocalyptic part: 'Reliqua huius visionis nimis sunt obscura, nec patent meo intellectui.' II, 30, p. 103.

43. Göttingen Hilka, 135, p. 30.

44. III, 40. The thirteenth century Heisterbach manuscript is Düsseldorf Landesbibl. C 26, A in Strange, who did not realize it was from the abbey and dated it later.

45. V, 21, in *Heresy, Crusade and Inquisition in Southern France* (1100-1250), (London, 1974) 195-99.

46. Hilka, p. 132.
47. I hope to be able to continue on these lines and one day to
     write a book on Caesar and his world. Since this article was
     written in 1978, *Analecta Cisterciensia* has published two more
     detailed studies of mine: 'Written Sources and Cistercian In-
     spiration in Caesarius of Heisterbach,' AC 35 (1979) 227–82,
     and 'Friends and Tales in the Cloister: Oral **Sources** in Caesarius
     of Heisterbach,' AC 36 (1980) 167–247.
48. As in the striking narration of Hildegund, a female virgin who
     died as a monk at Schönau and was responsible for many miracles
     there, which attracted pilgrims: I, 40, p. 52: 'Et nos fratres
     cum illis gratias referamus Salvatori nostro qui haec fieri vo-
     luit *nostris temporibus in ordine nostro,* ad gloriam suam et
     aedificationem nostram....' These lines restate the message of
     Caesar as he already expressed it in his prologue.

THE ALLEGED GREEK SOURCES OF WILLIAM OF ST THIERRY

David N. Bell

In 1940 Dom Jean-Marie Déchanet published a brief collection of three papers dealing with the sources of the spirituality of William of St Thierry.[1] The dominant theme of all three papers was the profound extent to which William had been influenced by Greek sources, and the way in which he had assimilated completely Greek theological conceptions. Dom Déchanet's main arguments involved William's use of Origen (in the translation of Rufinus) and Gregory of Nyssa (in the translation of Eriugena[2]), and his examination of the influence of these two notable names on William led him to the conclusion that the latter had been conquered by 'the philosophy and theology of the Orient,' and that 'his last-- but by no means his least--works carry the unmistakable imprint of eastern thought.'[3] From that time onwards (and for our present purposes we need not examine the views of earlier writers), the idea of the 'orientalism' of William of St Thierry has tended to be accepted as an obvious fact, and only very recently have there appeared studies in which this virtually canonical doctrine has been questioned.[4] The excellent work of John D. Anderson on *The Enigma of Faith*[5] is a particularly sound example of this more critical spirit, and his own conclusion is that although William certainly knew the work of Origen and Gregory (and that is not in question), 'the extent to which William uses the Greek Fathers must be...reappraised.'[6] 'The study of William's sources,' he continues, 'might progress considerably if a moratorium were declared on searching for these sources among the Greeks and greater effort were exerted on the Latin masters of Western thought: Augustine, Boethius, and others.'[7] With this viewpoint I am in total agreement, and my own study of William, completed at the University of Oxford in 1975,[8] was an attempt to re-assess the relative importance of eastern and western thought in William's spirituality and re-direct our attention back to the work of Augustine of Hippo.

In the few pages we have at our disposal here, it is obviously impossible to deal comprehensively with the question of William's sources, but we may still--even in speaking generally--bring to the reader's attention sufficient material to question the validity of Déchanet's estimate of the importance of oriental thought in William's theology. Let us begin, therefore, by examining the three main areas in which Déchanet sees this influence as being of particular significance.[9]

The first and the most important area is the matter of the image *(imago)* and the likeness *(similitudo)*, for it is upon these concepts that the whole of William's mystical theology is based.[10] Déchanet defines the image as 'a living imprint of the Trinity in the soul, an affinity of nature and God, a capacity for the divine and supernatural life,'[11] and he looks above all to Gregory of Nyssa for the source of this idea.[12] It cannot, he says, be derived from Augustine, for the latter's conception of the image is very different from this. For Augustine, the image is only an 'analogy,'[13] something 'far distant from the Deity; no more than a vague likeness to the God who is Three and One.'[14] William's conception has nothing in common 'with the analogical resemblance which Augustine's psychology discovered and consecrated. It is 'imprinted' in the literal meaning of the word, an indelible mark, the seal of the three divine persons, taking possession of the powers of the human soul from the moment of creation, so that before the Fall the soul found itself drawn, by its own natural structure, into the ineffable trinitarian movement.'[15] Louis Bouyer, who follows Déchanet in this matter, also speaks disparagingly of Augustine's concept of the image. He calls it a 'facile explanation' which reduces 'the doctrine of the Trinity to an application to the Divinity of the facts of human psychology by simple transposition.'[16] William, he says, leaves this explanation entirely aside, and draws from the Greek Fathers a conception of the image which is far more spiritual and far more effective.[17]

Bouyer is, of course, quite correct; William does indeed leave aside this explanation. But in so doing he is not rejecting Augustine, but rather Bouyer's grossly inaccurate summary of what Augustine understood by the image of God. And the same is true in the case of Déchanet. Augustine's conception of the *imago Dei* (and of the related, but distinct, *imago Trinitatis*[18]) is actually something much more wide-ranging and much more spiritual, and the failure of Déchanet and Bouyer to recognize this fact leads inevitably--as we shall see--to their somewhat unbalanced views of William's sources. Augustine's actual conception of the image is (basically)

--that it is our participation in God the Trinity;

--that this participation involves *esse, vivere,* and *intelligere,* but that man alone participates in the last factor of this triad[19];

--that this participation in God always remains (for if it did not, we would cease to be), though normally in a dormant or latent condition[20]; and

--that this latent participation may be realized or actualized, and that by this actualization we may share more fully in the being of the Trinity.[21]

'The image of God,' says Robert Javelet in his analysis of Augustine's conception, 'is a capacity for God, a possibility of participation in Divinity; even if it is deformed, it yet remains a potential.'[22] In other words, for Augustine as for Gregory of Nyssa (and for William of St Thierry), our creation *ad imaginem Dei* involves an ontological link between God and the soul, and the fact that in the operations of our rational mind we may perceive (though remotely) an *imago Trinitatis* is only a part of this greater and more general participation.

As a result of their misconceptions of what Augustine meant by creation *ad imaginem Dei,* it follows naturally that Déchanet and Bouyer must also look elsewhere for the important idea of *similitudo*. 'The image,' Déchanet says, 'is essentially an aptitude, a capacity. Man is the image of God that he might live the life of God, share in the good things of God, and be able to realize--with the aid of grace--his assimilation to the divine, his "flight" to the celestial homeland.'[23] And the 'likeness' is precisely this realization and assimilation, 'the actualization of the supernatural potentialities which comprise the image.'[24] But--once again--we need not look to Gregory of Nyssa for this conception. It is to be found clearly set out in Augustine. By creation *ad imaginem Dei* we are *capax Dei;* by fulfilling the potential inherent in this **capacity** our likeness to God is perfected. It is this, says Augustine, which is the very essence of 'image-ness', 'that it is a capacity for God and can participate in him *(quo eius capax est, eiusque particeps esse potest);* and this great good is **possible** only because it *is* his image.'[25] This doctrine which, as Déchanet realizes, forms the centre of the spirituality of the Bishop of Hippo.

The second major area which Déchanet considers must be traced to eastern influence is the 'whole theory of how God is known in and through love,'[27] and, once again, Gregory of Nyssa is adduced as the source of the concept.[28] Once again, however, whilst not denying that William read and used certain texts of Gregory, we would suggest that **Augustine** is the more likely source for the fundamental principles of this important doctrine. Two ideas must be taken into account:

--the relationship between our love for God and God's **Love** in the person of the Holy Spirit; and

--the old platonic idea that by love the lover is transformed into that which is loved.

In the first case, although Augustine does not present a full and comprehensive and polished doctrine of the Holy Spirit,[29] it is perfectly clear (as Gustave Combès points out) that between our love and the **Love** which is God there is an essential link.[30] The Holy Spirit, as we know (and as William accepted[31]), is whatsoever is common to Father and Son, and is so substantially.[32] And of this mutual interaction, the mutual love of Father and Son is--for our sake--the most significant factor. The Holy Spirit is God-as-Love and God-the-Gift, and as the Gift (which is yet God) is diffused in our hearts and made our own.[33] But this is not to say (as Combès makes clear) that our love for God is the 'substantial and subsistent charity of the Holy Trinity.' Of course not. God's charity, which is God, takes the measure of our humanity, and although our love for God remains distinct (but not separate) from the Love which is God, it 'is not an image, nor a reflection, nor a symbol, but a real and living participation.'[35] Thus, says Augustine, 'Love, which is from God and which is God, is properly the Holy Spirit, through whom the love of God is diffused in our hearts, through which the whole Trinity dwells within us. Wherefore most rightly is the Holy Spirit, who is God, yet called the Gift of God. How then shall we properly conceive of that Gift save as love, which leads us to God, and without which no gift of God of any sort can lead us to him?'[36] By love, therefore, and in love we are led to God, and by love and in love God the Trinity indwells us. Our love for God is our participation in the God who is Love, God the Holy Spirit, and 'he that dwelleth in love dwelleth in God, and God in him.'[37] We need look no further than the Bishop of Hippo for the development of this tremendous doctrine.

To this idea we must add the platonic conception of the assimilatory power of love. Once again, the theory is not fully developed in Augustine, but the basic hypothesis is clear enough, and Augustine in the *De Trinitate* illustrates his thesis with two examples. First we have the case of the chameleon, which accomodates its own colours to the colours it sees; and secondly, that of the fetus which, he says, usually shows some traces of the mother's inclinations, and Augustine gives the example of Jacob putting various coloured rods by the watering-trough of his sheep and goats during their pregnancy with the intention of producing speckled offspring.[38] That William knew this theory is quite evident, and he uses precisely the same analogy to explain it,[39] but it is equally evident that he develops the idea to a greater degree of elaboration than did the Bishop of Hippo.[40] In *The Mirror of Faith*, for example, we find the assimilatory process divided into three stages: firstly, when the corporeal senses are transformed into the *sensibilia;* secondly, when the intellect or reason is transformed into the *rationabilia;* and thirdly, when the loving soul achieves unity of spirit with God.[41] But apart from this elaboration (and similar ones), it is clear that the basic principles of the thesis are the same for both Augustine and William. 'In the case of love,' says Gilson, in his excellent analysis of Augustine's thought, 'the object loved reacts in some way on the loving subject so as to transform it into its own image and thereby assimilate it. To love material and perishable things is to be materialized and doomed to perish; to love the eternal is to become eternal; to love God is to become God.'[42] By love, then, not only are we led to God; not only does the whole Trinity dwell within us, but (in a certain manner) we are transformed into That which we seek. And it is this principle (for which we need not look to Gregory of Nyssa) which leads ineluctably to the ideas contained in William's conception of *amor-intellectus*.

The thesis that love itself is knowledge represents the culmination of William's spirituality, and it is manifestly impossible

to consider the origins, development, ramifications, and difficulties of the doctrine here.[43] The principle behind the idea, however, is fairly simple: love of God leads to assimilation to God,
to greater likeness to God, to the mutual indwelling of God and the
soul, and to the actualization of that potential which comprises the
image of God, and thus leads us to a knowledge of God which, although
of a very different order from our normal conceptual thinking, is
nevertheless a real and **positive** understanding. It is a *connatural*
knowledge,[44] produced in and through love, and according to Dom Déchanet is a theory which William 'evidently derives from Plotinus
and the Greek Fathers but explains in terms of our own intellect
by an odd comparison with St Augustine's theory of the part played
by the senses in cognition.'[45]

Two points must be made here: firstly, I have examined elsewhere the question of whether Plotinus can be considered as one of
William's direct sources (that is to say, whether William was acquainted with plotinian materials other than those which form the
traditional 'plotinian corpus' of the Church Fathers) and have concluded that the available evidence does not warrant such an assumption;[46] and secondly, although it is true that the augustinian
theory of cognition plays an important part in William's doctrine
of *amor-intellectus* (a point well illustrated by the useful study
of Père Malevez[47]), the augustinian theory of love and the Holy
Spirit is even more significant. We have seen already that for
Augustine love leads to the assimilation of the lover and the beloved, and to the indwelling or 'inhering' of God and the soul.[48]
By love we are conformed to God and made like him.[49] And just as
it is love, the highest love *(summa caritas)*, which conjoins *(con-
jungere)* Father and Son in the person of the Holy Spirit, so too it
is love which subjoins *(subjungere)* us to them,[50] and makes us one
spirit with God. 'One spirit,' says Augustine, and adds that the
addition of the word 'spirit' is necessary because the spirit of
man and the Spirit of God are different natures, and man and God
do not become simply identical. Yet, he says, 'by inhering, one
spirit is made from two different ones, in such a way that without
the human spirit, the Spirit of God is **blessed** and perfect, but
the spirit of man is not blessed except with God.'[51] It follows
logically that in this unity of spirit, one's knowledge and understanding of the nature of God is far beyond our normal conceptual-
ization,[52] and that it is an 'inherent' knowledge, an 'assimilated'
knowledge, a 'connatural' knowledge, a knowledge of God (in love
and by love) which is gained from being 'in' God, a knowledge which
is a true participation in the being of the **Trinity**. And this is
precisely what William of St Thierry means when he says 'amor ipse
intellectus est,' love itself is knowledge.[53] It is true that William develops this doctrine to a degree far beyond that of Augustine,
and in so doing makes use of oriental materials, but for the basic

principles of the idea, for the essential blue-print of the idea,
the influence of the Bishop of Hippo should not be under-estimated.

I think that our discussion so far has made it clear that there
is much more to the mystical theology of Augustine than Déchanet (and
certainly Bouyer) has realized, and that the augustinian conceptions
of image, likeness, and love may be seen as laying a very firm and
very important foundation for the remarkable spirituality of William
of St Thierry. On the other hand, I am not trying to say that Augustine alone was William's source for these ideas. Such a statement
would be ridiculous, and, as we have noted earlier, there is not the
least doubt that William had read certain works of Origen (whose impact on the twelfth century in general was profound[54]) and the *De
hominis opificio* of Gregory of Nyssa. Since William had also read
some Eriugena (although the influence of the Irishman on his work has,
I think, been exaggerated[55]), it is also clear that he would have come
in contact with other representatives of the eastern tradition, and
there is not the least doubt that these theologians affected his work.
It is also clear, we might add, that he had read them in translation,
and I have attempted to show elsewhere that it is extremely unlikely
that William had a reading knowledge of Greek.[56] My own argument,
however, is that these eastern writers did *not* provide William with
the fundamental principles of his spirituality, but were rather used
by him to adorn and elaborate a primarily augustinian and western
basis.

It is true that in at least one case Déchanet himself recognized
at a later date that a previous assessment had been too biased. When
the work of Dom Odo Brooke demonstrated the strongly augustinian character of *The Enigma of Faith*[57], Déchanet corrected an earlier statement and observed that he was forced to reverse his conclusion. *The
Enigma of Faith,* he said, should now be considered as exhibiting 'augustinian climate in general with Oriental influences which are quite
numerous.'[58] But on this matter we may make two comments: (a) that
it is not only for the *Enigma* that such a re-assessment is necessary,
but for William's mystical theology in general; and (b) that the work
of John Anderson has shown that even the revised estimate of Déchanet
needs revision: the 'oriental influences' in the *Enigma* are not even
'quite numerous.' Apart from Origen/Rufinus, they hardly exist at all.[59]

What seems to have happened to Déchanet is that after his important discovery of William's use of Gregory of Nyssa, he became carried
away with the concept of William's supposed 'orientalism,' and began
to play the game of 'Seek the Greek' with a less than tolerable regard
to scholarly criticism. A continual concern with the eastern horizon
can sometimes blind one to what is actually under one's nose, and we
find in Déchanet not only a general (and, I feel, misjudged) predilection for **oriental** sources, but a number of cases of specific errors
--errors which, unfortunately, only provide further support for the
myth (if I may put it so) of 'Guillaume the Greek.' Anderson has ex-

emplified the sort of inaccuracies which occur: Hilary is mistaken
for Origen; Boethius is mistaken for Basil; a variety of Latin Fathers appear as 'ps-Dionysius', and so on.[60] And I have myself drawn
attention to similar mistakes elsewhere.[61] Nor are Déchanet's inaccuracies confined to mis-traced quotations. Let us for a moment consider one of his comments on William's *Exposition on the Song of Songs*:
'And then again the extent to which our author was then familiar with
eastern thought is attested by his learned accounts of words quite
alien to Latin vocabulary, words such as *extasis, excessus, principale
mentis vel cordis..., theoria, theophania....*'[62] Such a statement requires considerable revision. Although the terms are far from being
in common and frequent use amongst the western writers, there is no
doubt that they were very well known. Both *extasis* and *excessus* are
biblical,[63] and a glance at the relevant entries in Albert Blaise's
excellent dictionary of Christian Latin[64] will confirm that all these
terms appear in well-established western Fathers. A similar state of
affairs may be seen with those terms Déchanet adduces elsewhere as
being particularly characteristic of Plotinus, and which form part
of his argument that William was directly influenced by the *Enneads*:
*regio dissimilitudinis, summa iustitia, sepulcrum corporis, unus,
unitas, id quod est, contemplatio summi boni.*[65] Although in some
cases (such as *id quod est*) Plotinus may indeed be the ultimate
source, I have attempted to demonstrate in my own criticism of Déchanet's thesis that these terms may also be found in Augustine,
and that there is no need to suggest a direct knowledge of Plotinus
on the part of William to explain these plotinian reminiscences.[66]

What then may we conclude from these brief observations? There
are, I would suggest, two main points which may be stated with some
confidence. Firstly, Déchanet's estimate of the great importance
of Greek thought in laying the foundations of William's mystical
theology is partly a result of his misapprehension of Augustine's
conceptions of image, likeness, and love. A careful examination of
these doctrines reveals clearly that in them may be seen the roots
of William's spirituality, and, whilst not denying the obvious influence of eastern thinking on his work, I would suggest simply that
this influence was neither as important nor as vital as Déchanet
maintains. The second point is that Déchanet's arguments for the
importance of oriental thought are sometimes supported by spurious
evidence. In a number of cases, 'citations' from Greek theologians
are actually to be traced to Latin writers, and terminology which
Déchanet asserts to be distinctively eastern is, in fact, easily to
be found in the west. The tracing of sources may well be 'an affair of dull diligence' (the words are those of Henry Osborn Taylor[67]), but it is an unfortunate necessity. As Anderson informs
us, 'a comprehensive study of the sources used by William of St
Thierry has yet to be undertaken,'[68] but until it *is* undertaken,
and until the sort of inaccuracies which we find appearing in

Déchanet's work are corrected, it will not really be possible to
make a precise and accurate estimate of the exact balance of east
and west in William's thought. That Déchanet swung the scale too
far to the orient is not, I think, in doubt; the extent to which
it should be swung back again has not yet been precisely determined.

Memorial University of Newfoundland

NOTES

In the following notes the name of William of St Thierry/Guillaume de Saint-Thierry has been abbreviated to W. of S.T./G. de S.T.

1. J. M. Déchanet, *Aux sources de la spiritualité de G. de S.T.* (hereafter cited as *Aux sources*) (Bruges, 1940). All three papers had been published at earlier dates: see *ibid.*, 1 n. 1, 25 n. 1, 60 n. 1.

2. The Eriugenian translation of the *De hominis opificio* was discovered by Maïeul Cappuyns (see his *Jean Scot Érigène* [Louvain, 1933; rp. Brussels, 1964] 172-178), and the text has been published by the same author in *RTAM* 32 (1965) 205-262. On William's need for translations, see Note 56 below.

3. Déchanet, *Aux sources*, 73. The same opinion may be found in many places in his work.

4. See especially J. D. Anderson, 'The Use of Greek Sources by W. of S.T., especially in the *Enigma Fidei*,' in B. Pennington (ed.), *One Yet Two. Monastic Tradition East and West*, CS 29 (1976) 242-253 (see also Note 5 below); and E. R. Elder, 'W. of S.T. and the Greek Fathers: Evidence from Christology,' CS 29: 254-266.

5. J. D. Anderson (trans.), *The Works of W. of S.T., Vol. III: The Enigma of Faith*, CF 9 (1974). For the purposes of this paper I shall refer to English translations wherever possible.

6. CF 9: 16.

7. CF 9: 17.

8. D. N. Bell, *The Image and the Likeness. A Study of the Mystical Theology of W. of S.T. and Its Relation to that of St Augustine* (Oxford University, typescript, 1975). An abridged version of this study will be published by Cistercian Publications (Kalamazoo, Michigan) as soon as I and they can prepare it.

9. Déchanet himself does not list the areas in this fashion, but there is little difficulty in extracting them from his work.

10. 'William's spirituality, like St Bernard's, has the doctrine of the image and likeness running through the whole of it' (Déchanet's introduction to T. Berkeley's translation of *The Golden Epistle*; CF 12 (1971) xxii (= *Aux sources*, 14). See further my thesis, Chapter III. The same idea may be found stated in a number of places in Déchanet's work.

11. J. M. Déchanet, *Oeuvres choisies de G. de S.T.* (hereafter *Oeuvres choisies*) (Paris, 1944) 249. See also Note 23 below.

12. See *ibid.*, 249-250; and the same author's *Aux sources*, 34-37.

13. See *Aux sources*, 35. There are actually some problems with Déchanet's use of this term, and a discussion may be found in my thesis, 158-159.

14. *Aux sources*, 35.

15. Déchanet's introduction to CF 12: xxiii (= *Aux sources*, 15).

16.   L. Bouyer, *The Cistercian Heritage*, (London, 1958) 114.

17.   *Ibid.*, 114-124.

18.   On this distinction see the straightforward (but somewhat unin-
      spiring) account by J. E. Sullivan, *The Image of God: The Doc-
      trine of St Augustine and Its Influence* (Dubuque, Iowa, 1963),
      Chapter II 'The Image of the One God,' and Chapter IV, 'The
      Image of the Trinity.' See also Note 19 below.

19.   Hence Augustine's stress on the importance of human rationality,
      and his reference in *De Civitate Dei* XXII, 24, 2 (PL 41: 789)
      to 'the spark of reason, in which man was made to the image of
      God.' See also *De Trinitate* XII, vii, 12 (PL 42: 1004-5). See
      further Sullivan, *The Image*, 49-53. Cf. William, *Expositio super
      Cantica Canticorum* (PL 180: 503C; tr. c. Hart, *The Works of W.
      of S.T., Vol. II: Exposition on the Song of Songs*, CF 6 [1970]
      72-73 §§88-89); *Epistola ad Fratres de Monte-Dei* II, iv (PL 184,
      340B-341C; tr. CF 12: 79-81 §§198-204); and elsewhere. We may
      say (very generally) that whereas the *imago Dei* is human ration-
      ality (which of necessity includes life and being), the *imago
      Trinitatis* comprises those trinitarian analogies which may be
      seen in and by the operations of that rationality.

20.   This is certainly the doctrine of Augustine's maturity, and his
      earlier views (which he later revised) that the image (rather
      than the likeness) could be lost need not concern us here. For
      a discussion, see my thesis, Appendix III 'Augustine and the
      Lost Image.'

21.   I would stress here that this brief summary cannot do justice
      to the richness of Augustine's thought on this matter, and for
      a full discussion (with further references to the considerable
      secondary literature) the reader may be referred to my thesis,
      Chapter I 'The Image of God and the Basic Principles of August-
      ine's Mystical Theology.'

22.   R. Javelet, *Image et ressemblance au XIIe siècle*, Vol. 1 (Paris,
      1967) 62. See also Sullivan, *The Image*, 51-53, 141.

23.   *Oeuvres choisies*, 252. See also *Aux sources*, 38 n. 1.

24.   *Oeuvres choisies*, 253. Cf. *Aux sources*, 38 n. 1 'The likeness
      is the image actualized, or in the process of actualization.'

25.   *De Trinitate* XIV, viii, 11 (PL 42: 1044). See also E. Gilson,
      The Christian Philosophy of Saint Augustine, trans. L. E. M.
      Lynch (New York, 1967) 219.

26.   See Déchanet's introduction to CF 12: xxiv. Cf. also *Oeuvres
      choisies*, 249, where the doctrine of the image is called 'the
      key to his spirituality.'

27.   Déchanet, *W. of S.T., The Man and His Work*, trans. R. Strachan,
      CS 10 (1972) 50-51.

28.   *Ibid.* See also Déchanet's introduction to CF 6: xxi-xxii.
      See also Note 45 below.

29.   See J. Burnaby, *Amor Dei: A Study of the Religion of St Augustine*

(London, 1938) 175 (and elsewhere).

30. See G. Combès, *La charité d'après saint Augustin* (Paris, 1934)
    54-58, the section headed 'By charity we participate in the Di-
    vine Love.' See also Note 35 below.

31. See, for example, J. D. Anderson (trans.), *Enigma*, CF 9: 114-117
    (§§87-90); but for a full account, see my thesis, Chapter IV
    'Love and Assimilation in W. of S.T.'

32. See F. Cavallera, 'La doctrine de saint Augustin sur l'Esprit-
    saint à propos du *De Trinitate*,' Part I, in *RTAM* 2 (1930) 369,
    374, 380, 383-4, 386 (but the entire paper is relevant to this
    matter). A comprehensive collection of references to Augustine
    will be found therein.

33. Cavallera, 'La doctrine', Part II, in *RTAM* 3 (1931) 19. See also
    A. M. la Bonnardière, 'Le verset paulinien Rom. V.5 dans l'oeuvre de
    saint Augustin,' in *Augustinus Magister* (Congrès international
    augustinien, Paris, 21-24 Septembre 1954) Vol. 2 (Paris, 1954)
    657-665; and Combès, *La charité*, Chapter I.

34. Combès, *La charité*, 54.

35. *Ibid.*, 54 See also *ibid.*, 257; and Cavallera, 'La doctrine,'
    Part II, 19: 'Augustine never separates from created charity,
    which transforms our soul to the image of God, uncreated charity
    which is its source and which he loves to personify as the Holy
    Spirit.' See also Burnaby, *Amor Dei*, 173-177.

36. *De Trinitate* XV, xviii, 32; PL 42: 1083.

37. 1 Jn 4:16 quoted by Augustine in *De Trinitate* XV, xvii, 31; PL
    42: 1082. See Burnaby, 175.

38. See *De Trinitate* XI, ii, 5; PL 42: 987-988 (the Jacob story ap-
    pears in Genesis 30). The details of this process of assimila-
    tion are not altogether clear in Augustine, and are involved
    with certain other difficulties in his theory of cognition.
    We cannot and need not explain these problems here, for the
    basic fact that assimilation occurs is not in doubt.

39. See *Spec fid;* PL 180: 391C (tr. T. X. Davis, CF 15 [1979] 72 [§29]).

40. For a consideration of this matter, see my thesis, Chapter IV,
    'Love and Assimilation in W. of S.T.' (especially 195-196).

41. See *Spec fid;* PL 180: 391B (CF 15: 72 [§29]). For further dis-
    cussion, see my thesis, 196.

42. Gilson, *Christian Philosophy*, 8 (standard references to Augus-
    tine are provided there).

43. For a full discussion see my thesis, Chapter VI, '*Amor-Intellec-
    tus* and the Nature of Highest Ecstasy in W. of S.T.'

44. For an introduction to this concept, see O. Brooke, 'Towards a
    Theology of Connatural Knowledge,' in *Cîteaux* 18 (1967) 275-
    290 (= *Studies in Monastic Theology*, CS 37: 232-49).

45. Déchanet, *W. of S.T., The Man and His Work*, 74. See also Dé-
    chanet's introduction to CF 12: xxvii-xxx (= *Aux sources*,
    18-21); Déchanet's introduction to CF 6: **xlvii-xlviii**; and his

main discussion of the question in his '*Amor ipse intellectus est*. La doctrine de l'amour-intellection chez G. de S.T.,' in *Revue du moyen-âge latin* 1 (1945) 349-374.

46.   See my 'Greek, Plotinus, and the Education of W. of S.T.,' in *Cîteaux* 30 (1979) 221-48.

47.   See L. Malevez, 'La doctrine de l'image et de la connaissance mystique chez G. de S.T.,' in *Recherches de science religieuse* 22 (1932) 178-205 and 257-279 (especially 270-277). For a summary and a criticism of Malevez' views, see my *The Image and the Likeness*, 378-381.

48.   Cf. *De moribus ecclesiae catholicae* xvi, 26; PL 32: 1322, referring to Psalm 72:28 (Vulgate): 'Is not everything which can possibly be said about charity here contained in the one word 'inhere' (*adhaerere*)?'

49.   See *De moribus*, xiii, 23; PL 32:1321: 'Through charity, therefore, we are conformed to God....'

50.   See *De Trinitate* VII, iii, 6; PL 42: 938.

51.   *Ibid.*, VI, iii, 4; PL 42: 926.

52.   Augustine distinguishes three levels of vision: (i) the corporeal (=physical); (ii) the spiritual (=imaginative); and (iii) the intellectual (=extra-conceptual). Our highest knowledge and experience of God takes place, as we would expect, at the third of these levels, and cannot therefore be understood in terms of our normal conceptual thinking. For a full discussion, see the whole of Book XII of Augustine's *De Genesi ad litteram*; PL 34: 453-486.   There is no need to examine the idea in detail here.

53.   See (for example) *Expositio super Cantica canticorum*; PL 180: 491D, 494A, 499C, 524D-525A (= CF 6: 46 [§57], 52 [§64], 64 [§76], 115 [§144]). The basis of the expression **is** Gregory the Great's *amor ipse notitia est* (*Homilia XXVII in Evangelia* 4; PL 76:1207A), and William tells us so (see his *Disputatio adversus Petrum Abaelardum*; PL 180: 252C: '...as Blessed Gregory says, love itself is knowledge'--and here too William substitutes his own *intellectus* for Gregory's *notitia*).

54.   See J. Leclercq, 'Origène au XIIe siècle,' in *Irenikon* 24 (1951) 425-439.   Beryl Smalley (*The Study of the Bible in the Middle Ages* [Notre Dame, 1964[2]], 14) has observed that 'to write a history of Origenist influence on the west would be tantamount to writing a history of western exegesis.' On the other hand, some care must be taken with regard to the dates of the Origen/Rufinus manuscripts, especially as they relate to the first generation of Cistercians: see A. Squire, 'The Cistercians and the Eastern Fathers,' in *One Yet Two*, CS 29: 172, n. 4. See also E. R. Elder, CS 29: 258-260.

55.   We cannot examine this matter in detail here, and I hope to give some consideration to it in a further study. Déchanet's estimate of the importance of Eriugena at Laon is certainly exaggerated

(see my 'Greek, Plotinus, and the Education of W. of S.T.' 232-5),
as is his comment in CF 6: xl, that *The Enigma of Faith* 'owes
so much to Scotus Erigena for its speculative aspect.' A glance
at Anderson's translation and notes (see especially pp. 16-24)
will reveal immediately that some revision is necessary here.
(See also his comments in his 'The Use of Greek Sources by W. of
S.T.,' 252-253). See further B. McGinn, 'Pseudo-Dionysius and
the Early Cistercians,' in CS 29: 224-225; E. R. Elder, CS 29:
260-262; and my *The Image and the Likeness*, 442-443, n. 27.

56. See my 'Greek, Plotinus, and the Education of W. of S.T.' I
have suggested there that there is some little evidence which
indicates that William might have had an interest in the Greek
language (as distinct from his interest in Greek *ideas* in Latin
translation), but that it is most unlikely that he could actually read it.

57. See especially Odo Brooke's thesis, *The Trinity in G. de S.T.
against the Anthropological Background of His Doctrine of the
Ascent of the Soul to God* (Rome, typescript, 1957), but since
this is not easily available, the reader may be referred to the
extensive extracts from it (with revisions and expansions) which
have appeared in *RTAM* 26 (1959) 85-127; 27 (1960) 193-211; 28
(1961) 26-58; 30 (1963) 181-204; and 33 (1966) 287-318
(= *Studies in Monastic Theology*, CS 37 [1980] 12-122, 134-207).

58. Déchanet's introduction to CF 6: xli, n. 108. This comment
originally appeared in Déchanet's edition of *G. de S.T.*, *Exposé
sur le Cantique des Cantiques*, published in Paris by Les éditions
du Cerf in 1962, p. 43, n. 2.

59. See CF 9: 16-24.

60. See *ibid.*, especially 17-19. See also Anderson, 'The Use of
Greek Sources by W. of S.T.,' *passim*.

61. I have shown, for example, in my 'Greek, Plotinus, and the Educa-
tion of W. of S.T.' that in one case 'Plotinus' is actually
Augustine (see paragraph g in that article); in another case,
Ambrose (see paragraph e and Note 130); and in a third case,
Plato (see paragraph c). Further corrections of this nature will
be found in the revised edition of my *The Image and the Likeness*.

62. Déchanet, *G. de S.T.*, *l'homme et son oeuvre* (Bruges, 1942) 63.
I have not followed the Strachan translation of this work here
since I prefer 'quite alien to' for Déchanet's 'bien étrangers,'
rather than Strachan's 'quite unheard-of' (p. 51).

63. For *extasis*, see Psalm 30:1 (Vulgate) and Acts 3:10; for *excessus*,
see Psalms 30:23; 67:28; 115:11 (all in Vulgate enumeration);
Luke 9:31; Acts 10:10.

64. A. Blaise, *Dictionnaire latin-français des auteurs chrétiens*
(Turnhout, 1954). *Theophania*, of course, is an important word
for Eriugena, but as Rozanne Elder observes, 'That William
writes of *theophania* or of an *ordo charitatis* no more proves

a knowledge of Eriugena or of Origen than *satisfacere* proves
he read Anselm' (CS 29: 257). It is rare--though not unknown--
that the evidence of a single word is conclusive.

65. See Déchanet, 'Guillaume et Plotin,' in *Revue du moyen-âge latin*
2 (1946) 241-260 (especially 243, 254).

66. See my 'Greek, Plotinus, and the Education of W. of S.T.' 239-245.

67. H. O. Taylor, *The Mediaeval Mind*, Vol. II (London, 1911) 148.

68. CF 6: 16.

A TWELFTH-CENTURY VIEW OF THE IMAGINATION:
AELRED OF RIEVAULX

Marie Anne Mayeski CSJ

The recent revival of scholarly interest in the early Cistercian Fathers has made the name of Aelred of Rievaulx moderately well known. This charming English Cistercian, who died while. Abbot of Rievaulx, in 1167, is perhaps most popular because of his treatise on spiritual friendship, a unique re-casting of ciceronian ideas within the context of the christian search for holiness. This paper, however, will synthesize from all his works Aelred's ideas regarding the imagination, a faculty whose use he explored to lead his monks to holiness.. Those works which are most rich on the imagination are the *Speculum caritatis,* a handbook for novices; the *De Iesu puero duodenni,* a tract on prayer for a younger monk; and the *De institutione inclusarum,* a rule of life and some paradigmatic meditations constructed for his sister, a hermitess.[1]

Aelred inherited the augustinian anthropological tradition, which understood man with his powers of memory, understanding, and will as the image of the trinitarian God, but an image whose likeness to God was marred by sin. In this tradition, the purpose of life was seen as being to return to God through the integrated use of each specifically human power. This proper use healed the ravages of şin and restored the image to its true likeness through union with God. All this was the work of grace, the healing power of the presence of the Trinity within the soul.[2]

As Aelred, first novice-master and then abbot, studied the practical ways in which each human faculty could be integrated within this return to God, he came to focus his interest on the power of the imagination and he explored in his writings its functions in the development of the person. The following attempts to look at Aelred's ideas on the imagination, studying first how he understood the nature of the imagination and then the practical functions he assigned this faculty. Finally, some conclusions of possible contemporary interest will be explored.

Aelred's interest in the imagination is understandably pragmatic and existential. He seeks to understand its dynamism so that he can put it to use in the service of prayer and moral development. He does not incline greatly to a philosophical analysis of the *nature* of the imagination,[3] but an understanding of its nature is implicit in his analysis of its function. As Aelred understands it, the imagination plays a mediating role in the process of knowing as well as in the structuring of motivation. His understanding of the nature of imagination may be clarified by answers to three pertinent questions. How did Aelred envisage the imagination within the knowing process?

What was Aelred's understanding of the relation between the imagination and other human faculties? What purposes, if any, did Aelred
assign specifically to the imagination?

The first question is a difficult one: how is the imagination
part of the process of knowing. The question of the structure of
knowledge is, of course, a complex philosophical problem with a long
history of controversy; yet Aelred was neither a skilled speculative
theologian nor by temperament or need a protagonist. Nonetheless,
his description of the imaginative process suggests that he saw it
as part of the act of knowing in two ways. In the fine augustinian
tradition, knowing is also a matter of loving; the one who loves is
the one who best knows, a theory borne out by simple human experience.
But loving, in itself, is a complex activity in which will and emotions, reason and *sensus* (one of Aelred's favorite words) play irre-
placeable roles. This is where the image comes into play. Because
the imagination can stimulate the *sensus*, affectivity, and the will,
it is a powerful stimulus to that love which leads to knowledge. In
this way, the imagination is truly part of the knowing process.[4]

The imagination enters still more intimately into the knowing
process by its aptitude for analogy. As Aelred describes it, imagination is precisely that faculty which expresses its insight into reality by analogies; and analogy is the result of a perception that
is simultaneously a grasp of concrete reality and of the meaning both
contained within and yet beyond the concrete. The meaning within an
analogical insight, however, is not abstract; it cannot be communicated except through another concrete reality. The juxtaposition of
two concretes in analogy is the perception of a point of similarity
or identity between them on the level of meaning and it cannot be
equated with any abstract concept. By deduction, the faculty that
deals in analogy must be a faculty that perceives significance in
the concrete,[5] significance vis-à-vis the perceiver and containing
a call to volition and/or intentionality. The use of the word 'meaning' or 'significance' is deliberately personal: meaning is always
meaning *for someone*, even while it flows from the ontological existence of that reality which 'has' the meaning.[6] If analogy is a
valid vehicle of knowledge, then imagination, the faculty which ap-
prehends analogy, is part of the structure of knowing, not merely
propaedeutic to it.

It is clear from this that Aelred viewed the imagination as
active only within the total complex of human dynamisms; its specific activity can be described only in relation to the activity of
these other faculties. We come, then, to the second question posed
above. First of all, the imagination is dependent upon both sensa-
tion and memory. The raw material with which the imagination either
retains or constructs its images is material brought to it by the
senses. Its relationship with memory is reciprocal; it uses the
sense data stored in the memory to construct images but it also

provides new images which are stored in the memory where they, in
turn, feed its life. Similarly the imagination is preliminary to
the intellect; the world of concrete realities must be presented to
the intellect in the form of images constructed by the imagination
before the intellect can abstract concepts by its proper activity.
At the same time, the activity of the imagination is parallel to
that of the intellect; through the process of analogy, the imagination **pursues** insights into the meaning of concrete reality that can
neither replace abstraction nor be replaced by it. It is a comple-
mentary insight into reality. In its relation to the emotions **and**
the will, the imagination functions as a stimulus. The validity of
things, the truth of things, if made attractive by the images constructed by the imagination, is desired and sought for more energetic-
ally through the emotions as they reinforce the will. In some sense
it is true to say that the imagination, in Aelred's thought, is the
mediating faculty: it mediates sense data to the memory and intellect;
it mediates the truth of rational deduction to the emotions and will.
As a mediating faculty it would seem to operate as the principle of
integration in the activity of the participant self as it faces the
world in the experience of knowing. As mediator and principle of integration, the imagination would be particularly congenial to the
thought of Aelred and indeed to that of the cistercian school.[7]
We come now to the question of how the imagination may properly
be used in growth toward union with God. Aelred assigns special
functions to the faculty of imagination, particularly in the area of
prayer, but functions entering in fact into the total structure of
the person's relationship with God. First of all, Aelred envisions
the imagination as able to construct a variety of possible meanings
for any event in Scripture and, on the basis of these possible meanings, to formulate new questions. New questions always have poten-
tially new insights, and therefore in positing these questions the
imagination, according to Aelred, can be a positive and creative force
in the interpretation of Scripture.[8] Aelred also exploits the power
of the imagination to elaborate upon the content of the scriptural
mysteries and through this elaboration to make them more vivid, more
enduring, more accessible to contemplation.
The interpretation of Scripture and the experiences of contemplation are seen by Aelred to have a two-fold effect: they are means to
a knowledge which surpasses all investigation; and they provide us
with the proper interior attitudes to sustain our life of virtuous
activity.[9] In order to bring about these effects in prayer, Aelred
envisages the participant self as fulfilling a very active role. Over
and over again, both to his sister and to his young monastic disciple,
Aelred describes the way by which they are to enter the scene of the
meditation (taken for the most part from the Gospels) and become an
actor in the drama taking place before the mind's eye. Through the
power of the imagination the self is to listen and to look, so that

every detail is absorbed and then responded to appropriately (i.e.
with tears, kisses, acts of faith). Prayer, thus described, is one's
attempt to explore and understand the mystery that one contemplates
by the use of all one's human faculties. The imagination is called
upon to elaborate in great detail the material content of the mystery, particularly the physical beauty and charm of Christ, so that
the emotional response to the human meaning of the mystery will be
reproduced. 'Follow the holy Virgin to Bethlehem,' Aelred tells
his sister:

> and with complete devotion go aside with her into the shel-
> ter where you can be present and assist at the childbirth.
> Having placed the infant in the manger break into a joyful
> cry. Sing with Isaiah: 'A child is born to us, a son is
> given to us.' Embrace the crib gently, letting love conquer
> timidity and affection cast out fear, so that you may kiss
> the sacred feet.'[10]

This stimulation of the emotions is not an end in itself but
the means to insight, because underlying Aelred's methodology is the
assumption that emotional responses to Jesus facilitate a personal
identification with him (we feel as he did; we understand his feelings) that opens the possibility of deeper understanding. The process can be stated thus: we imagine in order to feel; we feel in
order to understand. Imaginative elaboration also has the result of
extending the presence of the mystery to us. As self dwells imaginatively upon one detail after another, it makes the presence of the
mystery more vivid and more enduring so that the content of the mystery can be absorbed. As the imagination is filled gradually with
the mystery in its multi-dimensionality, other realities are blocked
out, the mystery is concentrated on at length and the delight that
its meaning can stimulate is savored as the step to understanding.
     A second area of significance for the imagination is moral de-
velopment. In his advice to his sister, Aelred describes the negative impact which the imagination can have upon moral development:
filling the imagination with immoral and worldly possibilities creates
the overwhelming desire for that behavior.'[9] The opposite is also
true, as Aelred points out when he is elaborating upon Jesus as model.
Filling the imagination with the possibilities of virtue, as exemplified by Jesus, is a powerful means for stimulating motivation for behavioral change. As one imagines the possible ways of being poor and
being obedient, as one envisions oneself living in a particular moral
stance, the conviction that this is indeed possible as well as desir-
able grows, and behavioral change is facilitated. In recognizing the
power of the imagination to construct possibilities for the future,[12]
Aelred has anticipated one of the finest insights of contemporary psychology. A recent statement by Paul Ricoeur, though it employs some

language foreign to Aelred and his contemporaries, reflects Aelred's insight. Its remarkable aptness justifies lengthy quotation.

> The imagination has a metaphysical function which we are
> not able to reduce to a simple projection of vital, un-
> conscious or repressed desires. The imagination has a
> function of projection and exploration in regard to that
> which is **still** possible to man. It is *par excellence* the
> institution and the constitution of the humanly possible.
> It is in imagining his potentialities that man exercises
> prophecy with respect to his own existence. We can then
> begin to understand in what sense we can speak of a re-
> demption through imagination; it is in the midst of dreams
> of innocence and reconciliation that hope works the very
> dough of the human.[13]

Aelred has high regard for the power of the imagination to construct possibilities and thereby to expand the limitations of one's own life. On the one hand, it can set up possibilities of meaning in the sacred text; these possible meanings lead to new questions which in turn open up new meaning. Thus the imagination can expand the sense of the sacred text to encompass the growing, changing reality of one's own life. On the other hand, imagination can also construct new possibilities of behavior; in this respect it is a future-oriented **faculty**. By means of imagination the individual can explore his own capabilities, can envision himself living differently, doing different things. Because of the impact of the imagination upon will and emotions, this imagining also stimulates motivation and then further possibilities are actively sought. The imagination can thus play a positive role in the ascetical process of conversion of life.

Aelred was equally impressed with the power of the imagination in **stimu**lating the will. For him, imagination is a powerful attraction to love, and therefore to that particular kind of knowledge which flows from love. It is to be cultivated, therefore, as an aid to charity. But it is also to be carefully disciplined as a source of disquiet. Because of its power over emotions, reason, and will, imagination must be used with great care. Few human beings live out their religious lives on the level of concepts; rather, these concepts are usually mediated to the individual through images (of God, of man, of the human ideal). Aelred warns that the imagination can construct false images of God, images that are not consistent with what is **known** about God from revelation. Since one's personal relationship to God is heavily influenced by the images one has of him, false images are very destructive of that relationship. If one's **dominant** image of God, for instance, is that of severe judge, one's relationship with him will be primarily be in terms of fear and, often, of resentment. If, on the other hand, one's image of God is merely that of a tender friend one can be deprived of moral challenge. The necessity for a balanced spectrum of images in spirituality is obvious. Aelred's teaching, therefore, offers contemporary man the practical challenge of using his imagination to explore the full meaning of God's revelation, continually to re-evaluate his life in terms of unactivated possibilities, and to evaluate the images of God by which he lives in terms of the content of revelation.

The importance which Aelred ascribes to the imagination leads to further reflections upon the connection between it and revelation. First of all, his thought does suggest that the imagination is part of the knowing process, and that it is, in fact, a form of knowledge. He also indicates that the kind of knowledge which the imagination yields is best expressed in analogy. There is a great deal of biblical revelation which takes place on the level of analogy--symbols, types, events that dramatize this or that transcendent reality. Revelation, then, is frequently a kind of illumination into the meaning of symbols or symbolic events. Since ordinarily the meaning of symbols is unlocked partly through the power of the imagination, it follows that revelation may take place partly in the imagination. If the imagination is the faculty that perceives significance in the concrete, and if so much of revelation is concrete action, then the imagination must be part of the locus of revelation.

Further, revelation always reveals the revealer: what is contained in a message is not just the meaning of that message but also the nature of the one who is the source of the message. Is it not fair to say, then, that the imaginative quality of much of scriptural revelation testifies to an imaginative God? We speak of the 'mind of God' and of the 'will of God,' knowing that we use the terms analogously. It would seem no less accurate or less respectful to speak of the 'imagination of God' in the same way.

Aelred of Rievaulx sees the imagination as a powerful human faculty which has more than one role to play in religious life. It must be integrated into prayer and moral development, especially as that faculty through which one's understanding of God is mediated. The role of imagination in a theology of revelation needs to be explored further. There is every indication that a better understanding of the faculty of imagination would help us greatly in comprehending the nature of revelation and would yield greater insight into the God who reveals. If this end is someday achieved, then Aelred of Rievaulx deserves thanks for providing a starting-point.

Loyola Marymount University

NOTES

1. The critical edition of these is *Aelredi Rievallensis: Opera Omnia I: Opera Ascetica*, CC, CM, edited by Anselm Hoste and C. H. Talbot (Turnholt: Brepols, 1971).

2. This is, of course, an oversimplification of a rich and complex tradition. For a more complete study, see John Edward Sullivan, *The Image of God* (Dubuque, Iowa, 1963).

3. He did leave an unfinished *De anima* but it is sketchy and unoriginal. [Published as *Dialogue on the Soul*, translated by C. H. Talbot. Cistercian Fathers Series, 22--ed.]

4. An example of this insight is found in the *Speculum caritatis*, Part I, Chapters 5 to 7.

5. The same insight is carefully and metaphysically demonstrated by Karl Rahner in 'The Theology of the Symbol,' *Theological Investigations* VI, 225-52.

6. The importance of analogy in comprehending reality is highlighted by Heidegger's recent tendency 'to identify philosophical with poetic thought.' See Quentin Lauer, *Phenomenology: Its Genesis and Prospect* (New York, 1958) p. 173.

7. See Geoffrey Webb, *An Introduction to the Cistercian* De **Anima**; Aquinas Paper #36 (London: Aquin Press, 1961): 'Ultimately they (i.e., the Cistercians) were moralists, their principle aim being the achievement of union with God by means of the ascetic life. Now the imagination theory helps us to locate a central point between creation and God where flesh can be transformed under the influence of spirit in some way,' p. 18.

8. *De Iesu puero* I, 1; *Opera* I: 28-31; I, 3: 55-56.

9. *Ibid.*, III, 22: 115-16, III, 28: 291-300.

10. *De institutione inclusarum* par. 29; *Opera* I: 931-37.

11. *Ibid.*, par. 26.

12. See *Speculum caritatis* III, 14; *Opera* I: 673-77.

13. Paul Ricoeur, 'The Image of God and the Epic of Man,' *Cross Currents*, 11 (Winter, 1961) 49.

CONRAD OF BAVARIA--THE PILGRIM PRINCE

Conrad Greenia, OCSO

Who was Conrad of Bavaria? He was a Guelph **prince**, a member of
the dynasty which gave Europe two Holy Roman Emperors,[1] four kings
of Burgundy,[2] six sovereigns of Great Britain,[3] one Russian Czar,[4]
and innumerable dukes, counts, and viscounts. He was also a cistercian monk in the dawn of the Order, when it was bursting with vital
force and bright promise. Furthermore, he was one of those rare
cistercian hermits who became a monk first and a hermit second;
usually it was the other way around.

Born around 1105, probably at the Guelf stronghold of Ravensburg in upper Swabia, he was a nephew of Duke Welf V of Bavaria,
the son of his brother Henry IX, who became Duke in his turn in
1120. Conrad would have been about fifteen years old at his father's
accession, and we **know** that he was sent to Cologne to pursue higher
ecclesiastical studies at sometime during this period of his life.
He did well at Cologne, but early in 1123 he turned his back on his
excellent prospects for a rich benefice and eloped from his guardian,
the archbishop, to become a monk. He entered the Cistercian Order
at Morimond, on the western **Border** of the Holy Roman Empire **in** what
is now part of France. Sometime in the summer of the following year
(1124) he left Morimond with Abbot Arnold and several other young
monks who proposed to establish the first cistercian monastery in
the Holy Land. Arnold died unexpectedly and the others returned to
Morimond without leaving the Rhineland. Conrad proceeded to Palestine
without them. He lived there as a hermit for an unspecified time
with one older companion, but he returned to Europe when his **health**
gave out and died near Bari in Apulia, where he is still venerated
as a local patron.[5]

What I **propose** to discuss here are several details of Conrad's
career which seem well established as a result of already published
material,[6] but which have not received the attention they deserve.
For instance, it is now universally accepted that Conrad of Bavaria
is the person mentioned in St Bernard's letter number six, and that
he certainly entered the Cistercian Order at Morimond; yet most accounts of his life erroneously state that he entered religious life
at Clairvaux. We may also take it as probable that he never received
permission from St Bernard to become a hermit, and that he probably
died in his twenties rather than in his fifties, again in spite of
contrary assertions in most accounts of his life.

In 1836, J. M.. Giovene gave us what is still the best life of
Conrad available,[7] clearly detailing his sources and warning readers
when he occasionally indulged in that perennial hagiographer's hang-
up, guessing. He has the merit of being the first to recognize that

Conrad of Bavaria and the Conrad of St Bernard's letter six had to
be the same person,[8] but he lacked the courage to say that the people who identified Conrad as a monk of Clairvaux were mistaken. Instead, he comes up with the ingenious but incredible suggestion that
Conrad may have transferred stability from Morimond to Clairvaux before setting out for the Holy Land.[9] Most subsequent biographers
have accepted this as a 'fact.' Clever as this seems, Giovene was
contradicting the chronicler, who has Conrad *entering* religious life
at Clairvaux.[10] The new critical edition of Bernard's letters accepts the identification of Conrad of Bavaria with Conrad of Morimond.[11]

The permission to become a hermit supposedly granted Conrad by
St Bernard is nothing but a deduction based on the supposition that
he had been a Clairvaux **monk**, and that no good monk would undertake
such a project without his abbot's approval. Carefully sifting
through the detailed bibliography which I have compiled on Conrad,
I find the earliest hint of this idea occurring in a 1599 manuscript
by the **Cistercian hagiographer**, Philip Seguin.[12] This was more than
450 years after the supposed permission had been granted, and Seguin
does not **name** the abbot of Clairvaux concerned. Still sixty-three
years later, in 1662, the author of an anonymous Latin 'History of
Bavaria'[13] identifies Bernard as the abbot who gave the permission
in question. I think it is now morally certain that St Bernard
never granted any such permission.

If Bernard did not grant it, who did? He himself answers this
question for us in his letter to the monk Adam (letter 7). Like Conrad, Adam had been a member of the group of Palestinian pioneers se-
lected in 1124 by abbot Arnold of Morimond. Bernard comments at some
length on the command given to these monks by their abbot. He holds
that it is no longer binding now that the superior in question is
dead. But Conrad may already have set out for the south before this.
Even if he had not, he may well have felt justified in proceeding on
the strength of the authorization granted to abbot Arnold by Pope
Callixtus II. Bernard alludes to this papal permission repeatedly
in his letter, and he ends by mocking it in his own inimitable fashion;
'When God said, "**See** that you do not despise one of **these** little ones
who believe in **me**," he did not add, "unless you have permission from
the Pope!'[14]

Although I think it probable that Conrad died in his twenties
rather than in his fifties, I must admit that I am less sure of this
now than I was nine years ago.[15] One source alleges that it was determined in 1832 that Conrad's relics were 'the bones of a man in
his fifties.'[16] In spite of persistent efforts, I am unable at this
writing either to confirm or to refute this unsettling allegation.
If I am hesitant about accepting the idea of Conrad's survival after
the year 1130, this is mainly because of the lack of any reliable
historical evidence as to his whereabouts and activities in the

period 1130-1150. I am, however, equally hesitant about placing
his death as early as 1126, as many authors have done.[17] His early
death is just barely possible, but it reduces his stay in Palestine
to less than a year, and his convalescence, relapse, and death in
Apulia must be compressed into an even shorter period. The evidence
suggests to me that Conrad died between 1127 and 1130, and that any
further precision is unjustified.

When I visited the Bari area in 1974, I was pleasantly surprised to discover that the chapel at Modugno in the Bari suburbs (where
tradition tells us that Conrad died and was originally buried) had
been recently acquired by the Rogationist Fathers, who operate a
'Boy's Town' institution in Bari, itself. Father Nicolo Bollino,
the energetic young superior, was unfortunately absent at the time
of this visit, but I was able to see for myself some very interesting
archeological work in progress at the shrine. Early in 1975, I read
the pamphlet which Fr Bollino had just published detailing his finds,
and later that year I was able to confer with him in Rome and to visit
the Modugno chapel in his company.

Bollino lists ten findings in his sixteen-page booklet,[18] but I
think we can sum up the essence of it in just two points: traces of
byzantine frescoes on the walls, and two tombs under the floor in
front of the altar. The **frescoes** and other archeological traces indicate that the place was a small **basilian** monastery, such as were
quite numerous in southern Italy throughout most of the Middle Ages.
Conrad seems to have lived for a time as a recluse in a grotto ad-
jacent to the chapel--there are archeological traces of this type of
occupancy--but there was probably a small community of perhaps four
or five basilian monks under the same roof. This would seem to settle speculation on the part of local historians as to whether Conrad
lived there in complete solitude, or whether the place housed a benedictine or cistercian community.[19]

Of the two tombs in front of the altar, one was empty, with indications that it had been broken open by force and the contents hur-
riedly removed, doubtless at the time when the new cathedral in nearby Molfetta was nearing completion and its builders were looking for
suitable relics to enshrine there. We know the enshrinement occurred
on 9 February, the day on which the feast of the 'Translation of St
Conrad, confessor and hermit,' is still **celebrated** at Molfetta, but
we do not know the year.[20] This may be because **many** ecclesiastical
documents kept at Molfetta were destroyed in 1529, when the city was
sacked by mercenary troops. There is also a **venerable** local tradition that Conrad died on 17 March, and I see no reason why we should
reject this, even if documentary proof is lacking.[21]

The second tomb found by Bollino under the floor of the Modugno
chapel contained the intact and undisturbed skeleton of a full-grown
man, but no scientific examination has as yet been made to determine
his age at the time of death. Both tombs probably date from the

twelfth century, so it would be interesting if we could find out
more about them. One was doubtlessly Conrad's, but we have no clue
at present as to who might have been buried in the other.

When I visited Conrad's birthplace in Germany in 1975, my big-
gest surprise was the discovery that it is not really in Bavaria,
and that consequently he was not a Bavarian, although he was a close
relative of most of the Dukes of Bavaria who ruled between 1070 and
1180. He has been known as Conrad of Bavaria for some three hundred
years, however, and it looks like the name is going to stick.[22]

Conrad's biographers who mention his birthplace usually give
it as Ratisbon (Regensburg) in Bavaria, where the twelfth-century
dukes had their official residence. This is another instance of
a deduction based on a false fact gradually becoming part of the
legend. A seventeenth century author gives Conrad's birthplace as
Munich:[23] his father was Duke of Bavaria, wasn't he; that's where
the Dukes lived, didn't they? Later, another author discovered that
Munich did not yet exist in the first half of the twelfth century, so
he substituted Ratisbon for Munich.[24] In both cases, nobody stopped
to consider that at the time of Conrad's birth, his father was not
yet duke, and would not become such for some fifteen years. Consequently, we may be morally certain that Conrad was born at the family
castle of Ravensburg, in upper Swabia (modern Württemberg).

Another instance of hagiographical incompetence is the treatment of this question by Adolf Dietrich, S. O. Cist., in his 1914
German life. He knew that the family residence was located at Ravens-
berg and that Conrad's father did not become Duke until some years
after Conrad's birth. Not daring to contradict the earlier authorities who said that Conrad was born at Ratisbon, however, he gravely
informs us that Conrad was born there while his mother happened to
be in town on a visit to her brother-in-law, the Duke![25] Ingenious,
perhaps, but must we accept this sort of juggling as serious biography?

I'm not sure whether or not I will have the privilege of writing
it, but I do hope that we will have a good critical biography of Conrad of Bavaria before many more years have passed. God grant it,
through the intercession of St Conrad!

Mepkin Abbey, South Carolina

NOTES

1. Otto IV (d. 1218) and Frederick of Brunswick (d. 1400). Frederick's claim is disputed and his name omitted from most lists of Emperors.

2. Rudolf I (d. 912), Rudolf II (d. 937), Conrad the Peaceful (d. 993) and **Rudolf** III (d. 1032). St Bernard's mother, Alice de Montbard, is said to have been descended from these kings. (See Commission d'histoire de l'Order de Citeaux (Aiguebelle), *Bernard de Clairvaux*, (Paris, 1953) p. 134, notes 85, 86, 87.

3. The 'House of Hannover,' George I (d. 1727), George II (d. 1760), George III (d. 1820), George IV (d. 1830), William IV (d. 1837) and Victoria (d. 1901). There is also a Guelf link with the last of the Saxon kings of England, since Tostig of Northumbria (d. 1066) had made an unsuccessful bid for the throne of his brother, King Harold (d. 1066). Conrad's grandmother, Judith of Flanders (d. 1094) was Tostig's widow when she married Welf IV of Bavaria in 1071, and the old Guelf Chronicles style her as 'former queen of England' and 'widow of King Tostig' (See Burchard of Biberach, *Chronicon Urspergensis* (Basel, 1569) p. 175; also J. Hennings, *Genealogiae* (1587) p. 114.

4. Ivan VI (d. 1764). Czar from October 1740 to December 1741, as an infant, he spent the rest of his life in captivity, dying at the age of twenty-four.

5. Our only primary sources for Conrad's life are the letters of St Bernard (letters 4, 5, 6 & 359) and the *Historia Welforum*, a family chronicle of the Guelfs written about 1170 *MGH SS* in Folio, *Band* 21, p. 463).

6. See L. Grill, S.O.Cist. 'Der hl. Bernhard von Clairvaux und Morimond,' in *Festschrift zum 800-Jahrgedachtnis des Todes Bernahards von C.* (Vienna-Munich, 1953); (French translation in *Bernard de Clairvaux* [Paris, 1953] p. 127-136); C. Greenia, 'Blessed Conrad the Hermit,' in *Cistercian Studies* 4 (1969) 159-162.

7. G. M. Giovene, *B. Conradi Bavari Vita*, (Naples, 1836).

8. Ibid., p. 17, 69, and xi, ff.

9. Ibid., p. 18, ff.

10. Cf. *MGH*, *SS*, 21:463; also Giovene, p. 58-59, etc.

11. *SBOp* 7:30, n. 13; 8:305, n. 10.

12. This manuscript work has never been published in full, but the material on Conrad is given by Giovene (p. 66) and by C. Henriquez in *Menologium Cistercium* (Antwerp, 1630) 86-87.

13. Text in Giovene, 63.

14. St Bernard, Ep 7.9; *SBOp* 7:37.

15. In my article cited in note 6 above.

16. See G. Capursi, *Culto Tributato a S. Corrado Bavaro*, (Molfetta, 1970) p. 17. (Giovene, p. xxxi, says simply, *in virili aetate mortuum*).

17. Cf. Grill, (note 6 above).

18. N. Bollino and F. Campanale, *Antico Santuario Madonna Della Grotta e Speco Di S. Corrado* (Bari, 1975) pp. 16.

19. See F. Samarelli, *S. Corrado, Patrono di Molfetta* (Molfetta, 1935) 22; also G. Capursi, pp. 19-20.

20. The fourteenth-fifteenth century 'Missal of S. Conrad' in the episcopal archives of Molfetta contains a calendar on the fly-leaf with the entry, *VII id. Feb. Traslacio S.ti Conradi cf.* See Giovene, *Kalendaria Vetera* (Naples, 1828) p. xxi.

21. The earliest document I can clearly trace is from 1630. C. Henriquez seems, however, to be following an already long established tradition.

22. Some recent authors refer to him as 'Conrad the Guelf,' but this could lead to confusing him with his great-uncle, Saint Conrad of Constance, who was also a Guelf (d. 26 November 975).

23. A. Damiani, *S. Corrado il Grande* (Naples, 1670) p. 19.

24. F. P. Catacchio, *Notizie sulla vita...di S. Corrado* (Molfetta, 1902 & 1962) p. 15. See also F. Samarelli, p. 15 for more of the same. Samarelli claims to have gotten his information about Ratisbon from G. Buccelin, OSB, who lists Conrad in his *Menologium Benedictinum* (Antwerp, 1655) p. 203. I have consulted this text, however, and find no allusion to Conrad's birthplace.

25. A. Dietrich, O. Cist., 'Der selige Konrad von Bayern,' in *Cistercienser-Chronick* for the year 1914, p. 37.

BALDWIN OF FORD AND TWELFTH-CENTURY THEOLOGY

David N. Bell

In a short but important paper published in 1911/12, P. Guébin observed that the second successor of Thomas Becket had been studied more in his life than in his writings,[1] and in the six--well-nigh seven--decades which have passed since this observation was made, little has been done to remedy the situation. Dom Jean Leclercq pub-published an account of Baldwin's eucharistic doctrine in the introduction to the critical edition of the *De sacramento altaris* (published in 1963),[2] but apart from that, and apart from isolated comments and an occasional brief paper,[3] the theological importance of this learned and austere archbishop has been strangely neglected. It is the hope of the present writer to make some small contribution to this neglected area in two ways: firstly by producing an annotated translation of Baldwin's. sixteen *Tractates*[4] (to be published by Cistercian Publications), and secondly by publishing a number of articles on various aspects of Baldwin's theology and its relationship both to that of his contemporaries and to the patristic tradition of which he was unquestionably a significant representative. This present paper, therefore, may be regarded as a fairly general introduction to a much wider field, and in it we shall be concerned not with detailed examinations of **individual** points of Baldwin's thought, but with assessing his importance in the course and development of twelfth-century theology as a whole.

It may be useful to preface our remarks with a brief survey of Baldwin's distinguished ecclesiastical career,[5] and to say a word or two about the *corpus* of his works. He was born in the diocese of Exeter and descended, as Collier puts it, 'from a private unfurnished family.'[6] He received a very sound education at the cathedral school of Exeter and may himself, at a later date, have become the Master of the school.[7] He certainly travelled abroad (we meet him in Italy sometime after 1150[8]), but was equally certainly back in England in the early 1160s, for Bartholomew of Exeter, soon after his consecration in 1161, appointed him archdeacon of Totnes. He served in this capacity for some eight or nine years, but in 1169/70[9] (at the height of the Becket controversy) he retired to the cistercian abbey of Ford where, by 1175, he was abbot. In 1180 he was elevated to the bishopric of Worcester, and then, four years later, succeeded Richard of Dover as archbishop of Canterbury. His years at Canterbury were disturbed by the long and bitter dispute over the building of a collegiate church at Hackington, a dispute which involved princes both secular and **ecclesiastical**, kings, and a succession of popes.[10] He occupied **the** see for over five years before leaving England in' March 1190 to accompany Richard I on the Third Crusade. It was an unfortunate move

on his part, for having arrived in the Holy Land he fell sick (partly,
one gathers, as a result of his deep concern over the dissolute conduct of the army[11]) and died at Acre (not at Tyre, *pace* Canivez, Leclercq, and Thomas[12]) on (or about) 19 November 1190.[13]

A considerable proportion of his theological works were published in 1662 by Bertrand Tissier in his *Bibliotheca Patrum Cisterciensium*, and these are reproduced in Volume 204 of the Migne *Patrology*.[14]
There is no doubt that this collection is not complete, but it is
more complete than is often suspected. The catalogue of Baldwin's
works given by Tissier,[15] for example, and reproduced (with minor
amendments) by Canivez,[16] can be misleading, for some of the works it
lists as distinct and separate entities are actually the same thing.
The sixteen *Tractates (Tractatus diversi)*, for instance, are certainly an abridgement and rearrangement of the thirty-three sermons *(Sermones triginta tres)*; the *De unitate caritatis* is almost certainly
Tractatus XV; and there are other examples.[17] And although it is true
that there still remain works to be discovered *(De orthodoxis dogmati-
bus*, for example, or the four books *Super historiis regum*, and a number
of other treatises), they are not to be found either in the manuscripts
listed by Canivez,[18] or in other manuscripts of Baldwin's works which
must be added to this list.[19] In fact, in the twenty-two manuscripts
which the present writer has examined, the only materials *not* published in the Migne/Tissier collection are two sermons[20] and a few sentences.[21] The other works--if they have not perished--still await discovery.[22] The Migne/Tissier collection, therefore, although it is not
complete, is almost as complete as it can be, given the present state
of our knowledge.

That Baldwin of Canterbury was vastly learned has never been in
doubt. The primary **sources** testify to it (we know, for example, that
whilst at Ford--where most of his theological works were composed--
his reputation for learning and religion had spread throughout the
whole cistercian order[23]) and the secondary sources echo it: 'an emi-
nent canonist,'[24] 'one of the most distinguished scholars of his time,'[25]
'ecrivain érudit,'[26] and so on. Yet this admiration is sometimes tem-
pered with criticism of what appears to be Baldwin's lack of originality. His theological learning, says Dom David Knowles, 'was thoroughly abreast of the times,' but his works 'have little originality
or spiritual value.'[27] C. J. Holdsworth is of the opinion that he
was 'a man of a capable and **thorough, if unadventurous, turn** of mind,'[28]
and W. Hunt considers that 'while [his] works do not display any great
learning, they prove that Baldwin had a wide acquaintance with the text
of Scripture.'[29] Let us therefore consider the accuracy of these comments, and make a beginning by examining the basis for Knowles' statement that Baldwin's theological awareness was 'thoroughly abreast of
the times.'

A careful examination of his works reveals a small but important
number of passages in which Baldwin applies himself to problems and
disputes of contemporary concern. One of the most obvious of these
areas is the azymitic controversy which, although it was actually the

outward manifestation of deeper theological concerns, played a significant part in the Great Schism of 1054.[30] Baldwin was well aware
of what was going on, and that the main Greek objection to the use of unleavened bread was that it was 'judaizing' (Baldwin uses the verb *judai-
zare*[31]) and implied a refusal to move from the Old Covenant to the
New.[32] His counter-arguments (not without parallel in other Latin
writers concerned with the controversy) are firstly that Christ used
unleavened bread and that the Latin church follows his example, and
secondly, that even though the Truth has come, signs still have a
role to play, and unleavened bread is one of these signs.[33] The precise significance of this *signum* is not for the moment our concern.

A second clear example of Baldwin's concern with contemporary
theology is his defence of the term 'transubstantiation' *(transsubstantio)* in speaking of the eucharist.[34] **Again**, he is aware that
not everyone was happy with the **term**, and makes two basic points in
arguing for it: firstly, there *are* other words which may be used
('changed'--*mutatur*--or 'converted'--*convertitur*--for example[35]), but
although there are many descriptive terms, there is still only one
faith. Secondly, we should not be put off from using such a word
because it does not appear in Scripture and may seem to be a '**pro-
fane novelty**' (Baldwin is echoing 1 Timothy 6:20). The same was true
of the important terms *homoousios* and *persona* 'which were adopted by
the holy Fathers for the affirmation of the truth and the proclamation
of the faith.'[36] *Transsubstantio* may be unscriptural, but yet accurate and acceptable, and, as is well known, it achieved final definition at the Fourth Lateran Council of 1215, some forty years after
Baldwin had completed his *De sacramento altaris*.[37]

Other examples which show Baldwin's appreciation of the theological movements of his day may be passed over more briefly. In *Tractatus* XV, for instance, we find an allusion to the dispute over appropriation,[38] a question which had been much discussed at the Council
of Sens in 1140 (about thirty years before Baldwin produced this *Tractate*[39]), but which was still a problem to the twelfth-century theologians.[40] It is possible too that we find a criticism of Abelard in
Baldwin's statement in the *De commendatione fidei* (also written **at**
Ford[41]) that it is clearly shown by Scripture (always Baldwin's final
authority) that there is no separation between the 'opinion' of faith
(existimatio fidei) and the certainty of knowledge *(certitudo scien-
tiae)*.[42] The ambiguity of the term *existimatio* (and *aestimatio*) in
Abelard's definition of faith--*existimatio rerum non apparentium*[43]--
had produced major problems, and led such writers as Hugh of St Victor to offer (implicitly) a correction and improvement to such a dangerous statement. Faith, says Hugh, is *certitudo* **rather** than *existimatio: certitudo rerum absentium supra opinionem et infra scientiam
constituta*.[44] Baldwin goes further: faith is not only *certitudo*, but
also *scientia*! Scripture does not merely say that Abraham *knew (sciens)* that God could do what he had promised (Baldwin is referring to

Romans 4:20-21, but that he **knew** most fully *(plenissime sciens)*. How
then can we doubt that faith can be *scientia*? And Baldwin goes on to
provide a further series of scriptural examples in which the verb
scire plays the most important part.[45]

We know too that he kept a close eye on the theological specu-
lations of his friends and pupils, for when Roger of Ford began to
think dubious thoughts about the bodily assumption of the Virgin,
Baldwin was not slow to advise **caution** and care.[46] And if we may
draw attention to the most obvious case of all, the whole of the
De sacramento altaris, with its continual stress on the reality of
the substantial transformation of the bread into the body of Christ
(non transfiguratur, sed transsubstantiatur!)[47], is a rejection and
denial of the heretical views of Berengarius (or, more precisely, of
the heretical views attributed to him), although it is characteristic of Baldwin that in the whole of this lengthy treatise neither the
name of Berengarius nor the precise nature of his ideas is ever mentioned.[48] Why **not**? Simply because Baldwin was not really interested
in discussing dialectical and scholastic problems. His concern, as
Leclercq has pointed out, was not *how* the eucharistic mystery takes
place, but what the mystery is and how it affects us.[49] He had no
intention of indulging in flights of dialectical fancy, and when Jar-
oslav Pelikan tells us that in a later chapter of the *De sacramento
altaris* its author found 'that he could not altogether avoid dealing
with such **philo**sophical concepts as form and matter or species and
substance,'[50] he is being somewhat misleading. Baldwin 'deals with'
these concepts by refusing to deal with them! All sorts of things
have been said about them and all sorts of theories and definitions
propounded, **and** as far as Baldwin is concerned, it has all been a
waste of time. He has his faith, a faith 'founded unshakeably on
the words of God himself,'[51] and it is enough for him that the eucharistic elements do become the body and blood of Christ, and that they
bring about all that they do bring about.

For **Baldwin** of Ford, theology was a matter neither of dialectics
nor of high-flown speculation, and unless this is continually borne
in mind, it is all too easy to characterize him as 'unoriginal' and
'unadventurous.' If we compare him, say, with an Abelard (or certain
other of the great scholastics) there is no doubt that the terms may
be applied, but to compare Baldwin with Abelard can be dangerous and
misleading. Both men were certainly concerned with the rational investigation and understanding of God's revelation, but in Baldwin's
view, rational investigation can only be carried so far, and the use
of human reason is circumscribed by very definite boundaries. Abelard's problem was that he went too far and ended up (like Peter of
Poitiers in the eyes of Senatus of Worcester) in 'treating audaciously
of the Trinity and disputing irreverently about god.'[52] The wisdom
of the world, says Baldwin, 'being ignorant of the limits to which it
could go, has dared to attempt an examination of the things above it,

things to which it could never attain if left on its own. It has
busied itself with difficult and profound investigations into the
nature of God, the origin of the world, the condition of the soul,
and the quality of righteousness and blessedness, and [in so doing]
has been able neither to find the way of truth nor to attain to the
wisdom of God which is hidden in mystery.'53

What then is the use of human reason, the *scintilla rationis*54
which marks us out as the image of God and which enables us to participate in blessedness?55 Baldwin leaves us in no doubt on this
point: reason should be used in two main ways--firstly (and most importantly) to make reasoned decisions between good and evil, righteousness and wickedness, truth and falsehood, so that we can choose
the right course and do it; and secondly, to understand clearly and
in detail what it is that God has said.56 Reason, in other words,
must be used strictly within the bounds of the faith, within the
bounds of God's revelation, and it is not for us to enquire into
what God has not wished to reveal.57

We may ask, for example, *when* transubstantiation takes place,
but not *if* it takes place.58 We may discuss the problems of chronological inconsistencies in the gospel narratives. Such questioning
and such discussion is not 'impious doubt' and is dangerous neither
to the piety of faith nor the faith of the Gospel 'so long as we believe without any doubt *(indubitanter)* the words and deeds there
reported.'59 Reason, therefore, occupies a vitally important place
in Baldwin's thought, but it must always be bounded by the truth of
the faith. If it begins to investigate and question the truth of the
faith itself, then we are indeed in peril. The whole of Baldwin's
thought centers on God's revelation in Scripture: 'The defences *(mu-
nimenta)* of our faith reduce to the authority of holy Scripture: if
this is true, the witnesses of the faith are true, the testimonies
of the faith are true, and consequently the faith itself is true.'60
If, then, we look in Baldwin for 'originality' or 'adventurousness'
in hair-raising speculation on the nature of God, we shall be disap-
pointed; and if we think of theology in terms of scholastic, speculative inquiry into things which (in Baldwin's eyes) should be well
left alone, then to criticize him for being 'unoriginal' and 'unadventurous' would not be untrue, but it would certainly be unjust.
One cannot condemn a man for not doing what he never intended to do.

Baldwin's theology is *monastic* theology, not *scholastic* theol-
ogy.61 For him, as for Evagrius, a theologian is one who truly prays,
and one who truly prays is a theologian.62 Or, as Bede put it more
succinctly, theology is the contemplation of God.63 What is commonly
understood by 'theology' today, therefore, was not Baldwin's view,
and he was not particularly interested in it. When he wanted to write
'theologically' he could do so, and his style is clear and lucid,64
but this is far from his main concern, and it is for this reason that
his consideration of such problems as the azymitic controversy, or

appropriation, or the other matters we mentioned above, occupy such
a small place in his work. The heart of Baldwin's theology is firstly, God's revelation in the Scripture and in Christ, a revelation which
he never tires of praising, a revelation which is wonderful and admir-
able and stupendous;[65] and secondly, our action in accordance with
this revelation.

The monastic theological tradition, as Leclercq has clearly pointed out, was essentially the patristic tradition,[66] and for Baldwin, as
for his monastic contemporaries, the content of the faith was defined
by Scripture and the exegesis of the 'orthodox Fathers.'[67] It would
be fitting, therefore, to bring this brief enquiry to a close by considering for a moment the identity of those 'orthodox Fathers' who
influenced Baldwin, and thereby gain a glimpse of the breadth of his
reading and the extent of his patristic learning.[68] First and fore-
most, of course, comes the impact of Augustine. Baldwin cites him
eleven times by name,[69] but his influence is all-pervasive, and it
would not be too much of an exaggeration to say that at this period
the patristic tradition and the augustinian tradition were one and the
same thing. Other than Augustine, and amongst the Latin writers, our
author names Ambrose,[70] Gregory the Great,[71] Hilary,[72] and Jerome[73]
--all standard and sound authorities--and amongst the Greeks we find
him citing Origen[74] and, in a remarkable passage, pseudo-Dionysius.[75]
This last citation is of considerable interest, for it appears to derive from Eriugena's translation of the *Celestial Hierarchy*,[76] and
leads us to suspect that some eriugenian works might have been available in an English cistercian monastery,[77] and that the conservative
and cautious Baldwin had been reading some very unconservative writings.
It is typical of our author, however, that his interpretation of this
dionysian passage is sound, scriptural, and augustinian and, in Baldwin's case, the impact of 'light from the East' is essentially re-
stricted to the exegetical influence of Origen.

Apart from these several authorities which Baldwin cites by name
(and apart from the canonical authorities with which he was unquestionably intimately familiar) the influence of other writers--both
earlier and contemporary--may also clearly be seen. In some cases
there is no doubt at all that their writings affected him (such is
the case with Bernard of Clairvaux, Aelred of Rievaulx, and the *Rule*
of St Benedict); in other cases, their influence is not quite so certain, and ranges from the possible to the very probable (and here I
would include Cassiodorus, Bede, Isidore of Seville, Leo the Great,
Hugh and Richard of St Victor--the Victorines, it seems, were well
represented in the library of Ford[78]--Anselm of Canterbury, and
Peter of Blois).[79] Such names, of course, do not necessarily
reflect the library holdings of the abbey, for many of them could have
been transmitted by the liturgy, a liturgy which, at the time, was a
rich and varied source of patristic information.[80] We should also
note that Baldwin's knowledge of these renowned authorities was neither

shallow nor superficial. As Leclercq has observed, 'Baldwin has assimilated them to his memory and his style; he has made them his own
and has transmitted them to us in an original and new combination.'[81]
Baldwin never makes a show of his erudition (this, perhaps, explains
Hunt's comment cited above that his works 'do not display any great
learning'), but it is impossible to read his writings carefully without appreciating that he is speaking from a formidably solid scriptural and patristic foundation.

     Among the secular writers, Baldwin quotes from three pagan poets
--Virgil,[82] Ovid,[83] and Lucan[84] (all of them anonymously)--and once,
in passing, he mentions the name of Plato.[85] His attitude to the
last is, as we might expect, severe and condemnatory. Plato is simply
an example of those concerned with worldly wisdom, a wisdom which is
far from the *via disciplinae* which God gave to Jacob. True wisdom,
the wisdom of God, comes not from the Academics or the Stoics, and
cannot be investigated by human subtlety. The wisdom of God comes from
heaven and its teaching is simple and straightforward: love the things
of heaven and despise the things of earth![86] It is this which leads
to salvation; and that alone is Baldwin's concern.

     In order to assess his place in the theological movements of the
twelfth century, therefore, it is first necessary to stipulate what
sort of theology one is talking about. As a 'scholastic' theologian,
Baldwin has little to say. As we have indicated, he was well aware
of what was going on, and the style of many passages in his work
leaves us in no doubt that he was living and thinking and writing in
a post-lombardic world. But this was not his real interest, and as
far as he was concerned, he had better things to do with his rationality. As a 'monastic' theologian, however, as a late witness to a
patristic tradition which by his time was becoming all to uncommon,
he is of very considerable importance. Beryl Smalley has noted that
'his many writings as monk and abbot of Ford show a combination of
theological doctrine and monastic spirituality which was becoming
rare in the second half of the twelfth century,'[87] and we may see in
Baldwin one of the last true representatives of a rich monastic theological tradition which was soon to be swallowed up in the inexorable
advance of philosophical scholasticism. He merits therefore an honor-
able and recognized place amongst the monastic theologians of his time,
and rightly deserves, as Leclercq has noted,[88] to occupy a due and proper position amongst the great cistercian writers of the twelfth century.

Memorial University of Newfoundland

NOTES

1. P. Guébin, 'Deux sermons inédits de Baldwin, archevêque de Canterbury 1184-1190,' in *Journal of Theological Studies* O. S. 13 (1911-12) 571.

2. *Baudouin de Ford, Le sacrement de l'autel,* ed. J. Morson; trans. E. de Solms, SCh 93-94 (Paris, 1963). Two volumes with continuous pagination.

3. A. Landgraf, 'The Commentary on St Paul of the Codex Paris Arsenal Lat. 534 and Baldwin of Canterbury,' in *Catholic Biblical Quarterly* 10 (1948) 55-62; C. Hallet, 'La communion des personnes d'après une oeuvre de Baudouin de Ford,' in *RAM* 42 (1966) 405-422; C. Hallet, 'Notes sur le vocabulaire du *De Vita Coenobitica* de Baudouin de Ford,' in *Analecta Cisterciensia* 22 (1966) 272-278; M. Pellegrino, 'Reminiscenze bibliche, liturgiche e agostiniane nel *De Sacramento Altaris* di Baldovino di Ford,' in *Revue des études augustiniennes* 10 (1964) 39-44; J. Morson, 'Baldwin of Ford: A Contemplative,' in *Collectanea O. C. R.* 27 (1965) 160-164; J. C. **Didier**, 'Baudouin de Ford et la dévotion au Sacré Coeur de Jésus,' in *Cîteaux* 26 (1975) 222-225.

4. The text in PL 204:403-572 is defective. A much better edition has been prepared by Robert Thomas, *Baudouin de Ford, Traités;* PC 35-40 (Chimay, 1973-75) six volumes. Fr Thomas provides both the Latin text and a sound French translation, but he does not offer any account of Baldwin's theological significance.

5. There is no full-length biography of Baldwin. A brief but sound **bibliography** may be found conveniently in Charles Duggan's article 'Baldwin of Canterbury' in volume two of the *New Catholic Encyclopedia*. To this must be added C. J. Holdsworth's doctoral dissertation, *Learning and Literature of English Cistercians, 1167-1214, with special reference to John of Ford* (typescript, Cambridge University, 1960), and Adrian Morey, *Bartholomew of Exeter, Bishop and Canonist* (Cambridge, 1937) 105-109, 120-121. For earlier works see J. M. Canivez, 'Baudouin...de Cantorbéry,' in *DHGE* 6: 1415-16, and the same author's 'Baudouin de Ford,' in the *Dictionnaire de spiritualité* 1: 1285-86.

6. J. **Collier**, *An Ecclesiastical History of Great Britain,* new edition, (London, 1852) 2: 370.

7. Giraldus Cambrensis, *Speculum Ecclesiae* II, xxv (ed. J. S. Brewer, RS 21/4 [1873] 81) speaks of him as *scholarum magister egregius,* but Giraldus is not always reliable.

8. See R. L. Poole, 'The Early Lives of Robert Pullen and Nicholas Breakspear,' in A. G. Little & F. M. Powicke (eds.), *Essays in Medieval History presented to T. F. Tout* (1925; rp. New York, 1967) 69. Poole's authority is John of Salisbury, *Letter* 292.

9. The date has been established by Morey, 121.

10. For a detailed account, see W. Stubbs' introduction to his

*Chronicles and Memorials of the Reign of Richard I: Vol. II,
Epistolae Cantuarienses* (RS 38, 1865)

11. See the *Itinerarium Regis Ricardi* (ed. W. Stubbs, in *Chronicles
     and Memorials...*, *Vol. I*, RS 38, [1865]), *cap.* lxv (Stubbs 123-4).
     See also *Letter* 346 in Stubbs' *Epistolae Cantuarienses* (Stubbs
     328-9).

12. **Canivez'** articles as cited in Note 5 above; J. Leclercq in the
     SCh edition of *De sacramento altaris*, 8; R. Thomas, PC 35, 1: 9.
     There is not the least doubt that Baldwin died at Acre.

13. The month and the year are not in doubt, but there is some ques-
     tion as to the day. The date given by the *Annales de Theokes-
     beria* (ed. H. R. Luard, RS 36/1 [1864] 54)--23 November--can be
     discounted, but the 20th rather than the 19th is still a **real
     possibility.** Gervase of Canterbury, normally a reliable source,
     gives 19 November *(Gervasii Cantuariensis Opera Historica,* ed.
     W. Stubbs, RS 73 [1879-80] 1: 488) and this is the most commonly
     cited date.

14. PL 204: 401-774. For Baldwin's letters, see PL 202: 1533, and
     Stubbs, *Epistolae Cantuarienses*. There are critical editions of
     the *Tractates* (see Note 4 above) and the *De sacramento altaris*
     (see Note 2 above).

15. Reproduced in PL 204: 401-404.

16. In his two articles cited in Note 5 above.

17. A detailed consideration of this important question must be left
     for a future, and more comprehensive, study.

18. **Canivez** gives the same list of nine manuscripts in both his arti-
     cles.

19. The Sch edition of the *De sacramento altaris*, 61-63, lists ten fur-
     ther manuscripts (or eleven, if one counts the fragmentary MS Ox-
     ford, Bodleian Lib. 172), and to this list must be further added
     Oxford, **Bodleian** Lib. 681, and Cambridge, Pembroke Coll. 159.

20. See Guébin, 571-574. The same two sermons also appear in Cambridge,
     Pembroke Coll. 159.

21. See John Morson's description of the peculiar manuscript Oxford,
     Laud Misc. 91 in the SCh edition of *De sacramento altaris*, 62.

22. Apart from the works listed by Tissier, both W. Hunt (in the *Dic-
     tionary of National Biography,* s.v. Baldwin, 954) and Stubbs *(Epis-
     tolae Cantuarienses,* xxxiv) attribute to Baldwin a Penitential.
     This is to be found in London, Lambeth Palace MS 235, but is actu-
     ally the Penitential of Bartholomew of Exeter edited by Morey in
     his *Bartholomew of Exeter* (see Morey, 164-166). The Lambeth manu-
     script itself attributes the work to both writers: *Hic incipit pen-
     itentiale magistrorum Baldweyni Cantuar. Archiepiscopi et Barth-
     olomei Exoniensis* (Morey, 165), and there is every likelihood that
     Bartholomew would have consulted Baldwin, a renowned **canonist as**
     well as a friend, in the compilation of such a work.

23. In a letter to Alexander III in 1178, one of his cardinals writes

that 'Master Baldwin, the abbot of Ford--although we have not seen him--is commended above all others by the whole cistercian order on account of his manifold learning, integrity, and religion' (see Morey, 106, n. 4). See also P. Glorieux, 'Candidats pour la pourpre en 1178,' in *Mélanges de science religieuse* 11 (1954) 17-19.

24. Duggan's article in the *New Catholic Encyclopedia* (see Note 5 above).

25. Stubbs, *Epistolae Cantuarienses*, xxxiii.

26. Canivez' article in *DHGE* 6: 1415.

27. D. Knowles, *The Monastic Order in England* (Cambridge, 1950) 317, n. 5.

28. C. J. Holdsworth, 'John of Ford and English Cistercian Writing 1167-1214,' in *Transactions of the Royal Historical Society*, Series V, 11 (1961) 125.

29. Hunt's account in the *Dictionary of National Biography* (see Note 22 above) 954.

30. See especially M. H. Smith, *And Taking Bread...Cerularius and the Azyme Controversy* (Paris, 1978), and J. H. Erickson, 'Leavened and Unleavened: Some Theological Implications of the Schism of 1054,' in *St Vladimir's Theological Quarterly* 14/3 (1970) 3-24. For a useful brief summary of the dispute, see J. Pelikan, *The Christian Tradition: II, The Spirit of Eastern Christendom (600-1700)* (Chicago, 1974) 176-179.

31. *De sacramento altaris* PL 204:652A (SCh 110). It is not a neologism--the verb occurs in Galatians 2:14.

32. See Pelikan, II: 177-178.

33. See generally *De sacramento altaris* 651C-652D (SCh 110-114).

34. For a useful account of the development of this term (illustrated with a large selection of texts), see *DTC* 5: 1287-1293.

35. See especially *De sacramento altaris* 662A-D (SCh 146-150). Baldwin's own favourite term is *mutatio*.

36. *Ibid.*, 662C-D (SCh 148).

37. We know that Baldwin wrote the *De sacramento altaris* at Ford because he says so. He refers to himself in the dedicatory letter as 'Fordensis monasterii servus' (641A; SCh 70), which means that the treatise was written sometime between 1170 and 1180. For the definition of the Fourth Lateran Council, see *DTC* 5: 1302.

38. See *Tractatus* XV; PL 204: 546D-547A (PC 40, 19).

39. There can be no doubt that this *Tractate*--a most important contribution to the theology of the monastic life--was produced while Baldwin was at Ford.

40. For a most useful collection of references, see J. Châtillon's edition of *Achard de Saint-Victor, Sermons inédits* (Paris, 1970) 136, n. 14.

41. This has been established by Holdsworth on the basis of certain statements which appear in the Oxford manuscript, Laud Misc. 91.

       See his article (Note 28) 122-123.
42.   *De commendatione fidei*; PL 204: 584C (and see generally *ibid.*,
      583B-584C 'De fidei certitudine').
43.   Abelard, *Theologia 'scholarium'* I, 1; PL 178:981C.
44.   Hugh, *De sacramentis* I, x, 2; PL 176:331B. For some useful com-
      ments, see D. E. Luscombe, *The School of Peter Abelard* (Cambridge,
      1970) 185-187.
45.   See *De commendatione fidei* 584A-C. See also *Tractatus* I; 408B-C
      (PC 35, 50). I hope to publish a full account of Baldwin's thought
      on faith, knowledge, and reason in the near future.
46.   See C. H. Talbot, 'The Verses of Roger of Ford on Our Lady,' *Coll-
      ectanea O. C. R.* 6 (1939) 44-54, and Holdsworth, 125-126.
47.   *De sacramento altaris* 678A (SCh 204).
48.   The name of Berengarius does appear in the scholastic appendix to
      the *De sacramento altaris* which forms the final part of the work
      in the PL edition (769C-774C; Berengarius is mentioned at 771B).
      De Ghellinck, in his articles in *DTC*, (see *DCT* 5: 1247; 10: 1051),
      accepted this as genuine Baldwin, but there is no doubt that he
      was incorrect. See the discussions in the SCh edition of the
      text, 23 n. 1 (by Leclercq) and 59-60 (by Morson).
49.   See J. Leclercq (trans. C. Misrahi) *The Love of Learning and the
      Desire for God* (New York, 1962) 212. See also his comments in
      the SCh edition of *De sacramento altaris*, 12, 15, 23-24.
50.   J. Pelikan, *The Christian Tradition: III, The Growth of Medieval
      Theology (600-1300)* (Chicago, 1978) 257.
51.   *De sacramento altaris* 679B (SCh 208), and many other places. See
      generally *ibid.*, 678D-680A (SCh 206-210).
52.   For Senatus' comments, see R. W. Hunt, 'English Learning in the
      Late Twelfth Century,'in *Transactions of the Royal Historical
      Society* Series IV, 19 (1936) 29-30. See also Leclercq, *Love of
      Learning*, 192-193.
53.   *Tractatus* VI; 454A-B (PC 37, 36).
54.   An augustinian term--see *De Civitate Dei* XXII, 24, 2; PL 41:789--
      used by Baldwin in *Tractatus* VI; 464D (PC 37, 90).
55.   See *Tractatus* IX; 505C (PC 38, 170).
56.   There is a large amount of material on this question in Baldwin,
      and I hope to consider it more fully in a later paper. For the
      present, the following references will suffice: *Tractatus* VI;
      454A-C (PC 37:36-38) and *De sacramento altaris*; 666D-667B (SCh
      164-6). Abelard would not disagree with Baldwin's view; the
      differences between them must be seen in terms of approach and
      emphasis, not in terms of truth and heresy.
57.   *De commendatione fidei* 607A:'Omittamus inquirere quod Deus noluit
      revelare.'
58.   See *De sacramento altaris* 654A-656B (SCh 118-126). Such passages
      are clear reminders that Baldwin was writing in the period of
      developing scholasticism.

59. See *ibid.*, 669A-670A (Sch 172-174). This is what Baldwin calls else-
     where *pia inquisitio* (693D [SCh 264]).
60. *De commendatione fidei*; 621A. Scripture is true, says Baldwin,
     because it is God's word, and it may be shown to be God's word
     in a number of ways, the most important of which is by a consider-
     ation of biblical prophecies and their fulfilment. Hence Bald-
     win's long discussion on this matter (see *ibid.*, 621A-629A).
61. For a thorough account of the difference, see Leclercq, *Love of
     Learning*, Chapter IX. These two forms of theology are not, of
     course, separate, but they are distinct (see especially *ibid.*,
     189-203).
62. Evagrius, *De oratione* 60; PG 79: 1180B (there attributed incor-
     rectly to St Nilus). See also Leclercq, *Love of Learning*, 228.
63. Bede, *In Lucae evangelium expositio* III, x; PL 92:471D: 'Una
     ergo et sola est theologia, id est, contemplatio **Dei**.'
64. Compare, for example, his discussion of the Trinity (a **thoroughly**
     augustinian approach) in *Tractatus* XV; 546D-547A (PC 40, 19-21),
     and 549B-D (PC 40, 29-33). As Canivez has observed *(Dictionnaire
     de spiritualité* 1: 1285), Baldwin's writings (for the most part)
     are remarkable for their 'belle latinité.'
65. See, for example, *De sacramento altaris* (655C-D [SCh 122-124],
     702C [SCh 296]*), De commendatione fidei* (606B-C, 613C-D), and a
     host of other examples. See also Leclercq's introduction to *De
     sacramento altaris*, 47-51, and his *Love of Learning*, 227-228.
66. See generally Leclercq, *Love of Learning*, Chapter VI. 'More and
     more,' he says in Chapter IX, 'it appears to be a prolongation
     of patristic theology' (189)--an observation also supported by
     Landgraf(see *ibid.*, 316, n. 2).
67. See, for instance, *De commendatione fidei* (620C) and *De sacramento
     altaris* (661C [SCh 144], 662B [SCh 148], 662C [SCh 148], 738A
     [SCh 444]). There are a number of other examples.
68. This final part of our presentation will be no more than a brief
     summary of much more extensive materials. A comprehensive and
     detailed survey of Baldwin's sources would involve a number of
     articles, and I hope to discuss the matter further in future publi-
     cations.
69. *Tractatus* I; 412A (PC 35, 66), *Tractatus* IV; 435C (PC 36, 48),
     Tractatus VII; 469D (PC 37, 124), *De sacramento altaris*; 659D
     (SCh 138-140), 689C (SCh 246), 695C (SCh 272), 698C (SCh 282),
     698D (SCh 284), 703C (SCh 300), 732C (SCh 424), 747C (SCh 484).
70. *Ibid.*, 650C (SCh 106).
71. *De commendatione fidei*; 598D.
72. *De sacramento altaris*; 689C (SCh 248), 699A (SCh 284).
73. *Ibid.*, 652A (SCh 110), 749D (SCh 484); *De commendatione fidei*;
     600B.
74. *De sacramento altaris*; 744D (SCh 486). See also Morson's dis-
     cussion in SCh 64-67.

75. *De sacramento altaris;* 720B (SCh 374).
76. See PL 122: 1046C: 'Esse omnium est super esse divinitas.' The version of Hugh of St Victor *(Commentariorum in Hierarchiam Coelestem S. Dionysii Areopagitae* V; PL 175: 1003C, 1008B) reads 'Esse omnium est superesse divinitatis.'
77. The question of the availability of eriugenian works in cistercian monasteries is important, interesting, and difficult. The matter has been considered by M. D. **Chenu**, 'Érigène à Cîteaux: Expérience intérieure et spiritualité objective,' in *La philosophie et ses problèmes. Receuil d'études de doctrine et d'histoire offert à Mgr Jolivet* (Lyon/Paris, 1960) 99–107 (which is primarily concerned with **Garnier** of Rochefort) and I. P. Sheldon-Williams, 'Eriugena and Cîteaux,' in *Studia Monastica* 19 (1977) 75–92. There are also a number of comments in the present writer's 'William of St Thierry and John Scot Eriugena' which is due to be published in *Cîteaux* in 1981.
78. See Holdsworth, 127. John of Ford was certainly influenced by Richard of St Victor: see *ibid.* 124, n. 3.
79. See A. Landgraf, (Note 3) 61–62.
80. See my introduction to *William of St Thierry, The Nature and Dignity of Love* (CF 30) 20–21.
81. Leclercq's introduction to the SCh edition of *De sacramento altaris,* 44.
82. *Tractatus* VIII; 479D (PC 38, 24) quoting *Enneads* IV, 1–2; *Tractatus* IX; 500B (PC 38, 142) quoting *Georgica* IV, 1 (and the phrase *roscida mella*, 'honey, dropping like dew,' which appears immediately before this last quotation, would appear to be taken from *Eclogae* IV, 30).
83. *Tractatus* XIV; 539B (PC 39, 178) quoting *Metamorphoses* I, 523; *Tractatus* XVI; 566A (PC 40, 115) quoting *Remedia amoris* 443; *De commendatione fidei;* 590D quoting *Fasti* I, 298.
84. *Tractatus* XV; 559C (PC 40, 77) **quoting** *Pharsalia* 2, 383. Not all of these quotations are quite in accord with the standard texts, but we will not stop to examine the differences here.
85. See *De commendatione fidei;* 591A.
86. *Ibid.*; 591A-B. The same idea occurs elsewhere.
87. B. Smalley, *The Becket Conflict and the Schools* (Totowa, N.J., 1973) 218.
88. Leclercq's introduction to the SCh edition of *De sacramento altaris,* 7.

CLASSICAL REMINISCENCES IN GILBERT OF HOYLAND

Lawrence C. Braceland, SJ

In addition to his forty-eight *Sermones* which continue the Commentary on the Canticle by St Bernard of Clairvaux, Gilbert of Hoyland has left us one short *Sermo*, four Epistles, and seven Treatises.[1] Here are some reflections of a classicist recently acquainted with Gilbert's Latin.[2]

The Sermo

The short *Sermo* has two paragraphs:[3] the first is full of pleasantries, while the second, in varied triplets, rings all the changes on the word of God as a seed fallen by the wayside, among rocks or among thorns. Deprecatingly Gilbert commends his audience for their keeness and humility in expecting to hear the word of God from one as ill-equipped and as unprepared as he is: 'From you I received the order; from you I learned the topic, as if in any soil I could divine rich veins of living water and make seeds sprout upon all its rivulets, and as if within the hour words would blossom for me at will': (*A vobis accepi mandatum, a vobis materiam, quasi in omni possim solo viventis aquae venas reperire et seminare super omnes aquas, et* '[quasi] *sub hora verba mihi ad votum exuberent*). Even in this short sentence one notes Gilbert's versatility: the two sets of anaphora: *a vobis* and the misleading *et*; the alliterative *m, s, v*; the imaginative water-diviner; the quotation from Isaiah; and is there a lurking reference to Lucretius? Lucretius' line, *e terraque exorta repente arbusta salirent*, occurs in a passage where he attempts to disprove that anything can spring up from nothing; he comments on the need for soil, water, seed, a time and a place, exactly what Gilbert says he lacks.[4]

Gilbert continues: 'Oh then be it done unto me according to your faith, and may all my limbs dissolve into speech, and may I be able to say with the prophet: "All my bones will proclaim: who is like unto you, O Lord?"' (*Utinam tum mihi fiat juxta fidem vestram, et membra mea omnia in linguam laxentur, et cum propheta dicere possim: 'omnia ossa mea dicent, Domine, quis similis tui?'*). One again notices the assonance, Gilbert's classical *tui* for the *tibi* of the Vulgate, the transformation of the audience's credulity into a faith like that of the Virgin, and the concluding quotation from the Psalms.[5] But is Gilbert's imagination again at work in this sentence? Is he thinking of Echo in the *Metamorphoses* of Ovid? In Ovid, poor Echo is transformed until only her bones and voice remain, then only her voice: *et tenuant vigiles corpus miserabile curae / adducitque cutem macies et in aera sucus / corporis omnis abit; vox tantum atque ossa supersunt: / vox manet, ossa ferunt lapidis traxisse figuram.*[6] Gilbert is as imaginatively rich as his translator may be poor. How does one suggest the delightful metamorphoses, the reversal of roles? *Fiat mihi secundum fidem tuum* makes Gilbert the angel with the word and his audience like Mary receiving the word, thanks to their *fidem* which is transformed from credulity into faith in Gilbert in the role of Gabriel communicating the **word**.

First Epistle[7]

Though Migne's reprint of Mabillon's text notes only one quotation from Seneca, he seems to be quoted at least five times in this and four times in the second Epistle. The first quotation, a paradoxical *sententia* which might have been culled from some collection, Gilbert calls a proverb and turns into indirect discourse: 'all things should be weighed with a friend, but he should be weighed first of all' (*omnia cum amico deliberanda esse, de ipso tamen prius*).[8] Gilbert's next paragraph quotes Seneca four times. 'Even after a bad crop, one must sow again,' is quoted exactly and called *illud philosophicum: et post malam segetem serendum est*.[9] Gilbert continues: 'You seem to me to burn so avidly for the exchanges of friendship, that where a little while ago you suffered shipwreck, you may recoup your losses by putting out to sea again': *ut ubi paulo ante naufragium pertuleris, navigatione iterata [commercium] restaures*, whereas Seneca had written: *post naufragium, maria tentantur*, perhaps another *sententia* culled from a collection.[10] 'Of course with prudence,' adds Gilbert, 'perhaps the more successful results of a single hour may balance the losses of a longer time': *prudenter plane unius forsitan horae felicior proventus longi temporis recompensabit incommoda*, apparently an adaptation of Seneca: *saepe quicquid perierat adsidua infelicis soli sterilitate, unius anni restituit ubertas*.[11]

After so much from *Seneca Noster*, Gilbert hastens 'to insert a statement from our familiar philosophy [*ut de domestica aliquid philosophia ingeram*], in you I am conscious of the saying of Peter, "charity covers a multitude of sins."'[12] Later in the paragraph without acknowledgement, Gilbert adapts Seneca again: 'Gifts of a wise man cannot but be eloquent': *Nesciunt muta esse munera sapientis;* in an earlier Epistle, Seneca noted that 'each of the wise men will have different gifts...one being more prompt in eloquence': *Habebit unusquisque ex eis [sapientibus] proprias dotes: alius erit adfabilior, alius expeditior, alius promptior in eloquendo*.[13]

Verbally, though not in idea, the last quotation from Gilbert recalls a passage in Ovid less flattering to the sage, who no less than the fool will accept a bribe and keep mum: *quid sapiens faciet? (stultus quoque munere gaudet) Ipse quoque accepto munere mutus erit*.[14] But an earlier passage in this letter: 'As it is profitless to sow seeds in sand...' is even more reminiscent of Ovid: *Quid facis, Oenone? Quid harenae semina mandas?*[15]

Thoughout this letter, Seneca at Gilbert's elbow is a friend
suggesting some happy, brief, felicitous turn of thought and phrase.
His is the advice Gilbert follows in writing to Richard, probably a
Cistercian brother abbot: 'that a prospective friend should be
tested before he is accepted.' Gilbert's procrastination irked
Richard, who none the less took the initiative in reconciliation;
Gilbert with apologies stands his ground but concludes his letter;
'Would that I could welcome you forever rather than for a time,
as an abiding rather than as a transient guest. Farewell.'

Second Epistle

Gilbert's second Epistle *Ad quemdam Adamum*, is a warm encouragement to a young friend, a scholarly cleric, to remember his intention
of entering the monastery of Swineshead. The letter reveals Gilbert's
attitude to the liberal arts and to philosophy as 'a step and a foothold...to more interior mysteries of wisdom.' It shows his interest
in attracting a young scholar with many followers, who later would be
able to assist in the development of studies proper to monks. To
rise to wisdom in the highest sense, is 'of all arts, the art, the
law, the norm, the form and the principle, the universal, uniform,
invariable exemplar.' Without this joyful wisdom, the mind 'battens
on banality and still-life painting,' (*pictis epulis*), which may have
been suggested by Horace's *pictis tabellis*.[16]
Later Gilbert continues: 'My words are meant precisely to pre-
vent your excusing yourself on the score of devotion to empty literature, lest you follow a shadow only to be deprived of the light,
lest distraught by the subtleties of Aristotle you find fault with
our silence and our **simplicity**.' Gilbert melted down into one sentence the **nuggets he found** in four paragraphs of a letter of Seneca:
*Tota rerum natura umbra est aut inanis aut fallax; Haec omnia in il-
lum supervacuum studiorum liberalium gregem coice; Illi non prae-
ferunt lumen, per quod acies derigatur ad verum; Audi, quantum mali
faciat nimia subtilitas et quam infesta veritati sit.*[17] So in both
letters, the liberal arts are only propaideutic: to moral philosophy in Seneca, to divine wisdom in Gilbert. Then with a reminiscence of metamorphosis and a happy mention of a namesake, Gilbert
pointedly asks Adam: 'Does our silence seem to you inactive and
artless...when in silence is taught and practiced the art of advanc-
ing towards God as it were in a straight line, and of transforming
and changing oneself into the new man, into the new Adam...?' After
a lengthy preterition, in which **Gilbert** prescinds from all other re-
wards and punishments in this world and the next, he invites Adam
to come for the first fruits, the joy of living and learning in the
school of monks, and to come at once: 'I am awaiting your reply in
person rather than in writing. Farewell.'

Third Epistle

In his third Epistle, Gilbert attempts to dissuade a pious
Brother William from returning to the court of some civil leader,
ad curiam...cum Duce. The letter, as long as a Treatise, resembles,
especially in satirical passages, the first half of the seventh
Treatise. Gilbert delicately warns William by criticising the vanity of a few others. 'Blush at the impudence of some, who though
they should expect all the necessities of life from the father of a
monastery,[18] by begging help from all sources, procure for themselves
some fine and rare hides, garish outfits, imported cloaks and other
items too numerous to mention, devices of vanity provocative of
pleasure for the nostrils, the eyes and the palate.' Gilbert carefully avoids offending William: 'That this blemish is wholly absent
from your character, your plea for prayers, so often repeated, is
proof enough and purifies the widespread pallor of this leprosy,'
but admits that he has been criticized himself: 'Herein I am harsh
and inhuman, they say, even though in other respects I am a handsome
fellow, but in this role my appearance has been made blacker than
lumps of coal, because I have learned to disburse only what I have
been accustomed to request.' **Gilbert** seems to echo two passages from
Horace's Satires: in the first Horace uses the metaphor of scattered blemishes to chastise avarice: *inspersos...naevos...avaritiam;*[19]
in the second, Horace (or a similar passage in Persius) seems necessary to complete the meaning. Though Gilbert is adapting Lamentations,
Denigrata est super carbones facies eorum, the line of Horace (or those
of Persius) is needed for the meaning: *Sani ut creta, an carbone no-
tati?*[20] Gilbert elsewhere, as noted by Mabillon-Migne, would quote
from this very satire of Horace,[21] and Horace's line means just what
Gilbert intends: after the Greek manner of voting, Horace's (and Gilbert's) critics cast into the ballot box, not chalk for acquittal but
charcoal for condemnation of him as insane; for the meaning then, one
must leave Lamentations for a line in Horace which is both difficult
for commentators and so memorable for a conscientious reader: Gilbert
is being blackballed.

Gilbert continues in a **passage** which with others shows that satire
did not die with Juvenal or Jerome:

> Let them rail at me to their heart's content. Let them
> construe their graft as my greed. From their softness
> let them forge a greater austerity on my anvil. I have
> indeed 'set my face as the hardest flint,' and though
> their mallet be **smashed,** I hope that 'I shall not be
> broken.'[22] Let me be branded as a poor sharer, as too
> tenacious. I would readily allow myself to be discolor-
> ed with this blemish, provided those hounds, or rather
> those delicate little whelps, do not devour the **bread**

of the children, provided the tatters of the poor do not
supply the superfluous fineries of others, provided I
do not seek to acquire an empty fame and false favors
for myself from the belching belly of a brother.

Rather in the Horatian manner, there is further satire in the
third Epistle, further searching questions about Brother William's
proposed religious life at court, some fears about a friend's return to life in a worldly milieu, with perhaps reminiscences of
Seneca.

Fourth Epistle

In this short letter to a friend, Gilbert shows how careful
he is in his written **replies.** It may not be farfetched to suspect an allusion to Vergil's *Aeneid I*, with Gilbert in the role of
Neptune whose realm has been disturbed by the Lord of Fountains in
the role of **Aeolus**, king of the winds. Gilbert wonders that the
Lord of Fountains had not been enlisted against him to force a
favorable reply, 'to overshadow me again with a cloud of imposing
intercessors...With deference, then and in my usual way, as in
other matters which I have made no decision to perform, I am post-
poning rather than formulating an answer, until we can confer together shortly. Farewell.'

First Treatise

Of the seven Treatises, all but the second and third were
adapted as letters. The first was addressed to a religious named
R, perhaps the Roger of Treatise VII who was probably the long-
lived Abbot Roger of Byland.[23] It's richly scriptural theology
is felicitously expressed in what Jean Leclercq has called 'written rhetoric.' Here is Gilbert at his best: alliteration and allusion, apostrophe, exclamation and prayer; balance and parallel;
metaphor, simile and symbolism; humor and wit; puns and rimes, and
the etymological interpretation of Hebrew proper names.[24] The treatise opens with friendly comments where, in metaphor, the art of
writing and the craft of weaving are almost intertwined:

Do you agree now that I have woven a discourse lengthy
enough to supply for what had been trimmed off in earlier
dispatches? Perhaps in my new role I have gone to excess
and now burdened you with my **prolixity,** though previously
you chided me for conciseness. Yes, you complained of my
brevity, my dear R, saying you received not correspondence
but phrases broken off like threads before they could form
a pattern. You added that you would be delighted if a

garrulous page would compensate for the rarity of our
friendly chats.

Gilbert exclaims: 'Blessed are they...who can attend and see
how sweet is the Lord'; then he laments: 'Woe is me, that my years
do not glide by on this one course unimpeded': *Heu me! quod non in
hoc ipsum libere labuntur tempora.* The words are bound to recall
Horace's wellknown lament: *Eheu fugaces, Postume, Postume, / labuntur anni...*[25]
After quoting Isaiah as watching by day and by night,[26] Gilbert
adds an imaginatively brilliant comment: 'His years were not slipping
by in vain. He wasn't a wandering minstrel eloping with time,
but kept his nights and days like treasure in a strong box, doling
them out in the custody of himself or in the watchtower of the Lord'
*non illi in vacuum diffluebant tempora, imo non ipse vagabatur et
volitabat cum tempore, qui tempora religata tenebat in sui custodia
vel in Domini specula illa expendens.* He regrets that he cannot give
uninterrupted time to fruitful contemplation on the heights, and describes
his state with lively humor in two similes and the etymology
of a Hebrew proper name:

> Who will give me the wings of a dove,[27] that I may fly
> to a retreat so secure and so fruitful, where there is
> rest and refreshment? For me, access to that retreat is
> rare, if indeed there be access at all, rare and perhaps
> also immediately interrupted and withdrawn like a shadow
> at sunset, until once more I am startled and suddenly
> jump off like a grasshopper.[28] A fine jump is that recorded
> in the Psalm, 'let me know my end, O Lord, and what
> is the number of my days.'[29] Isn't this Psalm entitled,
> 'For Idithun,' that is, for the broad-jumper? He had
> leaped beyond all that is transitory, crossing over in his
> mind to all that is real and permanent. [*Rarus, sed forte
> et interruptus statim, et sicut umbra cum declinat, ablatus;
> donec iterum locustarum more subitum excutiar in saltum.
> Bonus quidem saltus, de quo legis in Psalmo: ...Denique
> et pro Idithun, id est pro transiliente, hic psalmus
> inscribitur...*]

Then he comments on the verse of the Psalmist: 'They shall be
inebriated in the fruitfulness of your house...[30] Surely extraordinary
is this inebriation which proceeds from your light and not
from liquor, from sobriety and not from syllabub!' (*Inusitata
haec plane ebrietas, quae lumine fit, non liquore; sinceritate,
non sicera.*)[31]

Second Treatise

The second and third Treatises, not addressed to correspondents, are deeply and affectively prayerful. The second considers, in the quest for Christ, the difference between the contemplation of pilgrims and the vision of the blessed; the third explores the difference between the joy of the wayfarer and the happiness of one in the fatherland.

A single word in the second treatise prompts a comparison with St Bernard on one small point. *Subarrata,* here in the sense of pledged or redeemed, is found in **Sulpicius** Severus, Cassian, and Aldhelm.[32] In Gilbert's sixth Treatise, *Propinator,* found in a sermon of St Augustine, is recorded in Latham dated 1153, so probably from Gilbert but translated 'drinker';[33] Gilbert's context suggests a richer meaning; one who pledges a friend in a precious chalice of wine to be given later as a gift, perhaps a 'munificent toastmaster,' applied by Gilbert to the Lord. The two unusual words in Gilbert, rich in meaning, have an ancient ecclesiastical pedigree; by comparison, forty-five unusual words of St Bernard, from a larger *corpus* influenced by his secretaries, are recorded in an interesting list, *Nomenclator vocum exoticarum in S. Bernardo.*[34] Gilbert continues with two interesting laments as if he were discreetly deprecating and drawing a veil over the richness both of his words and of his experience: 'Woe is me that I do not pour out fully whatever abundance I receive! Woe for the dryness of my words and still more for the dryness of my affections.'[35]

Third Treatise

In the third treatise a problem **is** presented in the second paragraph: 'Who will guide my feet like the hoofs of a stag,[36] that lightarmed and lighthearted, I may pursue this gazelle, and that shedding the baggage of **my** household chores, I may range the forest in heavenly solitude': *Quis ponet pedes meos quasi cervorum, ut possim expeditus et alacer hunc hinnulum sequi? domesticas dediscere curas, et coelesti in solitudine silvescere?* Does Gilbert picture himself as the horse or the horseman? Is he thinking of Pegasus or of Bellerophon, of Actaeon or of **Apocalypse** 19:14: 'They follow him on white horses'? He continues: 'It is good to shed the heaviest burden, the burden of oneself, and to be reduced imperceptibly to the nimbleness of a deer': *Bonum est exonerari se ipso, onere gravissimo, et caprearum sensim in levitatem deficere.* Here Actaeon transformed into a deer is more than a parallel, for the myth illumines the meaning. If we admit that Gilbert had Echo in mind in the *Sermo* discussed above, we might argue to Actaeon here, for Echo and Actaeon occur only a few pages apart in Ovid's *Metamorphoses* (3:138-252 and 359-510). We might note one further point: there seems to be an accentual verse-couplet in: *Quae est tamen ista ratio / ascendentis cum lamento?* (T 3:2).

Fourth Treatise

Gilbert writes the fourth Treatise in the second person singular throughout, to a dear friend for us unnamed and unknown. Exploring the implications of theological dialogue and of meditation upon the divine, he rings the changes on two words, *fabula* and *confabulatio*, fable and confabulation or 'fable-talk,' which hide meanings deeper than the etymological pun. He contrasts the beatific vision face to face with our present knowledge of God in his work, his creatures, where he is seen in a mirror and in riddles: '...our reflections seem to me like a kind of fable, a parable full of figures intended to adumbrate the truth to come.' Our words: *confabulantes...confabulantibus...fabularentur...collationes de figuratis sermonibus*...indicate the problem of communication where we must have recourse to symbols and figurative language: 'Wherefore when collections of figurative passages are woven together, I would readily call them "fable-talk" as it were [*quasi confabulationes*] not because of the eternal truth adumbrated within but because of the **fig**ures of fancy displayed without, for **"what** is imperfect will be done away with."'[36]

Here Gilbert leaves us two problems: one is the origin of a comparison he makes, the other the source of a proverb he quotes. The comparison may be a simple observation of his own or a reminiscence from a cosmological passage in Lucretius or Cicero, Seneca or Pliny. He man be only reflecting on a fire in a grate: 'Just as solid and more corporeal matter with difficulty admits within it the power of fire, while matter that is fine and dry and light, is more quickly kindled and consumed in the devouring flame, so spiritual and **refined** meditations more quickly welcome but do not long endure the sweet violence of enkindled love...For my part I have regarded meditation as the tinder, and love as the flame.' And what is the proverb he refers to in his last sentence? 'Well I shall shut the door of my mouth at last, that according to the proverb, the shepherd's pipe [or quill] may be loaned to you, while I catch my breath': *Jam ergo ponam ostium ori meo, ut, juxta proverbium, tibi fistula accommodetur, dum ego respiro.*[37]

Fifth Treatise

The fifth Treatise is written to answer the enquiry of a friend about the meaning of the text of James: 'Every good gift and every perfect grant is from above, coming down from the Father of lights.'[38] Gilbert delayed his answer **because** of the difficulty of the text and the amount of time required to consult other commentators. Though

this Treatise breaks off after Gilbert has made some distinctions
about the text, his answer, one might think, could be retrieved by
consulting his remarks elsewhere on *donum, datum, perfectum, opti-
mum;* yet Gilbert may well have had some other comment in mind for
he has no penchant for repeating himself or anyone else. Gilbert's
delay, attributed to the difficulty of the text and the need to consult commentators, suggests a large number of authors available at
Swineshead or in the environs. Yet we can prove so little. He had
at hand St Bernard's Commentary on the Canticle, which he would not
tamper with, 'even with his little finger.'[39] He refers to St Jerome's *De scriptoribus ecclesiasticis* in his own commentary on the
Canticle,[40] and concludes his long letter to William with a request
for a copy of St Jerome's commentary on Isaiah.[41] Surprisingly, Gilbert introduces a quotation from the Rule of St Benedict, with the
word *Denique* which he reserves to introduce quotations from Scripture, an indication of his reverence for the Rule which he attempted
to follow faithfully in his **monastic** teaching.[42] He seems to have
followed St Augustine in his theology of original sin, grace, liberty,
and predestination, and to have been familiar with the work of John
Cassian and St Gregory the Great.[43] He was certainly a dedicated
friend of St Aelred, and of Roger of Byland, whose works he probably
had at hand.[44] Yet he gives the impression that for himself the best
commentary on Scripture was Scripture itself, and that if he consulted commentators it was to be sure of himself, not to plagiarize but
to contribute some original and independent development of his own.

Sixth Treatise

The sixth Treatise is written with warmth to a younger friend
otherwise unknown. Gilbert applauds his friend's zeal for learning,
declines the invitation to be his teacher or his physician in matters
divine, but here his reflections on the mysteries of the redemption
show great refinement, spiritual sensitivity, and sustained imagination. Gilbert's friend needs neither Gilbert's art for his healing
nor his bread for his sustenance, but rather 'drops of a more hidden
wisdom, drops refined and mellow, delicious and tasty.' These drops
are in the measureless ocean of the divine Majesty, which 'ebbs away
from the narrow straits of our hearts and our lips, and from this
ocean as if through tiny holes in a dyke, with difficulty some drops
seep toward us. Wonderful is his friend's thirst for these drops of
enebriating sweetness, but would that the Lord incarnate would quench
his thirst:

> would that he who is inebriated, as we read in Deuteronomy,
> might **welcome** the thirsty.[45] He is inebriated who is call-
> ed full of grace and truth. He is inebriated from whose
> fullness we have all received.[46] He is at once inebriated

> and inebriating; he is the chalice and he gives us to
> drink [*propinator*] [47] at once the winejar and the wine,
> wine pure and wine mixed, for wisdom mixed wine in his
> mixing bowl.[48] How sparkling you are, O inebriating mix-
> ing bowl! sparkling indeed, radiant in truth, intoxicat-
> ing in delight!

After some **paradoxes** on the Incarnation and **reflections** on our
human condition in relation to the Incarnation, he returns to the
drops in the chalice meant to inebriate us, but adds a surprising
dimension: 'So let the navel of your soul be like a mixing-bowl,
refined and purified and made subtle and capacious by the iron scal-
pel of penance and discipline, that you may be filled to the brim,
inebriated, that the verse may be applied to you: "your navel is
a round bowl that should never lack for mixed wine."'[49] He pursues
the metaphor with astonishing results:

> How many today on the day of their birth and in the first
> hour of conversion, **cut** their navel cord, but in later
> times act as if they were rejoined by the navel to the
> world, beginning in the spirit but ending in the flesh!
> So let your umbilical cord not only be cut but trimmed
> and rounded in perfect equality, in order that with all
> the corruption and corpulence excised, your well of liv-
> ing waters, as it were, may overflow with a continuous
> stream of spiritual drink, and for the future you need
> no longer come here to draw water from my **well**.[50]

So the drops of the ocean of divinity have been poured into the
chalice of the incarnate God who channels drops into the chastened
navel-cup of our hearts for our perpetual refreshment!

Seventh Treatise, First Part

The seventh Treatise is addressed to Roger, probably the abbot
of Byland; it has two parts: the first, attacking the ambitious
and the presumptuous, is dedicated to Roger; the second, warning of
the difficulties of high office, encourages Roger to retain his present position. Innocently enough, Gilbert took the occasion of a
request from Roger for advice, **to** send him the first part of this
treatise. Remove the opening sentences like a detachable dedica-
tion, one sentence of transition from the ambitious to the presumptuous, and the final sentence which lacks the usual word of farewell; you then have a treatise on **ambition** and presumption without
thought of Roger. The first part did not fare well! Though obviously everyone should be warned about these pitfalls, why should the
competent, popular, and successful Roger be singled out for special

attention? Gilbert hastened, in the second half, to outline the
difficulties of being an abbot and to reassure Roger that he had the
requisite qualities.

Gilbert states the problem: 'You ask, my dear Roger, that you
be persuaded to continue to hold your present office and that your
fear of the risks of power be diminished by my recommendations. Of
course "you are ordering me to throw oil on the fire," and on your
account alone to inflame with the bellows of my discourse [*sermo*]
the ambitions of many already white-hot within.' The quotation:
Oleum certe me jubes adjicere camino, is attributed to Horace:
Adde poemata nunc, hoc est, oleum adde camino.[51] In the few personal lines to Roger, Gilbert had no need to attribute to Horace
two words of what must have become a very common proverb. Nor does
he mean, as he did with his one reference to Seneca in the first
Epistle: look in Horace, as in Seneca, for further quotations in
this treatise. He does mean: look further in Horace's Satire to
see how absurd the poet considers ambition: according to Horace,
all but the wise are absurd, but especially the ambitious; indeed
Horace allows himself to be considered no less absurd: a puny mid-
get, who puffs himself up like a frog and writes poems, indeed
sermones.[52] If Gilbert were to contribute to the absurdity by
writing a *sermo* to encourage the ambitious and presumptuous, that
would indeed be to add fuel to the fire! Then in the same sentence,
perhaps to confuse readers after the Horatian manner, Gilbert makes
of his *sermo* no longer the fuel but the bellows! Gilbert always
weighed his advice and was chided for procrastination in forward-
ing it.[53] On the receipt of Roger's letter, he sent off what he
had at hand, a moral treatise on ambition and presumption as a
counter-weight to a later letter of recommendation still to be composed thoughtfully and perhaps painfully. The reference to Horace
was meant to set a context of good will and humor, but the epistolary treatise was interpreted as criticism of the beloved Roger.
The moral? Don't send a moral treatise as a letter, which Demetrius defined as 'the heart's good wishes in brief.'[54]

Gilbert argues against persuading people to be ambitious in a
bright passage about this temptation even among men in the desert.
He introduces a startling interrogation of Lucifer, which must have
startled Roger and his friends. He explains the meaning of three
Hebrew names: '*Sabama* means exulting in one's height, *Cis* means
harsh and *Saul* means petition.' He notes how symbolically, *quam
signanter*, Isaiah writes. With many another, he laments the changing times in Cicero's words: *O Tempora! O mores!*[55]

He writes some wry satire on anti-intellectual businessmen in
monks' clothing: 'not content with their own ignorance, they con-
temn the knowledge of others, they call the pursuit of wisdom ob-
tuseness, and they blacken with the smear of folly or of vainglory
what is cautious subtlety, while personally they labor for the food

which perishes and does not remain unto life eternal.'[56] When the
father feasts the prodigal now home from wishing to feed on the
husks of swine, some older monks like the older brother of the prodigal grunt like swine *(grunniunt)*. One wonders whether Gilbert is
thinking of Odysseus' men turned into swine by Circe.[57] When Gilbert **remarks**: 'A cursed thirst is the lust for wealth' *(mala sitis
ardor habendi)*, he may be remembering *auri sacra fames* of Virgil's
Aeneid or a closer passage of Horace: *quem tenet argenti sitis im-
portuna famesque*.[58] After the transitional sentence in paragraph
seven, for Roger's sake, Gilbert introduces an interesting dialogue
with the presumptuous man, which again would have taken Roger and
his friends by surprise. Gilbert concludes: 'Here I am reining in
my galloping discourse, for you are **already** being driven away to
other concerns, or rather, as often happens, you are distraught by
many concerns,'[59] an allusion to the Lord's remark to Martha. With
this ambiguous farewell, Gilbert omits his usual word: *Vale*.

Seventh Treatise, Second Part

In the second half of the Treatise, after commenting on the
storm aroused by the first half, Gilbert exposes the difficulties
and burdens of office, then commends Roger as one well endowed with
the qualities suitable for a prelate. Several satirical passages,
one on prelates and another on their subjects, may have reminiscences
of Horace: 'Why the very men who profess and preach abstinence, leading figures of our Order, how finicky they are in the houses of others! What an eye they have for banquets of rare foods prepared for
a gourmet! How they contract their eyebrows, turn up their noses,
look askance with their eyes, if anything is served with less taste
and less festivity!' *Ipsi abstinentiae professores et praedicatores,
ipsi primates Ordinis, quam fastidiosi sunt alienis in domibus! quam
exquisitas et elaboratas artificiose requirunt epulas! quomodo con-
trahunt frontem, corrugant nares, si quid minus lepide minus festive
apponatur*. The passage, perhaps no more than a common**place**, does
seem to echo four passages in Horace: *Siculae dapes/ dulcem elabora-
bunt saporem; explicuit vino contractae seria frontis; cenae sine
aulaeis et ostro/ sollicitam explicuere frontem; ne sordida mappa/
corruget nares....*[59]
A series of rhetorical figures punctuates the pages: *sententia:*
'but what humility may camouflage, achievement will herald'; *metaphor:* 'from the time the **Lord** harnessed you to plow in his place
and afterward to leave in furrows the unbroken soil of the valleys';
apostrophe: to Roger's City, a *metaphor* extending to lengthy *alle-
gory; quartet:* he gives many meanings to four words: snow, milk,
coral, sapphire; *wit:* 'Your auspicious success will persuade you
[not to resign] as well as your inauspicious successor'; *symbolism:*
you shuttle with discretion between Leah and Rachel, between the

active and the contemplative life; *etymology: Laban* means whitening,
Shechem means shoulders; *satire* with classical allusions: how the
new little brood trucks with **vanity** and superfluity!

> But your little brood who in recent times have begun
> to sprout, well-groomed, bright and whitewashed, are
> a kind of progeny of Laban, who is called Whitened,
> but otherwise are no match for the modesty of Rachel.
> For the appearance of worldly vanity she hid and con-
> cealed under the pretext of womanly weakness, but their
> traffic in worldliness and superfluity, men of **the new**
> brood overlay and cloak with the coloring of humanity;
> they do not purge out the old leaven but rather show
> off as merrymakers with imported dishes of food for a
> feast and are thought worthy of praise for the bountiful
> display of their banquets. It would be tedious work if
> I should wish to mention even cursorily the many species
> of vanity and weave **together** a list of their acts of os-
> tentation. Each of these characters you will recognize
> in gesture as a [swashbuckling] Thraso, an innkeeper in
> merry-making, a [parasitical] Gnatho in a brawl. Each
> wishes to appear as a Cato in chapter, a Cicero in court,
> a Virgil among the poets. Finally in conversation they
> are **mummers** but not monks. Their discourse overflows
> with facetious verbal wit....

Thraso and Gnatho, two characters in Terence's *Eunuchus*, seem to
have become standard names for the braggart, *miles gloriosus*, and the
parasite, *parasiticus*, perhaps a Falstaff and a Bardolph. Yet Horace mentions both Gnato and Cato in a single satire: *Terenti / fabula quem miserum Gnato vixisse fugato ducit...; 'Macte/ virtute esto'
inquit sententia dia Catonis.*[60]
   So on first looking into Gilbert's Latin, one classicist dis-
covers a kindred spirit who not only uses all the literary figures
described as 'written rhetoric,' but also shows an allusive and daring imagination to challenge his readers. Though this approach may
distort his personality and his deeply spiritual experience, it
may entice some to read him, preferably in the original, but even
in a translation. Sometimes at the expense of his own style, he
introduces an exuberant wealth of scriptural texts; he would be
most satisfied with scriptural threads woven into a tapestry where
only the work would be his, or with scriptural *tesserae* fitted into
a mosaic where only the cement would be his. In his use of the
classics, however, he was inhibited by his own advice: 'in the mouth
of a cleric or of a monk, sacred literature is much more fitting than
secular. Why do you wish to speak Egyptian in Jerusalem?'[61] Yet in
his writings, though he tended to hide her, his shy classical virgin

still peeps out unexpectedly through the veil of his pages to throw
light on their meaning.

The evidence of direct use of the classics, clear enough in general style, is not overwhelmingly obvious. Even dismissing the two
possible quotations from Ovid's *Ars amatoria* and *Heroides*, one must
admit that the recognition of his allusions to Echo and Actaeon clari-
fies his meaning, without however proving his direct use of Ovid's
Metamorphoses. But the idea of transformation or metamorphoses fas-
cinated him as one can see from his letters and from many passages
in his *Sermones*.[62]

The acknowledged quotations of Horace's *Ars poetica* and of his
Sermones,[63] plus many allusions and possible references make very
strong the case for Gilbert's use of Horace. The nine quotations
from Seneca, one acknowledged, make even stronger the case for his
use of at least the first eighty-eight *Epistolae morales*. One often
senses the humor and imagination redolent of Horace and the wit,
rhetorical figures, terse style, and practical wisdom characteristic
of Seneca.

When I had all but completed this first quest for Gilbert's
classical virgin, a student pointed out a remark of Joseph de Ghellinck: 'Apart from some texts of Virgil, one or two of Ovid, Persius, and Seneca, *sapiens quidem*, in his letter of 1146 (Epist. 256)
for the resumption of the crusade, he [Bernard of Clairvaux] almost
never cites the pagan authors. This is in striking contrast to his
correspondents and his disciples...especially Peter of Cluny, William of St Thierry and even Guigo the Carthusian and the Cistercian
Gilbert of Hoyland.'[64] This conclusion might seem to be contradict-
ed by superficial evidence; for example, in comparable works, in
Bernard's *Sermones supra Cantica* (143 columns in PL 183) there are
five acknowledged quotations from the classics, while in Gilbert's
Sermones in Canticum (241 columns in PL 184) there is only one. The
two works circulated together for centuries, so that wherever Bernard
went, Gilbert followed, and wherever Gilbert went, Bernard overshadow-
ed him. If Gilbert shows greater purity of diction, more hidden classical influence, he was so successful in hiding them in his commentary written 'in the style and manner' of Bernard, that he was able
to out-Bernard Bernard. Yet he was his own man, and Cornelius a
Lapide thought fit to quote him ten times where he seemed to develop
some valuable and interesting comment of his own on the Canticle.[65]
His other extant work, perhaps neglected because a little difficult,
merits the accolade of Etienne Gilson, 'well worth reading.'[66]

St Paul's College
The University of Manitoba

NOTES

1. Edmund Mikkers, 'De Vita et Operibus Gilberti de Hoylandia,'
   Cîteaux 14 (1963) 33-43 265-75.
2. All Gilbert's works are included in PL 184. I am referring in-
   frequently to the *Sermones in Canticum*, on which I reported to
   the Linguistic Circle of Manitoba and North Dakota, 'Gilbert of
   Hoyland (d. 1172), Disciple of St Bernard, Classical Literature
   and Contemplative Love,' of which a resumé has appeared in the
   Proceedings for October 1974.
3. PL 184:188B-D.
4. Lucretius 1:187, and see 220-30.
5. Lk 1:38, Ps 34:10.
6. Ovid, *Metamorphoses* 3:396-99.
7. For the *Epistles* see PL 184: 289A-98B; for the *Treatises*, PL 184:
   251D-90A.
8. Ep 1:1; PL 184: 289B. Seneca, *Epistolae Morales* 3:2.
9. Ep 1:2; PL 184: 289C. Seneca, *Ep Mor/* 81:1.
10. Ep 1:2; PL 184: 289C. Seneca, *Ep Mor/* 81:2.
11. Ep 1:2; PL 184: 289C. Seneca, *Ep Mor/* 81:1.
12. Ep. 1:2; PL 184: 289C. 1 P 4:8. For the use of the word *philo-
    sophia* from Cicero and Seneca to the end of the middle ages, see
    Jean Leclercq, 'Études sur le vocabulaire monastique du moyen
    âge,' *Studia Anselmiana* 48 (1961) 39-67.
13. Ep 1:2; PL 184: 290A. Seneca, *Ep Mor* 79:9.
14. Ep 1:2; PL 184: 290A. Ovid, *Ars amatoria* 3:656.
15. Ep 1:1; PL 184: 289B. Ovid, *Heroides* 5:15.
16. Ep 2:2; PL 184: 292A. Horace, *Sermones* 1:1:72.
17. Ep 2:4; PL 184: 292D. Seneca, *Ep Mor* 88:46; 88:45; 88:45; 88:43.
18. Ep 3:1; PL 184: 294A. *Rule of St Benedict* 33.
19. Ep 3:1; PL 184: 294B. Horace, *Serm* 1:6:65-69.
20. Ep 3:1; PL 184: 294B. Lm 4:8; Horace, *Serm* 2:3:246; Persius
    5:107-108.
21. T 7:1; PL 184: 276C. Horace, *Serm* 2:3:321.
22. Ep 3:1; PL 184: 294B. Is 50:7.
23. C. H. Talbot, 'A Letter of Roger, Abbot of Byland,' ASOC 7 (1951)
    218-231. Talbot thinks that Roger's letter addressed to G. is
    written indeed to Gilbert of Hoyland and that Gilbert's corres-
    pondent in T 7 is Roger of Byland. Edmund Mikkers agrees in his
    article cited in note 1 above, p. 273, n. 93. Roger's letter,
    will appear with Gilbert's treatises in Gilbert of Hoyland IV,
    CF 34.
24. When the Chronicler of Clairvaux recorded Gilbert's death in
    1172, he noted: *Hic reverendus, egregius atque devotissimus et
    doctissimus dominus Gislebertus...composuit sermones...super
    Cantica Canticorum valde notabiliter et scientifice in sequendo
    modum et stylum beati Bernardi* (PL 185: 1248C). The Chronicler

missed a small sign of Gilbert's independence: Bernard wrote
Sermones super Cantica, Gilbert *in Canticum.* For the style of
Bernard, see Christine Mohrmann, 'Observations sur la langue et
le style de Saint Bernard,' in the introduction to SBOp, 2:ix-
xxiii. For the style of St Aelred, Gilbert's contemporary in
England, see *Series Scriptorum S. Ordinis Cisterciensis, I,
Sermones inediti B. Aelredi Abbatis Rievallensis* (Rome: Cistercian Generalate, 1952) pp. 6-15, in the fine introduction of
the editor, C. H. Talbot.
25. T 1:2, PL 184: 253A. Horace, *Carmina* 2:14:1-2.
26. Is 21:8.
27. Ps 54:7.
28. Ps 103:23.
29. Ps 38:5.
30. Ps 35:9-10.
31. The Hebrew *sicera,* strong drink, is found in Lk 1:15 and six
other passages in Scripture; should we translate: 'our inebriation is from his **brilliance** and not from benedictine,' or 'from
his truth and not from vermouth,' or 'from clarity and not from
claret'? For *Sobria ebrietas* see Jean Leclercq, *La liturgie et
les paradoxes chrétiens,* (Paris: Cerf, 1963) pp. 37-57.
32. Sulpicius Severus, *Append Ep* 2:12; Cassian, *Coll* 7:6; Aldhelm,
Carm. de virginitate, 1935.
33. Augustine, *Serm* 361:7; R. E. Latham, *Revised Medieval Latin
Wordlist From British and Irish Sources* (London, Oxford, 1965).
Latham lists *subarro* with an obelisk, 'indicating a suspicion
that the form of the word is due to a misprint, a misreading,
or a **scribal** error,' gives the meaning 'to subjugate,' and the
date 1137. Latham lists *propinator,* translates 'drinker,' with
the date 1153, the date of Bernard's death when Gilbert **began**
to think of continuing Bernard's *Sermones supra Cantica.* But
the word occurs in St Augustine, has a richer meaning, and is
a transliteration from the Greek.
34. PL 183: 1307-308.
35. On the characteristics of Gilbert's religious experience, see
Pierre Miquel, 'Les Caractères de L'Expérience Religieuse d'après
Gilbert de Hoyland,' *Coll.* 27 (1965) 150-59.
36. 1 Co 13:10.
37. The proverb does not seem to be scriptural; it does not resemble
the only proverb on *fistula* quoted in Othlo's *Libellus Proverbi-
orum,* ed. G. C. Korfmacher (Chicago: Loyola, 1936): *sicut fistula absque inspirante nullum reddit sonum, ita et cor hominis
absque inspiratione divina nullum recipit bonum. Fistula* is
frequent for a pipe or a quill used for pastoral or inspired
songs; it is frequently referred to in the sense of a silver
or gold tube for use with the chalice in Communion, in liturgical and canonical writings, especially by Cistercians of the

twelfth century; see *fistula* in Du Cange, *Glossarium infimae et
mediae latinitastis* (1886, rpt. Gratz: Akademische Druck-Und
Verlagsanstalt, 1954). But what is *accommodetur*? fitted, ad-
justed, attuned, loaned? One is tempted to imagine a private
joke involving a ceremonial exchange of the bag-pipes. Jean
Leclercq assures me: 'I have written an article on *Fistula
illa caelistis* to appear soon on this theme,' see *Verbum et
Signum* 1 (1975) 59-68, Wm. Finle, Munich.

38. Jm 1:17.

39. SC 22:1; PL 184: 114C. SC 23:6; PL 184: 174D.

40. SC 36:3; PL 184: 189C.

41. Ep 3:6; PL 184: 197B.

42. Ep 3:1; PL 184: 294A. *Rule of St Benedict* 33.

43. See Jean Vuong-Dunh-Lam, article 'Gilbert de Hoyland,' in *Dictionnaire de Spiritualité*, 6:374. I have not had the opportunity of using Fr Lam's two-volume typescript thesis, *Doctrine
spirituelle de Gilbert de Hoyland* (Rome: Anselmianum, 1962);
he has contributed two articles from his **thesis**, 'Le Monastère:
Foyer de vie spirituelle d'après Gilbert de Hoyland,' and 'Les
Observances **Monastiques**: instruments de vie spirituelle d'après
Gilbert de Hoyland,' *Coll.* 26 (1964) 5-21, 179-89. Other articles continue to appear with pages on Gilbert in the *Dictionnaire*,
for example, 'Cantique des Cantiques,' 2:101; 'Contemplation,'
2:1950-55; 'Divinisation,' 3:1407-408.

44. See the moving eulogy of Aelred, SC 41:4-7; PL 184: 216C-218B;
and for Roger, note 23 above.

45. Dt 29:19 where PL cites 29:29. Gilbert writes *ebrius*; Vulg.
ebria pax.

46. Jn 1:14, 16.

47. *Propinator*, see note 33 above.

48. Pr 9:2.

49. Ez 16:4.

50. Jn 4:15.

51. T 7:1; PL 184: 276C. Horace, *Serm* 2:3:321.

52. Horace, *Serm* 2:3:314-322.

53. See Ep 2 and 4.

54. W. Rhys Roberts, *Demetrius on Style* (1902; rpt. Hildesheim,
1969) p. 177, n. 231. Demetrius, 223-35, would have saved
Gilbert grief.

55. T 7:1:5; PL 184: 279B. Cicero, *In Catilinam*, 1:2.

56. T 7:1:6; PL 184: 280A. Jo 6:27. See Alcuin's *Elegiacs for a
Scriptorium: Fodere quam uites melius est scribere libros, /
Ille suo uentri serviet, iste animae....*' Hrabanus Maurus had
the lines inscribed over the entrance of the doorway to the
Library at Fulda according to the editors of Lucretius, W. E.
Leonard and S. B. Smith, *T. Lucreti Cari de Rerum Natura* (1942
rpt., Madison, 1968) pp. 87-88.

57.   T 7:1:6; PL 184: 280A. Lk 15:25–32. *Grunniunt*, Bernard used
      the word of his monks grunting like hogs in disapproval of
      something in a *Sermo: Bene fecistis grunniendo significare
      quod minime ita sapiatis, imo quod non ita desipiatis, ne in
      eo quod planum est immoremur*, PL 183: 970D. See C. H. Talbot,
      Sermones inediti, p. 7, for some interesting remarks about monks'
      reactions to *Sermones*; for Talbot, see note 24 above.
58.   T 7:1:6; PL 184: 280B. Virgil's *Aeneid* 3:57; Horace, *Epistolae*
      1:18:23.
59.   T 7:2:4; PL 184: 283C–D. **Gilbert** seems to depend on four separate
      passages in Horace: *Carm* 3:1:18–19; *Serm* 2:2:125; *Carm* 3:29:15–16;
      Ep 1:5:23. The satirical tradition remained surprisingly strong:
      see Arthur Weston, *Latin Satirical Writing Subsequent to* **Juvenal**
      (Lancaster, Pennsylvania, 1915) and David S. Wieson, *St Jerome
      as a Satirist: A Study in Christian Latin Thought and Letters*
      (Ithaca, 1964).
60.   T 7:2:10; PL 184: 287C–D. Horace, *Serm* 1:2:20–21 and 31–32.
61.   SC 16:4; PL 184: 83C. See also 16:5.
62.   Ep 2:4; PL 184: 293A. See Ep 4:5; PL 184: 295D–96C. *Sermo* 1:1;
      PL 184: 288C.
63.   SC 31:4; PL 184: 163D. Horace *Epistola ad Pisones*, Ep 2:3:102–
      103. T. 7:1:1; PL 184: 276C. Horace *Serm* 2:3:321.
64.   J. de Ghellinck, S. J., *L'Essor de la Littérature Latine au
      XIIe Siècle* (Brussels, 1946) 1:181.
65.   Cornelius a Lapide, *Commentaria in Scripturam Sacram* (1638, rpt.
      Paris, 1890), 7:608; 8:69; 72, 77, 79, 80 twice, 116, 117, 118.
66.   Etienne Gilson, *The Mystical Theology of St Bernard* (1939, rpt.
      London, 1955) p. 247, n. 261.

Abbreviations

Canivez   Joseph M. Canivez, ed., *Statuta Capitulorum Generalium
             Ordinis Cisterciensis ab anno 1116 ad annum 1786.*
             Louvain: Bibliothèque de Revue d'Histoire Ecclésias-
             tique, 1933-1941.

CC CM   *Corpus Christianorum, Continuatio Medievalis.*
             Turnhout: Brepols, 1971- .

CCL   *Corpus Christianorum Latinorum.* Turnhout: Brepols,
             1953- .

CF   The Cistercian Fathers Series. Spencer, Washington,
             Kalamazoo: Cistercian Publications, 1969- .

CS   The Cistercian Studies Series. Cistercian Publica-
             tions, 1969- .

Dil   Bernard of **Clairvaux**, *De diligendo Deo (On Loving God).*

Ep(p)   *Epistola(e)* (Letters)

Ex. mag.   *Exordium Magnum Cisterciense,* ed. Bruno Griesser,
             Series Scriptorum S. Ordinis Cisterciensis. Rome, 1961.

PL   J.-P. Migne, ed., *Patrologiae cursus completus, series
             latina.* 221 volumes. Paris, 1844-1864.

RAM   *Revue d'Ascétique et de Mystique.* Toulouse, 1920- .

RTAM   *Recherches de théologie ancienne et médiévale.*
             Louvain, 1929- .

SBOp   Jean Leclercq, Henri Rochais, C. H. Talbot, *Sancti
             Bernardi Opera.* Rome: Editiones Cistercienses, 1957- .

SC   *Sermones in cantica canticorum (Sermons on the Song
             of Songs)*

SCh   *Sources chrétiennes.* Paris: Editions du Cerf, 1941- .

T   Treatise

CISTERCIAN PUBLICATIONS INC.
Titles Listing

THE CISTERCIAN FATHERS SERIES

THE WORKS OF BERNARD OF CLAIRVAUX

Treatises I: Apologia *to Abbot William, On Precept and Dispensation* CF 1
On the Song of Songs I CF 4
On the Song of Songs II CF 7
The Life and Death of Saint Malachy the Irishman CF 10
Treatises II: The Steps of Humility, On Loving God CF 13
Magnificat: Homilies in Praise of the Blessed Virgin Mary CF 18
Treatises III: On Grace and Free Choice, In Praise of the New Knighthood CF 19
On the Song of Songs III CF 31
Five Books on Consideration CF 37
On the Song of Songs IV CF 40

THE WORKS OF WILLIAM OF SAINT THIERRY

On Contemplating God, Prayer, and Meditations CF 3
Exposition on the Song of Songs CF 6
The Enigma of Faith CF 9
The Golden Epistle CF 12
The Mirror of Faith CF 15
Exposition on the Epistle to the Romans CF 27
The Nature and Dignity of Love CF 30

THE WORKS OF AELRED OF RIEVAULX

Treatises I: On Jesus at the Age of Twelve, Rule for a Recluse, The Pastoral Prayer CF 2*
Spiritual Friendship CF 5*
The Soul CF 22

THE WORKS OF GILBERT OF HOYLAND

Sermons on the Song of Songs I CF 14
Sermons on the Song of Songs II CF 20
Sermons on the Song of Songs III CF 26
Treatises and Epistles CF 34

OTHER EARLY CISTERCIAN WRITERS

The Letters of Adam of Perseigne I CF 21
John of Ford—Sermons on the Final Verses of the Song of Songs, I CF 29
Idung of Prüfening—Cistercians and Cluniacs: The Case for Cîteaux CF 33
The Way of Love CF 16
Works of Guerric of Igny—Liturgical Sermons I CF 8
Liturgical Sermons II CF 32
Three Treatises on Man: A Cistercian Anthropology CF 24
Isaac of Stella—Sermons on the Christian Year CF 11

THE CISTERCIAN STUDIES SERIES

EARLY MONASTIC TEXTS

Evagrius Ponticus—Praktikos and
Chapter on Prayer — CS 4
The Rule of the Master — CS 6
Dorotheos of Gaza—Discourses and
Sayings — CS 33
Pachomian Koinonia I:
The Lives — CS 45

CHRISTIAN SPIRITUALITY

The Spirituality of Western Christen-
dom — CS 30
Russian Mystics
(Sergius Bolshakoff) — CS 26
In Quest of the Absolute: The Life
and Works of Jules Monchanin
(J. G. Weber) — CS 51
The Name of Jesus
(Irénée Hausherr) — CS 44
Gregory of Nyssa: The Life of Moses
— CS 31
Entirely for God: A Life of Cyprian
Tansi (Elizabeth Isichei) — CS 43

MONASTIC STUDIES

The Abbot in Monastic Tradition
(Pierre Salmon) — CS 14
Why Monks?
(François Vandenbroucke) — CS 17
Silence in the Rule of St Benedict
(Ambrose Wathen) — CS 22
One Yet Two: Monastic Tradition
East and West — CS 29
Community and Abbot in the Rule
of St Benedict I
(Adalbert de Vogüé) — CS 5/1
Consider Your Call
(Daniel Rees) — CS 20
Households of God
(David Parry) — CS 39
The Rule of Iosif of
Volokolamsk — CS 36

CISTERCIAN STUDIES

The Cistercian Spirit
(M. Basil Pennington, ed.) — CS 3
The Eleventh-Century Background of
Cîteaux
(Bede K. Lackner) — CS 8
Contemplative Community
(M. Basil Pennington, ed.) — CS 21
Cistercian Sign Language
(Robert Barakat) — CS 11
Saint Bernard of Clairvaux: Essays
Commemorating the Eighth Cen-
tenary of his Canonization
— CS 28
William of St. Thierry: The Man &
His Work
(J. M. Déchanet) — CS 10

The Monastic Theology of Aelred
of Rievaulx
(Amédée Hallier) — CS 2
Christ the Way: The Christology of
Guerric of Igny
(John Morson) — CS 25
The Golden Chain: The Theological
Anthropology of Isaac of Stella
(Bernard McGinn) — CS 15
Studies in Medieval Cistercian
History I — CS 13
Studies in Medieval Cistercian
History II — CS 24
Cistercian Ideals and Reality
(Studies III) — CS 60
Simplicity and Ordinariness
(Studies IV) — CS 61
The Chimaera of His Age: Studies on
St Bernard (Studies V) — CS 63
Cistercians in the Late Middle Ages
(Studies VI) — CS 64

STUDIES BY DOM JEAN LECLERCQ

Bernard of Clairvaux and the Cister-
cian Spirit — CS 16
Aspects of Monasticism — CS 7
The Contemplative Life — CS 19
Bernard of Clairvaux: Studies Pre-
sented to Jean Leclercq — CS 23

THOMAS MERTON

Thomas Merton on St Bernard
— CS 9
The Climate of Monastic Prayer — CS 1
Thomas Merton's Shared Contempla-
tion: A Protestant Perspective
(Daniel J. Adams) — CS 62
Solitude in the Writings of Thomas
Merton (Richard Cashen) — CS 40

FAIRACRES PRESS, OXFORD

The Wisdom of the Desert Fathers
The Letters of St Antony the Great
The Letters of Ammonas, Successor
of St Antony
The Influence of St Bernard
Solitude and Communion
A Study of Wisdom

* out of print